Signposts
to the Past

Place-Names and the History of England

Margaret Gelling

Signposts
to the Past

Place-Names
and the History of England

J. M. Dent & Sons Ltd

London, Melbourne and Toronto

First published 1978
Reprinted 1979

Printed in Great Britain by
Biddles Ltd, Guildford, Surrey
and bound at the
Aldine Press, Letchworth, Herts
for J. M. Dent & Sons Ltd
Aldine House, Welbeck Street, London

This book is set in 11 on 13 pt Imprint 101

British Library Cataloguing Publication Data

Gelling, Margaret
    Signposts to the past.
    1. Names, Geographical—England
    I. Title
    914.2'001'4   DA645

    ISBN 0-460-04264-5

Contents

List of Maps

Maps 12, 13, 14, 15, 16, 18, 19, 20 and 21 are based upon Ordnance Survey maps with the permission of The Controller of Her Majesty's Stationery Office, Crown Copyright reserved.

Abbreviations

ABD	Aberdeenshire	ELO	East Lothian
AGL	Anglesey	ESX	Essex
ANG	Angus	FIF	Fife
ARG	Argyllshire	FLI	Flintshire
AYR	Ayrshire	GLA	Glamorgan
BDF	Bedfordshire	GLO	Gloucestershire
BNF	Banffshire	GTL	Greater London
BRE	Brecknockshire	HMP	Hampshire
BRK	Berkshire	HNT	Huntingdonshire
BTE	Bute	HRE	Herefordshire
BUC	Buckinghamshire	HRT	Hertfordshire
BWK	Berwickshire	INV	Inverness-shire
CAI	Caithness	IOM	Isle of Man
CAM	Cambridgeshire	IOW	Isle of Wight
CHE	Cheshire	KCB	Kirkcudbrightshire
CLA	Clackmannanshire	KCD	Kincardineshire
CMB	Cumberland	KNR	Kinross-shire
CNW	Cornwall	KNT	Kent
CRD	Cardiganshire	LAN	Lanarkshire
CRM	Carmarthenshire	LEI	Leicestershire
CRN	Caernarvonshire	LIN	Lincolnshire
DEN	Denbighshire	LNC	Lancashire
DEV	Devon	MDX	Middlesex
DMF	Dumfriesshire	MER	Merionethshire
DNB	Dunbartonshire	MLO	Midlothian
DOR	Dorset	MON	Monmouthshire
DRB	Derbyshire	MOR	Morayshire
DRH	Durham	MTG	Montgomeryshire

NAI	Nairnshire	SHR	Shropshire
NFK	Norfolk	SLK	Selkirkshire
NTB	Northumberland	SOM	Somerset
NTP	Northamptonshire	SSX	Sussex
NTT	Nottinghamshire	STF	Staffordshire
ORK	Orkney	STL	Stirlingshire
OXF	Oxfordshire	SUR	Surrey
PEB	Peebles-shire	SUT	Sutherland
PEM	Pembrokeshire	WAR	Warwickshire
PER	Perthshire	WIG	Wigtownshire
RAD	Radnorshire	WLO	West Lothian
RNF	Renfrewshire	WLT	Wiltshire
ROS	Ross and Cromarty	WML	Westmorland
ROX	Roxburghshire	WOR	Worcestershire
RUT	Rutland	YOE	Yorkshire (East Riding)
SFK	Suffolk	YON	Yorkshire (North Riding)
SHE	Shetland	YOW	Yorkshire (West Riding)

Other abbreviations

BAR *British Archaeological Reports*, ed. A. C. C. Brodribb, A. R. Hands, Y. M. Hands and D. R. Walker, 122 Banbury Road, Oxford.

EPNS English Place-Name Society, The University, Nottingham.

Asterisks before words (e.g. *dūnon*, *ecles*) and personal names (e.g. *Hycga*, *Cott*) indicate that the item is not recorded, but it is inferred from place-names or other philological evidence.

Introduction

The study of English place-names is a philological discipline which is based mainly on written evidence. This evidence consists of early spellings of names, and these have to be extracted from sources ranging in date from the earliest Greek and Latin texts which make reference to the British Isles to the first edition of the Ordnance Survey one-inch maps produced in the nineteenth century. The spellings are identified when possible with modern place-names, and the series of spellings for each item is presented in a manner which illustrates the development of the sounds in the spoken name, so that the philologist can study this development and reach conclusions about the original form and meaning.

This statement, while not exciting, needs to be made firmly at the outset, as the underlying method of the discipline will not be stressed later in this book. The main aim of the book is to discuss the bearing of place-name evidence on English history, and to suggest ways in which archaeologists and historians may draw on this copious store of material. It is a commonplace of Dark Age studies that philologists, historians and archaeologists do not always appreciate each other's points of view. Historians may feel that philologists are not particularly well equipped to evaluate the historical significance of their material, and archaeologists may feel that philologists lack the practical sense needed for the realistic interpretation of names bestowed by peasant farmers. Philologists, for their part, are acutely aware that historians and archaeologists are embarrassingly disaster-prone when discussing place-names. An earlier book on the interaction of the three disciplines in Dark Age studies, Wainwright 1962, was mainly concerned with the logical foundations of the three subjects and the possibility of a single scholar mastering all the fields sufficiently to achieve a satisfactory balance between co-ordination and specialization. My own aim is rather to set out the place-name evidence in such a way that archaeologists and local historians will understand its strengths and its weaknesses, and will be enabled to use it without catastrophic misunderstandings.

Assuming that Dr Wainwright's co-ordinating scholar is an ideal unlikely of attainment, the disciplines of history, archaeology and philology must remain to some extent distinct. There will continue to be demarcation problems, and accusations are sometimes made that the philologists operate a sort of closed shop. There is some truth in this, but long experience has convinced me that a closed shop is something of a necessity on the etymological side of place-name study. The subject is not exceptionally difficult, but it is full of pitfalls. Some of these are due to the extensive nature of the vocabulary involved in place-name formation, and the presence in it of items which superficially resemble each other but are of quite different meaning. Such pairs or groups of similar-looking words cause constant misunderstanding of place-names by historians and archaeologists. Since practical matters are the concern of this book, rather than underlying philosophical principles, the best way to make this point is by quoting some recent examples.

An excavation at Rivenhall ESX was the subject of a report in the 1973 volume of *The Antiquaries Journal*. The authors believed the name to mean '(place) by the rough hall', and suggested that this referred to a Roman aisled barn which their excavations had shown to be still standing in Saxon times. The President of the Society of Antiquaries unwittingly increased the confusion in his Anniversary Address for 1974, when he said that excavations at Rivenhall had possibly discovered the 'riven hall' of the place-name.

Rivenhall does not contain either the word *hall* or the word *riven*. The final element is Old English *halh* 'sheltered place', the usual source of -hall, -all, -hale, -ale at the end of a modern name. The similar but unrelated word *hall* does occur in place-names, but it is rare, and should only be assumed when a majority of early spellings has -*ll*-, as opposed to -*l*-, which is far from being the case in this instance. The first element of Rivenhall is probably Old English *hrēofan*, dative of *hrēof* 'rough, rugged', so the excavators' interpretation was not so badly out in this respect, though one could have dispensed with the later confusion with the past participle *riven*. Rivenhall appears to mean 'at the rough sheltered place'. Local investigators might be able to point to some special characteristic of the stream-valley here, or to discern some other *halh* such as a hollow near the church too slight to appear on maps. A wide range of speculation is possible as to the nature of the 'rough sheltered place', but it cannot be the Roman aisled barn, and the vocabulary of the name must be understood before profitable speculation can begin.

It is desirable that interested non-philologists should develop a sense of caution with regard to sets of similar-looking words which may have totally different meanings. The place-name element *hām* 'village' is the subject of some discussion at present for reasons set out in Chapter 5, and at recent conferences on Dark Age history historians and archaeologists have been heard expatiating on the special significance of places with names ending in -ham. The snag here is that there was another Old English word, *hamm*, which was a topographical term totally unconnected with *hām*, and which also becomes -ham at the end of a modern place-name spelling. Separating these two words is one of the more difficult tasks of place-name study, and philologists cannot always say for certain which of them is contained in a place-name, but there are many instances in which the necessary distinction can be firmly made. Non-philologists do not always recognize the existence of this problem, and are embarrassingly liable to weave historical theories round names they assume to contain *hām*, the early spellings for which demonstrate clearly that the other word, *hamm*, is the one involved in that particular instance. To cite a single example, claims have recently been put forward that Kingsholme near Gloucester means 'king's home', referring to the royal palace which apparently stood there; but this name, which was spelt *Kyngeshamme*, *Kyngeshomme* in the thirteenth century, can only mean 'water-meadow on the royal estate'. Another pair which have caused some trouble to archaeologists recently are *būr* 'bower' and *burh* 'fort'. The difference of meaning could hardly be greater, and it causes extreme embarrassment to the initiated to hear an archaeologist who suggests that a small building found on his excavation might be a *būr* being questioned by other archaeologists as to whether it was defended.

Because place-name etymology abounds with snares of this kind, it is not possible to invite general participation in the process of suggesting etymologies. The rules have been objectively established; they are not arbitrary, but they are intricate, and few non-specialists master them well enough to be on safe ground in this branch of the study. Knowledge of an extensive vocabulary (which varies in different parts of the country both as regards the words used and the precise forms of some of the words), attention to the early spellings of the name under consideration, and respect for the sound developments and spelling conventions of English are indispensable. It is therefore important at the outset to ask people who have no special competence in the history of the English language to accept specialist guidance about the meaning of place-names before building a theory on a supposed etymology. A casual glance at an isolated entry in a dictionary, especially by people with little practice in the use of dictionaries, is no basis for revision of an accepted derivation. Etymologies should be accepted from the philologists, or only revised with philological consent.

Another aspect of place-name study in which philologists must continue to operate something of a closed shop is that of identification. Most readers of Dark Age history are familiar with the perennial controversy about the location of the Battle of *Bedcanford*, by which, in AD 571, the rulers of Wessex obtained control of land extending from Eynsham OXF to Limbury BDF. This battle may or may not have happened in the general vicinity of Bedford. Historical interpretation of the nature and location of the fighting is one aspect of the problem, but place-name scholars have striven for half a century to explain to archaeologists and to some historians that there is no case to be made for the place-name *Bedcanford* being actually identical with the modern name Bedford. Bedford BDF is spelt *Bedanford* in Old English documents, and there is no evidence in pre-Conquest or in post-Conquest spellings for the -*c*- of *Bedcanford*. Decades of trying to explain this point do not avail; I have recently met the old equation of *Bedcanford* with Bedford when examining a Ph.D. thesis. A similar difficulty occurs with regard to the Battle of *Fethan leag* in 587, which ended the West Saxon expansion of which the victory at *Bedcanford* was part. Sir Frank Stenton (Stenton 1943, p. 29) identified this with a wood in Stoke Lyne OXF, which was called *Fethelee* in 1198. As far as philological correspondence is concerned this is perfect; Old English *Fethan leag* would naturally be spelt *Fethelee* in 1198. The only objection is that the wood in Stoke Lyne is never mentioned again, and one would have liked more than one spelling to support such an important identification. Other historians, however, guided in part by different views on the nature of the campaign of 587, continue to support rival identifications which are philologically unsound. Dr C. Hart (Hart 1975, p. 81) equates *Fethan leag* with a place near Stratford-on-Avon WAR for which we have Old English spellings *Faccanlea*, *Fachan leah*, *Fæhha leage*. This is impossible because the sound represented by the spellings -*cc*-, -*ch*-, -*hh*- does not interchange with that represented by -*th*- in the Old English period (it sometimes did later, as in the curious development of the name Keighley, but that is another story).

It is tedious to fight again these ancient campaigns (not the campaigns of the sixth century, but those of the twentieth century concerning the identification of the battlefields), and I feel that the time has come to put an end to the argument and to assert firmly that only investigators with some philological training should be regarded as competent to pronounce on these matters. We may have to endure charges of arrogance or obscurantism, but we have tried very hard to explain that these identifications need a sound philological basis, and we have not been able to make ourselves understood in all quarters.

If it be accepted that place-name etymologies and identifications must be of specialist origin or have specialist agreement, then the study may be whole-heartedly recommended to the specialist in other fields, or to the amateur. On the non-philological aspects of the subject there is scope for a great deal of useful work. The development of English place-name studies has been lopsided—place-name etymology has become a highly developed science, but work on the historical bearing of the material has not kept pace. On this aspect some more or less inspired guesses were made in the early years of the English Place-Name Society's existence. It was decided that certain types of name—those ending in -ing and -ingham, those which referred to pagan religious practices, those which contained words or personal names designated 'archaic'—belonged to the earliest stages of the Anglo-Saxon settlement, and a place-name chronology was evolved with these as a starting-point. Little attempt was made to discern a chronological pattern in the great mass of settlement-names which consist of a topographical statement about the site of a settlement without referring to the habitation itself. There are many reasons for rejecting these attitudes, and these are discussed in Chapter 5; but the theories postulated in the early stages of the English Place-Name Society's work were not seriously re-examined till the 1960s, nor were they checked against the increasing body of evidence accumulated by Dark Age archaeologists. Some of the theories, particularly the notorious one by which names in -ing and -ingham were considered to belong to the earliest English settlements, hardened into dogma. The eventual challenge to some of these theories came not from young scholars, as might perhaps have been expected, but from a small group of people who had been trained in the old tradition and had worked and thought within its framework for many years. It was a middle-aged revolution, getting under way about 1960. Those of us who put our shoulders to the wheel then, and who succeeded in getting the subject moving at last, felt that we were doing a bold thing in challenging the assumptions about place-name chronology which we had imbibed from the august teachers of our young days. The seal of respectability was put on the new attitudes in May 1976 when Professor Kenneth Cameron explained them to the British Academy in the Israel Gollancz Memorial Lecture (Cameron 1976).

The problem now is two-fold. We have radically revised our thinking about the historical bearing of place-name studies, and we have the great satisfaction of seeing a few younger scholars take up the work in accordance with the lines we have tentatively suggested. These new approaches to place-name studies are being recognized (albeit on a small scale, like everything else in this field) as suitable for post-graduate theses in the universities. But there are so few of us working on place-names that the detailed application of the new insights which we feel to be of such value is going to take a very long time. That is one aspect of the problem, and for this reason we will obviously welcome all the help we can get from scholars in other disciplines and from amateurs. Local historians, with their detailed topographical knowledge, should have a tremendous contribution to make.

The second aspect of the problem which faces those of us who are concerned with the health and future of English place-name studies is that of communication with the reading public. This problem was highlighted in the year 1973, which saw the celebration of the English Place-Name Society's fiftieth birthday. A number of well-intentioned articles appeared in that year, outlining the history and achievements of the Society, and we found to our surprise and chagrin that most of our well-wishers were totally unaware of all the articles published in specialized journals between 1965 and 1973 which we thought had brought about a fundamental revision in place-name thinking. The publication of Professor Cameron's Israel Gollancz Memorial Lecture should transform the situation as regards communication with scholars in related disciplines, but there is still the problem of reaching the general reader. A short article in *The Local Historian* (Gelling 1974a) produced a response which suggested that the general reader, while mystified, was at least prepared to be reached, and this article led to an invitation from Messrs J. M. Dent and Sons to write this book. In it I have tried to describe the work of the last fifteen years in less technical terms than those which are appropriate to learned journals. I have also tried to point the way forward, as it appears to me, and to indicate fields for research which I hope interested amateurs will think worth investigating.

As far as I know I am not in serious disagreement with any of my contemporary or younger colleagues, though obviously we do not concur in every detail. It is a great encouragement to know that Professor Kenneth Cameron, the Honorary Director of the English Place-Name Survey, approves of this venture. The book is different in scope and intention from his remarkably successful study (Cameron 1961). As a first introduction to the study his book is unlikely to be replaced or surpassed. I should be happy for my book to be seen as a sequel to it, providing extra information on particular topics (such as Romano-British place-names, and names of special interest to archaeologists) and suggesting ways in which local historians might make practical application of the knowledge of the subject which many of them will already have gained from it. The other colleague to whom I stand particularly indebted is John Dodgson, of whose work in the field of revised place-name chronology an account is given in Chapter 5. Younger colleagues whose friendship and support has been invaluable include Dr Gillian Fellows Jensen and Dr Barrie Cox. Their works, and those of others who have helped in the great revision, are cited in the following pages and listed in the bibliography. Most work on the subject published before the end of 1976 has been taken into account.

Chapter 1

The Languages

In a country such as England, where the current language is a relatively recent introduction, and other languages (Old Norse and Norman French) have had a limited currency at even more recent dates, the mixture of languages in the stock of place-names constitutes a vital part of the evidence for estimating the mixture of races in the composition of the nation. For the purposes of a study of place-names in relation to the history of England it is important to be clear at the outset about which languages are involved, and by whom they were spoken. In England there are six successive layers to be distinguished.

1. A non-Indo-European language, assumed to have been spoken before the coming of Celtic people to Britain. This obscure tongue differs from all the others involved in English place-names in being the only one which is not a member of the Indo-European family of languages. We know of two such languages in western Europe—Basque, which survives to the present day, and Pictish, which was used for monumental inscriptions, carved in the ogam script, in Scotland in the eighth and ninth centuries AD. The Pictish inscriptions can be transliterated, but are not understood, apart from a few Celtic words and personal names which are interspersed among the unintelligible sequences of letters. It seems clear that the Picts of this late date were actually speaking a Celtic dialect, but the more ancient language was still remembered, perhaps by a priestly caste, and was used for inscriptions.

If such a pre-Celtic language has left traces in English place-names, these are probably to be found in river-names, which are most likely everywhere to preserve remnants of older languages. It is very probable that some English river-names which are not easily explained as Celtic or Germanic belong to this ancient stratum. Since nothing is known of the vocabulary of this hypothetical pre-Celtic language in England (and there could have been more than one), there is nothing the place-name student can do about it except to remember that it may be responsible for some of our more intractable names.

2. *A Celtic language* for which the name British has been used in the most recent authoritative study, Jackson 1953. British is a descendant of Common Celtic, a branch of the Indo-European family of languages. The language known to philologists as Common Celtic divided into two main branches, Goidelic (the parent of Irish and Scottish Gaelic) and Gallo-Brittonic. The language called British, which is the ancestor of Welsh, is a division of Gallo-Brittonic.

During the earliest period from which written records are available this language, British, was being spoken throughout the main island of Britain with the probable exception of Scotland north of the Firths of Forth and Clyde. We do not know at what date the speakers of a Celtic language first came to Britain, but it is believed that the language was introduced, like the later Germanic language, by settlers from the Continent, and there is no doubt that it superseded the non-Indo-European language referred to under 1.

Our information about British begins with the first contact of Greeks and Romans with the island, the oldest source being Pytheas of Marseilles, *c.* 325 BC. Information becomes much fuller during the Roman domination of part of Britain from the mid first to the early fifth century AD. The place-names known to have been in use during those centuries are the subject of Chapter 2. Most of them are in the British language, and it is important to realize that this language, of which Cornish and Welsh are descendants, was spoken all over what is now England, and was in no way less charac-teristic of the districts later called Kent and Essex than of those later called Cornwall and Herefordshire. The identification of British place-names in all parts of England is one of the most important tasks of place-name study, and this is discussed in Chapter 4. Professor Jackson (Jackson 1953, p. 195 n.1) draws attention to the possibility that some prehistoric immi-grants to Britain may have been non-Celtic Indo-European speakers, and some other Indo-European tongue may have given rise to obscure place-names 'which have an IE. look'.

3. *Latin*, another Indo-European language, which was used in Britain at least for administrative purposes from the mid first to the mid fifth centuries AD. During this period Latin was the only written (as opposed to spoken) language in Britain, and it was the language of the western Church, which must have become a noteworthy linguistic influence in Britain during the fourth century, at any rate in the towns. The extent to which

Latin was spoken in non-official society in Roman Britain cannot be ascertained with certainty. There is a careful assessment of the evidence in Jackson 1953 (pp. 97–112). Professor Jackson concludes that there was no likelihood of a Romance language developing in Britain and superseding the British language, as Celtic languages were superseded on the Continent, where French, Italian and Spanish developed from Vulgar Latin and became the general speech. In Britain Latin was probably a language learnt in school rather than one acquired naturally. Professor D. Greene (Greene 1968) has suggested that Latin may have been more widespread and more colloquial in nature in Britain than Professor Jackson allowed, and there is obviously room for different opinions here. It does, however, seem unlikely that a Romance language such as French would have developed here; and this means that if the Anglo-Saxon settlement had not occurred, the Welsh form of Celtic speech would have been the language of the whole of Britain apart from those areas of the north and north-west into which the Gaelic form was introduced from Ireland. The rarity of Latin place-names in Britain, discussed in Chapter 2, supports Professor Jackson's view that the language was not much spoken in the countryside.

Although Latin was probably not widespread among peasant farmers in Britain, a number of Latin words were adopted by British speakers. A smaller number of Latin words found their way into Old English, some direct from Latin and some through the medium of British. Latin place-names are very rare in England, but names in British and Old English which incorporate Latin words are well evidenced, and are of considerable interest to the historian and archaeologist. With reference to the occurrence of Latin words in British or Old English place-names, it is necessary to appreciate the distinction between loan-words and cognates. In all the Indo-European languages there are words of cognate origin, that is words which descend from a common root which was in the ancestral language before the division occurred into the Greek, Latin, Celtic, Germanic and other branches. Cognate words in Latin and English do not superficially resemble each other very closely (*nest*, for instance is cognate with *nidus*, and *horn* with *cornu*), but in Latin and British some cognate words have very similar forms, e.g. British *moniịo-*, Welsh *mynydd*, which are connected with Latin *mons* 'mountain', British *cūlo-*, Welsh *cil*, 'nook', which are connected with Latin *cūlus* 'fundament', *Novio-* (in the British place-name *Noviomagus*, Chapter 2), which is connected with Latin *novus* 'new'. The occurrence of such words as these in place-names is not evidence for contact between British and Latin speakers. On the other hand there are many words in British (and in Modern Welsh) which were borrowed from Latin speakers after the coming of the Romans to Britain.

These include *cadeir* 'chair' (from *cathedra*), *eclesia* 'church' (from *ecclesia*), Modern Welsh *pysg* 'fish' (from *piscis*), Modern Welsh *pont* 'bridge' (from *pons*, *pontis*), Modern Welsh *terfyn* 'boundary' (from *terminus*). Place-names of British origin containing these words, and Old English names containing Latin loan-words such as *camp* from *campus*, *croh* from *crocus*, may sometimes have special historical significance; this point is discussed in detail in Chapter 3.

What is said here about the Latin element in English place-names is confined to the Romano-British period and its immediate aftermath. In the Middle Ages Latin was again the language of legal and administrative records, and this Medieval Latin has some influence on English place-names, especially in the prefixing or affixing of Latin words such as *magna* 'great' and *parva* 'small'. This use of Latin is particularly well evidenced in DOR, where it is found in Melbury Abbas, Whitchurch Canonicorum, and Toller Fratrum and Porcorum.

4. Old English. This is the name used by philologists for the language which replaced British in a large part of the island of Britain. Old English is a Germanic language, belonging to a different group of the Indo-European family from the Celtic languages. The circumstances of its success in Britain will always be to some extent mysterious. Germanic-speaking people who moved into other provinces of the Roman Empire in the fifth century AD did not invariably impose their language on the populations they dominated. French, Italian and Spanish are descended from Vulgar Latin, though in these countries also there were Germanic conquerors. The extent to which the change from British to Old English in this country can be claimed as evidence of a change of population is one of the great debating points of English history, and more will be said of this in Chapter 4.

The change of language in Britain was accompanied by the introduction of a vast number of Germanic place-names. The great majority of place-names now in use in England were coined in the Old English language, of which modern English is the much-modified descendant. For this reason English place-name studies have been carried out mainly by specialists in Old English. In so far as place-name studies have any part in university teaching, it is in English Language Departments that they are to be found.

5. Old Norse. This is another member of the Germanic branch of the Indo-European family of languages. In eastern England north of the Thames there are areas which have a large number of Old Norse place-names, and these names are related to the Danish invasions of the late ninth and late tenth centuries. In north-western England there are Old Norse place-names which must be connected with the Norwegian invasions of the early tenth century. It is with regard to the Danish place-names of eastern England that some of the most revolutionary work on the historical bearing of place-name evidence has been done in recent years, and this is described in Chapter 9.

6. *Norman French*. This was the language of William the Conqueror and the new aristocracy he established in England after 1066. The Normans were themselves partly of Germanic origin; their Dukedom originated in a gift of French land made by King Charles the Simple of France in AD 911 to Norwegian Vikings who had been ravaging his lands. Hence the name Norman, 'man of the North'. Unlike the Germanic settlers who brought the English language into Britain in the fifth century, the Normans did not impose their language on the people of their Dukedom; they themselves adopted French. Nor did they impose the French language on the English people after 1066. Norman French had a great influence on the development of English, but it did not replace it, and the descendants of the Norman aristocracy eventually became English-speaking.

The French element in English place-names is discussed in Chapter 9. It is instructive to note the contrast with the Old English and Old Norse elements. It seems clear that a new language spoken only or mainly by a ruling class does not affect place-names in the same way as a new language spoken by peasant settlers. This principle perhaps explains the rarity of Latin place-names in Roman Britain.

These six languages (or at any rate the five which we can recognize) must be borne in mind when English place-names are studied. It may be useful to add to this linguistic analysis some remarks about the relationship of place-names to the rest of the spoken language.

The place-names in current use may be in the language or languages currently spoken in a country, or in languages previously spoken but now extinct there. If they are in the language currently spoken, this does not mean that they are necessarily intelligible, as the language may have developed since the place-names were coined, and the names may have been fossilized at a relatively early stage of the development. Thus, though most place-names now used in England are in the English language, only a small proportion of them (such as Horspath, Newland, Newtown, Nettlebed, Redcastle) are immediately intelligible; the great majority are in various stages of fossilized Old or Middle English, with a great range of complications due to the interaction of spelling and pronunciation in the last few centuries.

In the British Isles, the areas where Celtic speech has continued to be used have a relatively high proportion of place-names intelligible in terms of the current Celtic languages. Cornish, Gaelic and Welsh have of course developed since prehistoric times, but it is probably safe to say that their development has been smoother than that of English, and there has been a greater tendency for place-names in these languages to develop with the language, not to become fossilized and cease to be meaningful as most English names did. For the last few centuries there has been widespread modification of Cornish, Welsh and Scottish Gaelic place-names by English speakers, and in recent years there are conscious efforts to limit this Anglicization, and to restore older spellings which do not reflect English mispronunciation. In Richards 1970, for instance, the late Professor Melville Richards discussed some Welsh town-names (such as Caerffili, Cricieth, Crucywel, Dinbych) under their 'correct' Welsh spellings, not under the familiar English spellings (Caerphilly, Criccieth, Crickhowell, Denbigh), though he accepted some Anglicized spellings, such as Cardiff, Cardigan, Tenby.

The English modification of Welsh names may be compared with the Norman French modification of English place-names after the Norman Conquest in 1066, but the latter process must be studied as an event of the distant past, and understood through the medium of written forms in official records. There was, of course, no attempt to check the process, such as there is now for Welsh and Gaelic names, and no deliberate restoration of 'correct' Old English spellings. Medieval place-name spellings represent only a desire to identify the place as clearly as possible.

We are able to study the effects of Norman French pronunciation on English place-names in the pages of the Domesday Survey, compiled in AD 1086. The old view that all the material for this record was obtained by government officials who travelled round the country asking questions which were answered by juries of local people has been much modified. It is now considered that use was made of some earlier written records, and that there were various stages in the editing of the final form of the survey. But whatever the precise stages by which the information reached the pages of the two volumes in the Public Record Office, the place-name spellings must to some extent represent an attempt by French-speaking clerks to render the pronunciation of English country people. Many of the names in the final version are certainly not copied direct from documents written by English speakers. The French rendering of English names might have been expected to result in chaos, but it did not. Some Domesday spellings are erratic, and have to be disregarded in the light of earlier and later forms, but most of them show a remarkably consistent treatment of English sounds. Some of the more important sound-changes and sound-substitutions which are reflected with considerable regularity in the spellings of 1086, and in official records for the following two centuries, are:

1. The simplification of *ch* to *c*. This has caused many names which might have ended in -chester to have -cester (as in Gloucester, Cirencester, Worcester), and is the reason for C- (instead of Ch-) in Cerne DOR, Cerney GLO, Cippenham BUC. Many names with Ch- or -ch- in which the English pronunciation has survived, have *C*- or -*c*- spellings in Domesday. Diss NFK would have become Ditch (which is its meaning) but for this Norman sound-substitution.

2. Consonant clusters at the beginning of names were simplified so as to be easier for French speakers. Names beginning with *S* followed by a consonant were liable to be affected by this process. Sometimes *S*- was dropped; but for this Nottingham NTT and Tutbury STF would be Snottingham and Stutbury. The combination *Shr*- was particularly difficult for French speakers, and attempts to cope with this in the name Shrewsbury are discussed later in this chapter. *Cn*- was made easier by the insertion of a vowel; but for this Cannock STF would be Knock, the development being comparable to that of *Knútr*, the Danish king's name, to Canute.

3. The initial sound in such names as Yealand LNC, Youlgrave DRB did not exist in Norman French, so the initial sound in such words as *judge* was substituted. In Yealand the English pronunciation has survived (though Domesday spells the name *Jalant*); the French pronunciation has been kept in other names, such as Jarrow DRH, Jesmond NTB, which would have become Yarrow, Yesmond if their development had not been subject to French influence.

4. The letters *l*, *n*, *r* interchange with each other in French spellings of English names. This is seen in the complicated development of Shrewsbury and Salisbury, discussed later in this chapter. Durham should have been Dunholm, and the change of the first syllable is due to this French confusion of *n* and *r*.

5. The initial sound in *thorn* was unknown to the Normans, and they replaced it by *T*-. This French pronunciation has survived in some names, such as Turnworth DOR (which contains *thorn*), and Tilsworth and Tingrith BDF, which would have developed to Thilsworth and Thingrith if English pronunciation alone had been involved.

These examples, which are far from giving a complete picture of the
changes imposed by French speakers on the pronunciation of English
names, are cited here in order to demonstrate that changes which might have
been expected to be chaotic are actually consistent and amenable to simple
classification. This is a vital point to establish, as it is fundamental to the
methods and principles of English place-name study. The clerks who
wrote out the Domesday Survey were not briefed about their spelling.
They found themselves faced with these problems in the field or in the
office, and their spontaneous responses were on the same general lines.
That there is this kind of pattern in place-name pronunciation, and that it
will be spontaneously reflected in the spelling of clerks, is the basis of
English place-name study.

In England, the study depends much more on written evidence and
much less on listening to local pronunciation than the study of Celtic
place-names in Wales and Scotland does. This is partly because a greater
number of English names have ceased to be part of the living language, and
partly because the operations of a new administrative class speaking a
different tongue began in 1066 in England, and can only be observed in
spellings, while in Celtic countries widespread English influence is more
recent, and a local pronunciation may still reflect an uncorrupted oral
tradition. (This does happen in England, but it cannot be expected as a
general phenomenon.) Also, England has known a bureaucratic administration for a long time, and the effect of written forms on spoken forms is
much more pronounced than in Celtic-speaking areas. For many centuries
in England a large proportion of the population has been aware of place-
names as sequences of written letters, not just as sequences of sound, and
this awareness has played havoc with oral tradition.

The interaction of the spoken and written forms of English place-
names does not appear to be consistent, or amenable to simple rules. The
process can be understood in regard to most names, but each name has to
be considered separately. This may seem to contradict what has just been
said about patterns in place-name pronunciation being consistently
reflected in official spellings; but this less consistent development is only a
widespread phenomenon in the last few centuries. It does not invalidate
the science of deducing etymologies from written forms, as most of those
on which reliance is placed are much earlier than the widespread literacy
which, while introducing a new and fascinating dimension into the study,
has played havoc with the evidence. It is a basic tenet of English place-
name study that etymologies should never be based on modern forms
unless these are supported by earlier ones.

With the general spread of literacy, a new element appears in place-name development. People feel a respect for the written form which is more insidious than the consistent conservatism of medieval clerks. The medieval clerk, being concerned only with the correct identification of the place in his records, can be expected to strike a balance between a spelling which bears an obvious resemblance to those of previous years' records, and one which reflects the sound of the name as he hears it spoken. At any rate, such a balance may be expected to emerge if we have a considerable number of medieval spellings for a name. The modern writer and pronouncer of place-names is subject to more insidious pressures than the need to identify the place clearly. He is also concerned to identify himself, as regards his social standing and his knowledge of 'correct' linguistic procedures. Because of this, a place whose name had developed naturally to Brummagem becomes Birmingham, because the conservative spelling is taken as 'correct' and dictates pronunciation, and Atcham SHR finds its stately home called Attingham, probably because the gentry know that that is how it was spelt in early records. Sometimes the fully developed form, like Brummagem or Atcham, survives in local speech, but sometimes it is rejected by local people after it has gained currency outside the area. In recent years the people of Ratlinghope SHR have been surprised to hear their village called Ratchope by visitors; they themselves, able to read maps and signposts, have apparently abandoned this erstwhile local form. The restoration of the longer form of Cirencester GLO for earlier *Cisetur*, contrasting with the retention of the short form of Leominster HRE, illustrates the chaos which now prevails.

In order to illustrate some of the possible complications of the interaction of spelling and pronunciation, it may be profitable to look in detail at a few names. Rugeley STF and Shrewsbury SHR may be instanced.

Rugeley, the first syllable of which now rhymes with *stooge*, is derived from Old English *hrycg* 'ridge' and *lēah* 'clearing', and might have been expected to become Rudgeley. In fact there are still traces among older people in the town of a pronunciation Rudgeley, so this is an instance in which the local oral tradition is trustworthy. The word *hrycg*, which became *ridge* in standard English, was spelt with -*u*- in the west Midlands till the end of the fourteenth century, and some place-names, including Rugeley, became fossilized while this vowel was in use, before the spread of -*i*- from standard English. Rudge SHR also shows this fossilized vowel, though the spelling of the consonants has developed further than in the Staffordshire name. Rudge SHR is *Rigge* 1086, *Ruge*, *Rugge* 1242; the spelling *Rudge* appears in parish registers in 1706. The -*g*-, -*gg*- of the Middle English spellings for both names represents the sound now spelt -*dge*. To account for the standard English pronunciation of Rugeley it is probably necessary to postulate the effects of literacy. People saw the fossilized spelling *Ruge-*, associated it with words like *huge*, and began to pronounce it in a way which bears no relationship to the origin of the name.

Shrewsbury has had a more complicated development, perhaps one of the most complicated of all English place-names. It is recorded in 1016 as *Scrobbesbyrig*, which may mean 'the fortified place of a district called The Scrub'. As mentioned above, the initial combination *scr-* was particularly difficult for Normans to pronounce. They simplified it to *sr-*, and then made it easier still by inserting a vowel, to give *sar-*. The name was also affected by Norman confusion of *-r-* and *-l-*, so *Sarop-* became *Salop-*. Spellings such as *Salopesberie* are overwhelmingly predominant in government records of the twelfth and thirteenth centuries, and this Norman form remained in official use and is the basis of the abbreviation Salop, used of the modern county. The local people, however, did not all adopt this Norman version of the name. An English form, which must have persisted in speech without getting written down much in the twelfth and thirteenth centuries, appears in the records in 1327, when Geoffrey *de Shrobesbury* is mentioned in the Patent Rolls. This is a perfectly regular development from *Scrobbesbyrig*. Normal also, though not inevitable, is the development of *-b-* to *-v-*, found in the slightly later spellings *Shrofbury* 1339 and *Shrouesbury* 1346. (This interchange has occurred in Pavenham BDF, which was *Pabenham* till 1492, Bavington NTB, which was *Babington* in Middle English, and Baverstock WLT, earlier *Baberstoke*.) After this in the Shrewsbury spellings we have an early instance of spelling influencing development. The letter *-u-* was employed in Middle English as a vowel and as a consonant (*-v-*), so that people seeing the name written *Shrouesbury* might take the *-u-* for a vowel. The diphthong *-ou-* could be written *-ow-*, and so we get forms like *Schrowesbury* 1391, though there were probably still people who knew that the *-u-* was a consonant in the fifteenth century. We find the spelling *Shrouesbury* in 1453 and 1461, but since the one letter did duty for vowel and consonant, we cannot be certain which was intended. The *Shrew-* spellings begin in the late fourteenth century (e.g. *Shrewesbury* 1386), and they alternate with the *Shrow-* spellings after that. The *Shrew-* spelling may originally have been due to nothing but the difficulty of distinguishing *-o-* and *-e-* in medieval handwriting. Eventually the two spellings would be accepted as akin to the variant forms of such words as *sew* (also spelt *sow*), *shew* (also spelt *show*). Thus, by the fifteenth century, the stage was set for the modern dilemma of whether to say *Shrewsbury* or *Shrowsbury*. The latter is the more 'correct', though this is contrary to the usual rule that the 'lower class' or 'local' pronunciation (in this case *Shrewsbury*) has more chance of preserving a genuine tradition.

The linguistic agility which enables modern English speakers to accept Salop as a form for Shropshire is paralleled by the ease with which Keighley is accepted as a spelling for a name pronounced *Keethley*, and Altrincham as a rendering of a name pronounced *Altringham*. All readers will know of instances even more bizarre than these. The divergence between spelling and pronunciation requires individual study in each case, and instances are only cited here to demonstrate that there is no simple guide to the origins of English place-names. Whereas in some Celtic-speaking areas it would be safe to say that the local pronunciation is the best guide, in England one cannot say categorically that either the local pronunciation or the accepted spelling is more likely to be reliable. A fossilized spelling may preserve valuable information (as in the W- of Wrockwardine and Wroxeter SHR, which is lost in pronunciation), or it may be responsible for distortion of the development, as in Rugeley. All sources of information have to be considered, and particular attention paid to the manner in which spelling and speech may have influenced each other.

Chapter 2

The Place-Names of Roman Britain

The Ordnance Survey Map of Roman Britain has an *Index of Roman Names* listing all the place-names recorded in the Romano-British period which are sufficiently well located to be placed on the Map. If the names of tribes, and some places in Ireland and France, are discounted, this list yields over 200 place-names. Other place-names mentioned in sources relating to Roman Britain which are not sufficiently well located to be shown on a map amount to nearly as many again—certainly another 150 items, probably more. Exact figures are not obtained easily, owing to such problems as that of textual corruption, which may produce 'ghost' names or make it uncertain whether slightly differing spellings in different sources refer to the same item. It seems safe to say that we know at least 350 names of rivers, islands, settlements and Roman forts in the area of England, Wales and Scotland. This must be a tiny proportion of the place-names which were in use from the first to the mid fifth century AD, but it is a sufficient number to enable some conclusions to be drawn about the types of name current in Roman Britain. The nature of these names will be analysed in some detail in this chapter, both because the subject is of interest in its own right, and because it is a necessary foundation for the study of the Germanic place-names which replaced most of the Romano-British ones. The contrast between British and Germanic nomenclature can only be fully appreciated if the nature of the British place-names is understood.

The material from Roman Britain can be used (albeit at some risk) by a person who is not a specialist in the Celtic languages because it has been the subject of expert study. Two articles in learned journals, Richmond, Crawford and Williams 1949, and Rivet and Jackson 1970, are the basic equipment. These articles incorporate linguistic comments on individual place-names by Professors I. Williams and K. Jackson, and armed with these and with Jackson 1953 some discussion of Romano-British names may be attempted.

Some of the names discussed by these authors are unsolved. The name *Alauna*, for instance, of which four instances appear in the Ordnance Survey list, one of them being now represented by the River Alne NTB, elicits from Professor Jackson the comment 'Meaning and etymology unknown'; and other well-recorded names, such as *Cunetione* and *Venta*, are left unsolved by the same authority. The tentative conclusions which follow in this chapter about the nature of Romano-British place-names are based on an analysis of those names for which a firm etymology is available.

First, it is interesting to note what proportion of these place-names is in the Latin language. The nature of the sources from which the information is derived might perhaps be expected to exaggerate the proportion of Latin names to vernacular ones, as only places of special concern to the Roman governing class are likely to be mentioned in documents or inscriptions. In fact, the proportion of Latin names among those recorded is small. The following are the certain or possible examples of Latin or part-Latin place-names recorded from Roman Britain—*Ad Ansam, Ad Pontem, Aquae Arnemetiae, Aquae Sulis, Caesaromago, Calcaria, Castra Exploratorum, Cataractoni, Fanococidi, Horrea Classis, Lindum Colonia, Pinnata Castra, Pons Aelius, Pontibus, Salinis* (two examples), *Spinis, Traiectus, Trimontium, Victoria, Villa Faustini.*

It may seem unreasonable to include *Trimontium* in this list while omitting *Tripontio*, especially as the Ordnance Survey list emends the latter name to **Tripontium*. Professor Jackson, using the spelling *Tripontio* which is the only one on record (in the Antonine Itinerary), comments that the ending is the British suffix *-jo-*, that *tri-* is the root for 'three' in both Latin and British, and that as the Latin word *pont-* was borrowed into British this name, which means 'three bridges', is not a hybrid, but a wholly British name. (The settlement at *Tripontio*, near Caves Inn on the boundary between Warwickshire and Northamptonshire, is now becoming a physical reality as excavation proceeds in advance of gravel working and road construction.)

Since the number of Latin or part-Latin names known from Roman Britain is so small, some comments may be offered on all the examples:

Ad Ansam. Latin *ansa* means 'handle' (e.g. of a jug) or 'loop of a sandal'. The place-name means 'at the loop', and may refer to a bend in a river. It occurs in the Antonine Itinerary, in Iter IX, which runs from *Venta Icinorum* (Caistor-by-Norwich) to London. *Ad Ansam* comes before *Camoloduno* (Colchester), and Professor Rivet locates it at Stratford St

Mary SFK, where the Roman road crosses the River Stour; but the actual settlement has not been found.

Ad Pontem, 'at the bridge', occurs in Iter VI of the Antonine Itinerary, which runs from London to Lincoln. It is next but one before Lincoln in the list of names on this route, and Professor Rivet locates it at East Stoke NTT. The one-inch map marks a Roman Fort beside the River Trent, but the Foss Way does not appear from modern maps to cross the river. The bridge may have been a causeway over marshy ground.

Aquae Arnemetiae (the form given in the Ordnance Survey list for the *Aquis Arnemeze* of the Ravenna Cosmography). This is identified with the Roman fort at Buxton DRB. It is a hybrid name, combining Latin *aquae* (which refers to the Roman thermal baths known to have existed here) with the name of a British goddess, *Arnemetia*.

Aquae Sulis, the Latin name of Bath SOM, recorded in a number of sources, including Ptolemy's Geography and the Antonine Itinerary. A parallel formation to the preceding name, 'the waters of Sulis'. *Sulis* was the name of a British goddess who was equated with Minerva.

Caesaromago, a hybrid name, apparently meaning 'the plain of Caesar', with British **magos* 'plain, field' as second element. This is recorded in several sources, including the Antonine Itinerary, and is applied to the Roman town at Moulsham, on the southern outskirts of Chelmsford ESX. A recent article, Drury 1975, sets out what is known of the Roman town from excavation, and discusses the significance of the name, preferring 'Caesar's market' to 'Caesar's plain'. Other places with this name are found on the Continent; it was the Roman name of Beauvais.

Calcaria, a Latin adjective meaning 'of limestone'. This is located at Tadcaster YOW. The Venerable Bede, writing *c.* AD 730, knew the Latin name, which he gave as *civitatem calcariam*. He said the English called the place *kælcacæstir*, 'chalkchester', but it is clear that this name had been replaced by the modern one, Tadcaster, by the date of the Norman Conquest.

Castra Exploratorum, 'fortress of the Scouts'. This occurs in Iter II of the Antonine Itinerary and is located north of Hadrian's Wall at Netherby CMB. It is surprising that only two of the Roman forts in the vicinity of Hadrian's Wall had Latin names (cf. *Pons Aelius*). Nearly always they were known by a British name describing the adjacent countryside.

Cataractoni, now Catterick YON. This name is recorded in a number of sources, starting with Ptolemy. The form *Cataractoni* is the one in the Antonine Itinerary, and Professor Jackson analyses this as from Latin *cataracta* 'waterfall, rapids' and a British suffix *-ono-*. The earliest Old English source in which the name occurs, the Venerable Bede, gives the simple Latin form *Cataracta*. The name refers to rapids on the River Swale near Richmond, and Professor Jackson suggests that it was originally the name of the river. This is an interesting example of a Latin place-name which has survived.

Fanococidi, from Latin *fanum* 'shrine, temple' and the name of a Romano-British war-god Cocidius, to whom there are eighteen surviving dedications carved on stone. It is not known which Romano-British fort or settlement is referred to by the place-name (which occurs in the Ravenna Cosmography), but the dedications to the god are so distributed as to suggest that his shrine was within the triangle between Bewcastle, Netherby and Stanwix in Cumberland.

Horrea Classis. This form is an emendation of *Poreoclassis* in the Ravenna Cosmography, and it is not certain that the name really existed. It would be Latin for 'the Fleet storehouses'. The place in the Ravenna Cosmography was in Scotland, north of the Antonine Wall, and may be Ptolemy's *Orrea*.

Lindum Colonia, now Lincoln. The British name *Lindo* occurs in Ptolemy, in the Antonine Itinerary, and in inscriptions; it means 'pool' or 'lake', and refers to the pool of the River Witham in the city. In the Ravenna Cosmography the Latin word *Colonia* is added, referring to the status of the town as a settlement of time-expired legionaries. Although it only appears in this late source, the Latin addition must have been in colloquial use as it has survived as the second part of the modern name.

Pinnatis. This name occurs in the Ravenna Cosmography, referring to a site in Scotland, north of the Antonine Wall. It is an adjective from Latin *pinnae*, perhaps 'merlons', referring to battlements on an earthwork, though as most camps had these the significance of such a name is not clear. The full name may have been *Pinnata Castra*, as a name like this was translated into Greek by Ptolemy.

Pons Aelius. This name occurs only in the Notitia Dignitatum. It is considered to refer to Newcastle NTB. *Aelius* is the family name of the Emperor Hadrian, so 'Hadrian's bridge'.

Pontibus, 'at the bridges'. This occurs in the Antonine Itinerary, and is located near Staines MDX.

Salinis. This Latin name occurs in the Ravenna Cosmography, apparently on a road leading north-eastwards from Gloucester. It means 'at the salt-pans', and is probably to be identified with the Romano-British settlement at Droitwich WOR, now being excavated by Birmingham University in advance of building work.

Salinis. A second example of the name 'at the salt-pans'. This is identified with Nantwich CHE. Another British *Salinae* occurs in Ptolemy's Geography in the territory of the Catuvellauni, but this has not been located, and it may be a confused siting of Droitwich. Ptolemy also mentions two places with this name on the Continent.

Spinis. A Latin name meaning 'at the thorn bushes' which occurs in the Antonine Itinerary and must be located near Speen BRK. Latin *spīnis* could not develop by ordinary phonological processes to Old English *spēne*, modern Speen, but there is no serious doubt that the English name is an adaptation of the Latin one. The Anglo-Saxons assimilated the unfamiliar *spīnis* to an English word *spēne*, 'place where there are chips of wood'.

Traiectus. This is a Latin word meaning 'ferry'. It occurs in Iter XIV of the Antonine Itinerary between *Abone* (Sea Mills) and *Aquis Sulis* (Bath). The route represented by this part of the Itinerary is uncertain. *Traiectus* cannot be the point at which the road leaves the River Severn, and Professor Rivet considers that the text may be corrupt at this point. It is not certain that *Traiectus* is a place-name.

Trimontium. A Latin name, meaning '(the place of) the triple peaks', which occurs in Ptolemy, in the Ravenna Cosmography, and on an inscription, and is identified with the Roman fort at Newstead, near Melrose ROX. The reference is to the triple-peaked Eildon Hills, which are a notable landmark.

Victoria, 'victory'. This was in Scotland, and is mentioned in Ptolemy (transliterated as *Ouiktoria*, not translated as *Nikē*) and in the Ravenna Cosmography. Professor Rivet, in a personal communication, suggests that it is Inchtuthil, named thus for Legio XX Victrix.

Villa Faustini, 'villa of Faustinus'. This occurs in Iter V of the Antonine

Itinerary, and may have been at Stoke Ash SFK. There are eight villa-names in the non-British sections of the Itinerary, but this is the only one recorded from Roman Britain.

The number of place-names listed and discussed above is twenty-one, which is only a small proportion of the number, between 350 and 400, which we know from the long period of Roman rule in Britain. To this small group there should probably be added Aust GLO, which is not recorded in any Romano-British source, but which seems inexplicable except as the Latin cognomen *Augusta*, which would develop to *Aust* in the British language before being passed on to the English. It has been conjectured (Smith 1964, 128) that there was a crossing of the River Severn here in Roman times (if so, the wheel has now come full circle) which was known as *Traiectus Augustus* from a connection with the Legio Augusta, stationed at Gloucester till moved to Caerleon on the Usk in AD 75. But Professor Rivet has pointed out to me that *Augusta* was common in Gaul as a place-name, and the connection with Legio II Augusta is very doubtful.

Considering that the sources available to us from Roman Britain are specially concerned with Roman settlements and forts, rather than with native farms and villages, the small number of Latin, as opposed to British, place-names on record from the period may fairly be taken as indicating that even the Latin-speaking administrative classes were for the most part using British place-names rather than new Latin coinages of their own creation. It is noteworthy that even in this short list the names are to some extent repetitive. Three of them refer to bridges (*Ad Pontem, Pons Aelius, Pontibus*), two refer to spas (*Aquae Arnemetiae* and *Aquae Sulis*), three refer to the exploitation of natural resources (*Calcaria* and the two examples of *Salinae*). *Fanococidi* and *Villa Faustini* refer to buildings, probably of Roman origin, and *Caesaromago, Horrea Classis, Traiectus* and *Victoria* are examples of deliberate name-giving. The only items which look as if they were spontaneous descriptions of the setting, without obvious reference to Roman installations, are *Ad Ansam, Cataractoni, Spinis* and *Trimontium*, and it may be significant that two of these survived and are still in use in the forms Catterick and Speen. The colloquial use of Latin *colonia* which led to its survival as the second element of Lincoln is also noteworthy; but the evidence suggests that Latin was rarely used in Britain for the spontaneous coinage of place-names.

The significance of this last statement would be clearer if it were possible to make detailed comparisons between the place-names recorded from Roman Britain and those recorded from other parts of the Empire. This cannot be attempted in the present book, but some effort has been made to provide a control for the analysis of the British material by reading the whole of the *Itinerarium Provinciarum Antonini Augusti*, popularly known as the Antonine Itinerary. This text is a collection of some 225 routes along the roads of the Roman Empire, which lists stopping-places on each route with a statement of the number of miles between each. It covers most of the Empire, from Spain to Turkey and from Britain to North Africa, and it constitutes a vast collection of place-names most of which were probably in use during the first three centuries AD. The criterion for inclusion was that a settlement was a recognized stopping-place on a Roman road.

From an unscientific analysis it seems to emerge that the proportion of Latin place-names along these routes varies greatly from one province to another. For the western Empire, the proportion of 10 per cent, which is about that of Latin or part-Latin to non-Latin names in the British section, is probably the lowest reached. Obvious Latin names are not in the majority anywhere, not even in Italy, but they do sometimes approach 50 per cent, and in several provinces they amount to about a third. To take one example, the section dealing with Sardinia mentions just over forty stopping-places, of which at least the following thirteen seem certain or likely to be Latin—*Aquis Neapolotanis* ('Neapolitan baths'), *Neapolis* is one of several Greek names in Sardinia), *Coclearia* (? 'place of snails'), *Cornos* ('horn'), *Ferraria* ('iron mines'), *Foro Traiani* ('Trajan's market'), *Gemellas* (also in Africa and Spain, perhaps referring to a town with two focal areas), *Ad Herculem* (presumably a dedication), *Ad Medias* ('central parts'), *Metalla* ('mines'), *Molaria* ('place of the mill'), *Sulcis* ('at the furrows'), *Tegula* ('tile'), *Ad Turrem* ('at the tower'). There is also an *Elefantaria*, apparently 'place of elephants', which is difficult to explain in Sardinia but might perhaps refer to an ivory market.

The Gaulish sections of the Itinerary are more relevant for comparison with Britain, but these cover a vast area in a not very orderly manner; difficulties of location make it hazardous to attempt any analysis, as it is not always clear whether one is meeting the same place several times or several examples of a particular name. It is clear, however, that some of the Latin place-names which recur on the Continent are not evidenced in Britain. These include *Fines*, *Finibus* ('boundary'), *Stabulum* ('stable'), *Tabernas* ('shops'), *Turres* ('towers'). Latin names of trees (*Fraxinum*, *Oleastrum*, *Olivam*, *Ulmos*) are fairly well evidenced elsewhere but do not seem to occur as place-names in Roman Britain.

Our knowledge of Latin place-names on the Continent is not wholly derived from sources recorded during the time of the Roman Empire. There are many names which must have been coined at a time when the language had not yet become Vulgar Latin, because they incorporate terms which disappeared after the time of the Empire. In France these include Castres, Châtre, Chestres, from *castrum* 'camp', Conflans, Confolens, from *confluentes* 'confluence', Fréjus, Feurs from *forum* 'market', Muizon from *mutationes* 'posting station'. None of these terms has been detected in place-names in Britain. The names Entraunes, Entrammes, Antrain, Entrains and Antran, all from *inter amnes* 'between the rivers', are considered to date from the Roman period because the word *amnis* did not survive in Gaul. Many other examples could be given.

In commenting on the scarcity of Latin place-names in Britain it should, however, be emphasized that Britain is not being contrasted with other parts of the Empire where Latin names were predominant. To judge by the Antonine Itinerary the Roman administrators everywhere used a high proportion of pre-existing vernacular place-names. But Latin names are scarcer in Britain than in most parts of the western Empire, and they include fewer specimens which may be spontaneous descriptions of the site by people whose native tongue was Latin.

In contrast to the Latin names, which have to be searched for, the written sources for Roman Britain offer relatively rich material for the study of the British names in use from the first to the fifth centuries AD. As mentioned above, a fair number of names from these sources, such as *Alauna, Clausentum, Corinium, Corstopitum, Venta, Verolamio, Vinovia*, are unsolved mysteries, and some of these may belong to a layer of place-names older than the use of Celtic speech in Britain. Unfortunately, the category of obscure names includes *Londinium*, modern London. This is often explained as 'place belonging to Londinos', from a supposed personal name meaning 'the wild one' and an adjectival ending; but this etymology is rejected in an emphatic footnote in Jackson 1953 (p. 308), and we have as yet nothing to put in its place. There are, however, a good number of place-names in these Romano-British sources for which experts in the British language are prepared to give a firm etymology. The safest ground in this difficult territory is that of the Antonine Itinerary, since Professor Jackson has recently provided comments on most of the names contained in it (Jackson 1970); and a rough analysis of those British names in the Itinerary which are amenable to etymology will be attempted in order to gain some idea of the types of place-name in use in Roman Britain.

There are 111 names in the British section of the Antonine Itinerary. All are stopping-places on roads, so that although some of them originated as river-names, they were all in use as settlement-names in the Roman period. Of these 111 names, there are 32 which Professor Jackson considers obscure (this is counting both instances of *Isca* and four instances of *Venta*). This leaves 79 names for which more or less firm etymologies are available. Twelve of these are Latin or partly Latin, and these have already been discussed, so there are 67 British names to be considered. These 67 intelligible British names can be divided into the following categories:

1. Topographical statements, a subdivision of this category being river-names which are used as settlement-names without the addition of a suffix: 34 names.
2. Names containing a word for a town or fort or other building construction: 18 names.
3. Names formed by the addition of a suffix to a personal name; there are 5 of these.
4. Names referring to an activity: 4 names.
5. Names not amenable to classification, of which there are 6.

The listing of all these 67 British place-names, in alphabetical order within the five categories, and the provision of fairly detailed notes on each one will take up a fair amount of space, and such treatment may seem out of proportion to the rest of this book. It is worth doing, however, because it is the first time this body of material has been studied in an attempt to ascertain what type of linguistic formation was felt to constitute a satisfactory place-name by the people of Roman Britain. In order to offer some conclusions about this it is necessary to have a corpus of names with reasonably firm etymologies which are firmly related to towns or forts in known topographical situations. In the article, Rivet and Jackson 1970, which is the basis of this analysis the identifications of the Romano-British place-names with towns and forts are the work of Professor Rivet, and the etymologies are the work of Professor Jackson. Correlating both parts of this work and trying to look with a fresh eye at the topography of each place is a relatively simple but time-consuming exercise, which the reader of this book cannot fairly be expected to do for himself; so it seems necessary to lay out this evidence in detail as the basis for some general conclusions about Romano-British place-names and the ways in which they differ from the Old English names by which most of them were replaced.

By far the largest category of British names in the Antonine Itinerary is that of place-names which consist of a topographical statement or a river-name. The following are considered to fall into this class:

Bremenio (the fort at High Rochester NTB). The stream here, now the Sills Burn, was probably called **Bremiā* 'roaring', and derivational suffixes were added to this to form a settlement-name.

Bremetonnaci (the fort at Ribchester LNC). The River Ribble was probably *Bremetona* 'roaring river', to which the adjectival suffix -*āco*- was added to make a settlement-name.

Brige (not precisely located, but occurring between Winchester and Old Sarum). Probably 'hills' from British *brigā*, but Professor Jackson comments that it is unusual for such a word to be used as a British place-name without the addition of a suffix. The Roman road runs over down-land.

Brocavo (the fort at Brougham WML). From the British word for a badger, which became Modern Welsh *broch*; this was one of the few British words to be borrowed by the Anglo-Saxons. A suffix has been added to give a meaning 'places of badgers'. The fort was beside the River Eamont.

Calleva (the Roman town at Silchester HMP). 'Place in the woods', formed by the addition of a suffix to the British word which is the ancestor of Modern Welsh *celli* 'grove'.

Camborico (not certainly located, but between Caistor St Edmunds, near Norwich, and Cambridge). Professor Jackson suggests emendation to *Camborito*, which would mean 'crooked ford'.

Canonio (Kelvedon ESX). Professor Jackson suggests a river-name *Cānonā*, 'reedy river', to which a suffix has been added to make a settlement-name. Kelvedon is on the River Blackwater, the British name of which was Pant (now restricted to part of the river), but the Domsey Brook, which joins the Blackwater near Kelvedon, could be the 'reedy river'.

Coccio (the Roman town at Wigan LNC). Formed from a British word meaning 'red' and a derivational suffix. No suggestion has been offered about what was red at Wigan.

Conbretovio (a Roman site at Baylham House SFK, north-west of Ipswich). Professor Jackson gives the etymology 'at the confluence', as if the name were identical in meaning with *Condate*. But Baylham is not situated at a confluence in the ordinary sense of the term. The River Gipping meanders here, and there may have been several channels, and the name refers to a coming together of these; or streams which now join the Gipping well to the north of Baylham may have flowed in here in earlier times.

Condate (near Northwich CHE). This name also means 'the confluence'; it is the origin of the surviving French place-names Condé, Condat, Condes. The site of the Romano-British settlement can only be deduced from the distances given from other towns, but it was probably in the township of Witton cum Twambrook, where a number of rivers—Dane, Weaver, Peover Eye and Wade Brook—flow together. The English name Twambrook means 'between the brooks'.

Eburacum (York). The survival of this name is discussed in the final section of this chapter. The meaning is probably 'yew grove', the name being formed by the addition of the adjectival suffix -*āco*- to the British word for a yew tree. It is possible that the suffix was added to a personal name **Eburos*, in which case York would belong in the third category into which these names are here sorted. Professor Jackson considers this less likely, but only on the grounds that this latter type of place-name is rare in Britain, though very common in Gaul.

Letoceto (the Roman town at Wall STF). The circumstances in which this became incorporated in the English name Lichfield are discussed in the final section of this chapter. The British name means 'grey wood', from two words which are the ancestors of Modern Welsh *llwyd* and *coed*. The same place-name has become Litchett HMP, Lytchett DOR, and there are a number of Cornish and Welsh instances. This may have been a compound appellative, describing a particular kind of wood.

Lindo (Lincoln). Discussed with Latin names at the beginning of the chapter.

Magnis (the Roman town near the village of Kenchester HRE, west of Hereford). Professor Jackson suggests 'the rocks', from a word which is the ancestor of modern Welsh *maen* 'stone'. There was another *Magnis* in Roman Britain, mentioned in other sources than the Antonine Itinerary, possibly to be located at Carvoran NTB, on Hadrian's Wall, where the topography is more dramatic than it is at Kenchester. The name may have been transferred to the Roman town in HRE from the adjacent hill-fort, on an abrupt hill overlooking the village of Credenhill; see the discussion of *Uriconium* later in this chapter for such a relationship between an Iron Age fort and a Roman town. The difficult problems posed by the apparent survival of *Magnis* in the modern name Maund are discussed in Chapter 4.

Mamucio (the Roman fort at Manchester LNC). Formed by the addition of suffixes to British *mammā* 'breast, breast-shaped hill'. One copy of the Antonine Itinerary has *Mancunio*, which is considered by modern scholars to be a corruption of *Mamucio*, but was at one time considered to be the correct form and so became the basis for the adjective *Mancunian*.

Mediolano (a Roman town at Whitchurch SHR). This name, which means 'central plain', is well-represented in Gaul, Milan being an example. The exact significance has not been established. Whitchurch lies in a flat region which is sufficiently raised to be a watershed between several major rivers.

Noviomago (a Roman town at Crayford KNT). This name means 'new field', from British words which are the ancestors of Modern Welsh *newydd* and *ma*. Chichester SSX was also called *Noviomago* in Romano-British times, and there are several examples in Gaul. In the Chichester instance, since no pre-Roman occupation is known, the name may have been coined in early Roman times. Newland is the equivalent English name. In the KNT example of *Noviomago* the reference may have been to land broken in from heath, like the adjacent Dartford and Bexley Heaths; at Chichester the reclamation would be from marsh.

Pennocrucio (the Roman town on Watling Street, south of Penkridge STF). Both elements of this name can mean 'hill', but when *penno-* (the ancestor of Modern Welsh *penn* 'head') occurs as a first element in a compound name of this date it is likely to mean 'chief, most important'. The second element, British *crouco-*, means 'hill, barrow, mound'. Professor Jackson gives the etymology 'chief mound' or 'hilly mound', which is inexplicable in terms of the modern topography. The crossroads by which *Pennocrucio* was situated is not on a hill. Here, Watling Street is descending a smooth, gentle slope from the high ground of Cannock Chase to the valley of the River Penk. It can only be suggested that there might have been a great tumulus called 'the chief mound' on the site of the town, of which no trace remains, or that the name was that of a large district and the mound lay elsewhere. The survival of *Pennocrucio* in the modern name Penkridge is discussed later in this chapter.

Rutunio (Professor Rivet locates this at Harcourt Mill, near Stanton upon Hine Heath SHR, on the River Roden). Formed by the addition of the *-io-* suffix to British *Rutunā*, perhaps 'swift flowing river', which has become Roden.

Segeloci (a Roman town at Littleborough NTT). Probably 'vigorous pool'.

The site is south of Gainsborough, where a Roman road crosses the River Trent, and the name may have referred to a pool in the river where there was a strong current.

Segontio (the Roman fort and settlement at Caernarvon). Formed with the -*io*- suffix from British *Segontī*, 'vigorous river', which has become the modern river-name Saint. The same first element is found in *Segeloci*.

Sitomagi (the position in Iter IX suggests a site near Dunwich SFK; the settlement has probably gone into the sea). The name means 'wide field', with the same second element as *Noviomago*.

Verteris (the Roman fort at Brough WML). Professor Jackson derives this from a British word meaning 'summit'. Possibly the name referred originally to the high moorland east of Brough.

Uxacona (the Roman fort and settlement at Red Hill SHR, between Wroxeter and Penkridge). Formed by the addition of suffixes to a base *uxo-, which means 'high'. Watling Street goes over the summit of an abrupt hill at this point.

The next list is of settlement-names adopted, without the addition of a suffix, from river-names. This category contains eleven items, and may be regarded as a subdivision of the large category of Romano-British place-names which consist of a topographical statement. Only names intelligible to the modern philologist are being considered here, as the point of the exercise is to form an idea of what was considered a satisfactory place-name in Romano-British times. For this reason the two instances of *Isca* are not included. It is well known that this river-name is the source of the Modern English and Scottish river-names Exe, Axe and Esk, but the difficulties of finding an etymology which accounts satisfactorily for them and for the Welsh River Usk are such that Professor Jackson concludes his discussion of *Isca* with the statement 'The question must be left open'. Similarly *Alone* (which occurs in several Romano-British names of towns and rivers and in the Welsh river-name Alun), *Isurium* and *Nido* (Neath GLA) have been omitted, because no firm etymology is available for them. The settlement-names of the British section of the Antonine Itinerary which were originally river-names, and for which an etymology is given by Professor Jackson are:

Abone (a Roman site at Sea Mills GLO). British *abonā*, Modern Welsh *afon*, 'river', whence the various Avon rivers, including the Bristol Avon, on which Sea Mills stands. If none of the examples of this name had been recorded in Roman sources, one might have suspected that the use of Avon as a river-name in many localities was due to a linguistic misunderstanding by the Anglo-Saxons; that is, they heard British-speaking people referring to 'the river', and did not realize that the word was a common noun, rather than a specific name. Since this instance is recorded from pre-English times, however, it must be accepted as a British river-name.

Conovio (the Roman fort at Caerhun CRN). The name of the River Conway. Other sources show that the Antonine Itinerary spelling is a mistake for *Can-*. The name means 'the reedy one' from **cāno-* 'reed' (Welsh *cawn*, found also in *Canonio supra*) and a suffix *-ouio-*.

Dano (the Roman fort at Doncaster YOW). The name of the River Don, from **dānu-* 'bold', probably 'rapid' in river-names. There is another River Don in DRH which is identical. The Continental names Danube and Rhone (the latter Celtic **Rodānus*) are related.

Derventione (the Roman fort and town at Malton YON). British **Deruentiū*, which Professor Jackson translates 'the river in the oak wood', whence English river-names Derwent, Darwen, Darent. Malton is on the Yorkshire Derwent.

Deva (the Roman fort and town at Chester). British **Dēuā* 'the Goddess', whence River Dee CHE, ABD, KCB.

Dubris (Dover KNT). One of the few Romano-British place-names to survive without the addition of Old English *ceaster*. The name, which occurs several times in England, means 'waters', and the plural of 'water' was probably felt to be a river-name, without implying that there was more than one stream at the place. Professor Jackson considers the British form to have been **Dubrās*. The derived Old English name *Dofras* is also plural, but this may have been because the English kept the *-as* of the British form, rather than because they knew the name was plural.

Galacum (Professor Rivet identifies this with Burrow in Lonsdale LNC, where there is a Roman fort at the junction of Leck Beck with the River Lune). Professor Jackson suggests derivation from British **galā* 'valour, vigour', with the *-āco-* adjectival suffix, to give a meaning 'vigorous stream'. *G-* may be an error for *C-*, however, in which case the name would mean 'noisy stream'. The reference must be to Leck Beck, which starts as a mountain stream.

Galava (the Roman fort and settlement south of Ambleside WML). From the same root as suggested for the preceding, with -*aᵤo*- suffix, the meaning being again 'vigorous stream'. A number of streams unite near Ambleside to flow into Windermere. The name *Galava* may have referred to the River Brathay, the modern name of which is Norse.

Lemanis (Lympne KNT). The river on which Lympne stands, the East Rother, was British **Leman(n)ā*, 'the river in the elm wood'. The fort-name is either a British plural, or a nominative singular form which the Romans took for a locative plural. The Anglo-Saxons called the river *Limen*, but the town *Liminas*, echoing the Latin plural. The development is closely parallel to that of Dover, and this name also survived without the addition of *ceaster*. There are a number of rivers in Britain with names from this stem, e.g. Leam NTP, Lemon DEV, Lymn LIN and Scottish Leven. Another example is Lac Leman in Switzerland.

Leucaro (where a Roman road crosses the River Loughor GLA). British **Leucarā*, 'bright river'. The modern river-name Loughor, Welsh Llychwr, is from a by-form of the Romano-British name.

Voreda (The Roman fort and settlement at Plumpton Wall CMB). Professor Jackson suggests a river-name **Ṿorēdā*, 'horse-stream'. This may have been the name of a tributary of the River Petteril.

The next largest class of intelligible names in the British section of the Antonine Itinerary comprises the eighteen items which incorporate a word for a building. The term 'building' is used very loosely here, and names referring to bridges and earth ramparts are included in this category, as well as the names in -*duno* and *Duro*-. These eighteen names are:

Camboduno (possibly near Dewsbury YOE). The first element is British **cambo*- 'crooked, curved' (Welsh *cam*) and the second is British **dūnon* 'fort' (Welsh *din*). The name occurs also in the Roman province of *Raetia*.

Camoloduno (Colchester ESX). 'Fort of Camulos', the latter being a war-god. There was another *Camulodunum*, named in Ptolemy and in the Ravenna Cosmography, which is tentatively located at Slack near Huddersfield YOW. The ESX *Camulodunum* was the capital of the British king

Cunobelinus, whose sons were defeated by the Roman invasion of AD 43. The Emperor Claudius received the submission of many British tribes here, and a new Roman city was built which kept the name of the old capital. The element **dūnon* in the British name may have seemed appropriate because of the linear earthworks west of the town, possibly built to defend the approach which was not protected by Roman River and the River Colne.

Durobrivis (Rochester KNT). The second element is the plural of British **brīu̯ā* 'bridge', presumably referring to the crossing of the River Medway. The first is **duro-*, described by Professor Jackson (1970, p. 72) as 'a common British and Gaulish place-name formant which appears to mean 'walled town, enclosed town with gateways', as distinct from 'fortress' proper, which is **dūno-*'. This word is well-represented in Romano-British place-names. It occurs in eight British names in the Antonine Itinerary, and in all but one (*Lactodoro*) it is the first element. This manner of forming a compound, by putting the main word first and the defining element second, which became normal in Welsh names during the fifth century AD, is not otherwise found among the British place-names recorded from Roman Britain. In other provinces, where **duro-* also occurs in names in the Itinerary, it is sometimes the first element (as in *Durocatalaunus*, modern Chalons-sur-Marne), but it is used as a second element much more often than in Britain. Professor Jackson comments that Gaulish *Brivodurum* is the same name as *Durobrivis* with the elements the other way round. This anomalous characteristic of British names in **duro-* is discussed later in this chapter. Another problem posed by these names is that in a number of the towns to which they refer the walls were not built until the late second century or after, though *Duroverno* (*infra*) was known by that name to Ptolemy *c*. AD 150, and it is probable that all the names are earlier than the Roman town defences. In an attempt to overcome this difficulty it has been suggested (Frere and Rivet 1971) that the *duro-* names were transferred to the towns from neighbouring comparatively short-lived forts of the early Roman period. The use of this term in Roman town-names is not fully understood, but as Frere and Rivet point out if the reference were to native earthworks one might have expected a name in *-dūnon*.

Durobrivis (the walled Roman town on Ermine Street, between Water Newton and Chesterton HNT). The same name as the preceding, the second element in this instance referring to the crossing of the River Nene.

Durocobrivis (a Roman town on the site of Dunstable BDF). Professor

Jackson rejects an etymology 'walled town of the joined bridges' partly on the grounds that Dunstable is not on a river. Watling Street does, however, cross two small streams north-west of the high ground on which Dunstable stands; the road is embanked here with material cut from the chalk to ease the gradient down to the lower ground (Margary 1955, 157), so from the topographical point of view 'walled town of the joined bridges' seems highly appropriate. More serious is Professor Jackson's other objection that this etymology demands *Durocombrĭu̯ās* not *Durocobrĭu̯ās*. Emendation of the form in the Itinerary would be necessary to make sense of this name.

Durocornovio (a Roman settlement near Wanborough WLT, east of Swindon). Apparently 'walled town of the Cornovii'. The territory of the tribe called *Cornovii* was in Shropshire, but a detached group could have been referred to in a place-name elsewhere. *Durocornovio* is cited in a number of reference books as a form for Cirencester GLO. Professor Rivet gives the location cited above, however, and it will simplify the complicated linguistic history of Cirencester if this form is eliminated.

Durolevo (an unlocated site between Sittingbourne and Faversham KNT). No suggestion is available about the second element.

Duroliponte (the walled Roman town at Cambridge). Professor Jackson suggests that the second element is a river-name *U̯lipontī* 'wet river', perhaps meaning 'overflowing, boggy river'. This would be an excellent name for the River Cam.

Durolito (Rodwell 1975, p. 86, locates this at Chigwell ESX). The second element may be *ritu-* 'ford', with dissimilation of *r-r* to *r-l*.

Duroverno (the walled Roman town at Canterbury KNT). 'Walled town by the alder swamp', second element *u̯erno-* (Welsh *gwern*). The Romano-British name remained in learned use till the end of the ninth century AD.

Lactodoro (the walled Roman town at Towcester NTP). This differs from the eight preceding names in having the defining element first, as is normal in Romano-British names except for those in *duro-*. Professor Jackson suggests 'walled town of the dairymen', with British *lacto-* 'milk' (Welsh *llaeth*) as first element.

Lavatris (the Roman fort at Bowes YON). The plural of British *lau̯atro-*

'water-trough, tub, bath'. Professor Jackson suggests that the name refers to a Roman bath-house, but this would not be a distinctive feature, as all forts had them. Perhaps there were water-troughs here before the fort was built.

Margiduno (the Roman walled town and fort at Castle Hill NTT, on the Foss Way east of Nottingham). Probably 'marly fort', referring to an earthwork made from marly soil.

Muriduno (Carmarthen). 'Sea fort', referring to the situation at the head of the estuary of the River Tywi.

Ratas, Ratis (the Roman cantonal capital at Leicester). British **rātis* 'earthen rampart, fortification'. This is not an appropriate name for the great town at Leicester, but it may have been transferred from an earlier tribal capital in an Iron Age fortification. The village of Ratby, west of Leicester, possibly has as first element the Romano-British name, and this may refer to the fort called Bury Camp, which lies in the parish of Ratby. If this is a pre-Roman site, the tribal capital and the name could have been moved from here to the site by the River Soar. This would be a parallel to the sequence of events postulated for *Uriconio*.

Sorvioduni (the Romano-British settlement at Old Sarum, the prehistoric hill-fort near Salisbury WLT). The first element is unexplained, but **dūnon* refers to the fort. The manner in which this name was adapted by the Anglo-Saxons is discussed later in the chapter.

Tripontio (the Romano-British settlement at Caves Inn near Rugby WAR). 'Three bridges'. Watling Street crosses a tributary of the River Avon.

Vindocladia (the Romano-British settlement at Badbury Rings, the prehistoric hill-fort between Blandford Forum and Wimborne Minster DOR). Professor Jackson translates this 'the town with the white ditches', and it is clearly a reference to the chalk of which the great fort is constructed.

A much smaller category of place-names in the British section of the Antonine Itinerary comprises those in which a suffix has been added to a personal name, giving a meaning 'estate belonging to x'. These names, which make use of several suffixes, are particularly well evidenced in France with Latin personal names as a base. For instance, *Albiniacum* from the Latin name *Albinius* gives modern Albigny, Arbigny, Aubigné,

Aubigny, and *Maximiacum* from *Maximius* gives Maissemy, Marsagnis, Marsagny, Massagnis, Massigny, Maymac, Messemé, Messimy, Meximieu. Formations of this type based on Celtic personal names are rare in France, however, as they were in Britain, and the contrast between the two countries lies in the absence in Britian of estate-names which have a Latin personal name as base.

The five British place-names in the Itinerary which consist of a Celtic personal name and a place-name-forming suffix are:

Blestio (a Romano-British settlement at Monmouth). Possibly from *Blestus*, which is recorded as a Gaulish personal name, and the *-io-* derivational suffix.

Burrio (the Roman fort at Usk MON). From a personal name **Burros*, 'sturdy', and the *-i̯o-* suffix.

Luguvalio (Carlisle CMB). From a personal name **Luguu̯alos* ('strong as the god Lugus') and *-i̯o-*. The survival of the Romano-British name is discussed later in this chapter.

Sulloniacis (the important Romano-British settlement at Brockley Hill HRT, on Watling Street, south of Elstree). 'Estate of Sullonios', from a personal name and the *-āco-* suffix which is common in France. *Eburacum* and *Brovonacis* may be names of this type though they have been tentatively classified in other categories.

Uriconio (the Roman cantonal capital at Wroxeter SHR). Professor Jackson considers it possible that this is 'town of Virico', the latter being a recorded Gaulish name. The survival of *Uriconio* in The Wrekin and Wroxeter is discussed later. It is noteworthy that four of these five place-names are in the west of Britain, though *Sulloniacis* is in the east.

A still smaller group of names in the British section of the Itinerary consists of the four which refer to an industrial or agricultural activity. These are:

Bovio (between Chester and Whitchurch, tentatively located at Holt DEN, where Roman remains are known). Professor Jackson suggests 'cow place', from British **bou̯-* with *-i̯o-* derivational suffix.

Bravonio (the important Romano-British settlement at Leintwardine HRE).

Probably 'quern place' from **braṇon-* 'quern' (Welsh *breuan*). Possibly quern stones were obtained from the hills east of the town.

Brovonacis (the Roman fort at Burwens in Kirkby Thore WML). Professor Jackson considers *Brov-* to be a mistake for *Brav-*. Possibly 'quern place', from the same root as preceding with *-āco-* suffix. But a personal name **Brāṇonịos*, 'quern man', is possible, in which case the place-name belongs in the same category as *Sulloniacis*.

Gobannio (Abergavenny MON). From British **gobann-* 'blacksmith' and *-ịo-*. There are Roman iron-workings in the neighbourhood. The name survived as that of the River Gafenni, at the mouth of which (Welsh *aber*) the town stands.

Finally, notes may be added on six names from the British section of the Itinerary which do not fit into any of the categories recognized above. These are:

Blatobulgio (the Roman fort at Birrens, between Ecclefechan and Eaglesfield DMF). The *-ịo-* suffix has been added to a compound which could mean either 'flowery hollow' or 'flour sack', and Professor Jackson suggests that the latter might refer to large and well-stocked granaries. Surviving Scottish names which appear to have the same origin are Blebo FIF, Blelack in Cromer ABD, and Blelock in Auchtergaven PER (Barrow 1973, p. 59).

Delgovicia (tentatively located near Millington ERY, north-east of Pocklington). Professor Jackson suggests a place-name formed with the *-ịo-* suffix from a tribal name **Delgoṇices*, which might mean 'spear-fighters'.

Manduessedo (Mancetter WAR). This name appears to mean 'horse chariot'. The survival of the first syllable in the English name Mancetter is discussed later in this chapter.

Regno (the Roman cantonal capital at Chichester SSX, called *Noviomagus* by Ptolemy, and *Navimago Regentium* in the Ravenna Cosmography). The tribe whose capital this town became were called *Regnoi* by Ptolemy. Assuming that *Regno* is an alternative name to *Noviomagus*, this appears to be an instance of a tribe-name used as a settlement-name. Professor Jackson considers that the tribe-name was British **Reginī* 'the proud ones, the stiff ones', which would be similar in meaning to the tribal name *Belgae*, from **belg-* 'to swell up'. He rejects the suggestion that the town-name is Latin *regnum* 'the kingdom'. It is not clear why the Ravenna Cosmography has *Regentium* where something like **Regnorum* might have been expected.

Verlucione (the Romano-British settlement at the hamlet of Sandy Lane WLT on the Roman road from Bath to Mildenhall, east of Lacock). Professor Jackson suggests derivation from **leuk-* 'light', with prepositional prefix **u̯er-* 'over, super-' and *-i̯on* suffix, giving a meaning 'very bright town'.

Vernemeto (a Romano-British settlement on the Foss Way, near Willoughby on the Wolds on the LEI/NTT border). 'Great sacred grove', a compound of **nemeto-* and **u̯er-*.

There is no reason why the sixty-seven British names discussed above should be other than typical of those place-names in Roman Britain which referred to the more important settlements. They provide a good deal of positive evidence for the types of place-name in use in the province. They also provide significant negative evidence, as some of the categories of place-name most typical of Anglo-Saxon England and of modern Wales are absent from the Antonine Itinerary and from other Romano-British sources.

One characteristic which emerges very clearly from a study of the intelligible British names of the Itinerary is the predominance of the type of settlement-name which consists of a topographical statement. Many of the names in this category are derived from rivers, and some of the river-names used have been made into settlement-names by the addition of a place-name-forming suffix, while others are used without any addition or modification. Uncompounded topographical terms other than river-names were generally felt to need a suffix if used as settlement-names, but there are exceptions, such as *Brige* and *Magnis*. Compound names for topographical features, such as *Letoceto*, *Mediolano*, *Noviomago*, were regularly used as settlement-names without a suffix. The use of place-name-forming suffixes with uncompounded elements and with some river-names is another notable characteristic of Romano-British place-names.

Apart from bridges and a possible water-trough (*Lavatris*), the only building-works referred to in the British names of the Itinerary are those of an outstanding nature, such as the great defensive earthworks of the pre-Roman period, and the walled sites thought to be designated by *duro-*.

There is no category of Romano-British place-names corresponding to the later English type for which the term 'habitative' has been coined (see Chapter 5). In fact, one of the most striking negative characteristics of these names is the absence of any word for an unfortified Romano-British village or farmstead. It may be that such places are not very likely to occur in our sources from Roman Britain, but it is probable that there was sometimes an accidental conjunction between a humble British habitation-site and a Roman station or fort. English place-names provide many examples of places of major importance (such as Berwick-on-Tweed) whose names indicate a much humbler beginning. This negative characteristic does not apply only to the Antonine Itinerary. A search through all the other place-names recorded from Roman Britain has failed to find any reliable evidence of a word equivalent to Welsh *tref*, Cornish *chy*, or any of the common Old English habitative terms such as *hām, tūn, worð*. It seems reasonable to conclude that if habitative place-names referring to ordinary settlements had been in use in Roman Britain a few specimens would have appeared in the records.

The evidence from Roman Britain suggests that the normal settlement-names of the province consisted of the following types:

1. A British topographical term with a place-name-forming suffix, e.g. *Calleva*.
2. An adjective with a suffix, e.g. *Coccio*.
3. A river-name with or without a suffix, e.g. *Rutunio, Deva*.
4. A compound name for a topographical feature, e.g. *Letoceto*.

Personal names are rare in Romano-British place-names, and this negative characteristic is strikingly in contrast with the nature of later Welsh and English place-names, and with contemporary Gaulish ones. Some of the place-names in the Ravenna Cosmography (e.g. *Branogenium*, and *Durcinate* if emended to *Curcinate*) may belong in the category, but the place-name type in which a suffix is added to a man's name to give a meaning 'estate of x' is certainly rare in our sources from Roman Britain, and no instances have been noted in which Latin personal names are used as the base for such place-names.

Another outstanding characteristic of the place-names of Roman Britain is that in a compound name the defining element normally comes first—as in *Letoceto* 'grey wood', *Mediolano* 'central plain', *Noviomago* 'new field'. Among wholly British place-names the major exception to this rule is constituted by the group of names in *Duro-*. It is noteworthy, however, that most of the compound Latin or partly Latin names known from the province—*Aquae Arnemetiae, Aquae Sulis, Castra Exploratorum,*

Fanococidi, Horrea Classis, Pons Aelius, Villa Faustini—have the noun first and the defining element second. This suggests that the anomalous placing of *duro-* in most British names in which it occurs may reflect a Latin manner of forming place-names. The *duro-* names which can be firmly located refer to major towns, where influence from Latin would be at its strongest.

The order of elements—descriptive word first, defined object second—which is usual in British place-names recorded from Roman Britain is an important characteristic, as it may be a way of differentiating older names from those coined (or perhaps in some cases remodelled) after the Roman period. The change from this order to the one usual in modern Celtic languages—defined object first, defining element second—is said (Jackson 1953, pp. 225–7) to have happened not later than the sixth century AD, on the grounds that the later type of compound name is ás common in Brittany as it is in Wales and Cornwall, which indicates that such names must have been prominent at the time of the British emigrations to Brittany. The question of the order of elements in a compound place-name is a difficult and complicated one. Discussions in recent years at conferences of the Council for Name Studies in Great Britain and Ireland (which some readers of this book may recall vividly) have brought out the difficulties and dangers of the subject without providing any clear guide-lines. The Romano-British material, some of which is set out above, clearly suggests that the great majority of the compound place-names in use before and during the Roman period are likely to have been the 'older' type of compound, and it seems to follow that place-names which are formed in the opposite manner may be expected to date from the sixth century or later, or at least to have been re-modelled in accordance with the new fashion. Welsh and Irish scholars will probably regard this as an over-simplification of a subtle and complicated linguistic problem, but the fact remains that we can only suppose the 'later' type of compound to have been common in Roman Britain if we assume that the place-names used by the British population in speech differed from those written down in the Roman road-books. The present writer, while humbly aware of having failed to comprehend the subtleties of argument which Celtic experts bring to this problem, feels justified in clinging to the general probability that compound names formed in the modern Welsh manner, like Denbigh 'fort small' and Trefriw 'farm hill', were coined later than the Roman period, and that those like Malvern WOR in which the adjective comes first, are probably as old as the Roman period even when they are not recorded till the eleventh century or later. This subject is discussed further in Chapter 4.

The final subject to be considered in connection with the recorded place-names of Roman Britain is that of their survival or disappearance. An important study of this (Hogg 1964) was published some years ago, but has received less attention from philologists than it merits, perhaps because it appeared in an archaeological journal. Mr Hogg has kindly agreed to the use of his study here, and to the reproduction, slightly emended, of his map (Fig. 1).

In Hogg 1964 the settlement-names of Roman Britain are shown to have undergone one of four possible processes:

1. The Roman name has fallen completely out of use.
2. Some element of the Roman name survives, combined with Welsh Caer- or English -chester, or another English or Welsh word.
3. The Roman name survives little altered, as in Penkridge STF and Speen BRK.
4. A Roman settlement-name survives as that of a district, but is either not applied to a settlement (as in Archenfield HRE, from *Ariconio*), or is applied to a settlement quite distinct from the Roman one (as probably in Maund HRE, from *Magnis*, see Chapter 4).

Mr Hogg's study embraces all the place-names recorded from Roman Britain south of Hadrian's Wall, which is a much larger body of material than the small selection of intelligible names from the Antonine Itinerary which are set out in the first half of this chapter.

The first category, that of the lost Romano-British names, is by far the largest. These are shown on the map by the symbols + and — according to whether their exact position is known or not. These lost names are too numerous to be listed here. If Romano-British names did survive, they were most frequently combined with Welsh *caer*, or with an English word. Names to which this happened are shown by the symbol ● on the map, and they are listed in alphabetical order below. The criterion for inclusion in this category is that a Romano-British name should have survived into the post-Roman period, so this list (and the following one) contain some names, like *Concangium* and *Anderita*, which do not survive today. Some of the sources in which the Romano-British names occur are indicated by Pt (Ptolemy), A (Antonine Itinerary), ND (Notitia Dignitatum) and R (Ravenna Cosmography).

The Romano-British settlement-names in the area south of Hadrian's Wall which survived as part of a later place-name are:

Alauna (R): Alchester in the parish of Wendlebury OXF.
Branodunum (ND): possibly Brancaster NFK.

Brocavo (A): Brougham WML (see below).

Concangium (ND, R): Chester le Street DRH (*Cuncaceastre, Cunceceastre c.* 1050).

Corinium (Pt, R): Cirencester GLO (see below).

Corstopitum (A, R): Corbridge NTB.

Dano (A, ND): Doncaster YOW.

Durnovaria (A): Dorchester DOR (see below).

Durobrivis (A, R): Rochester KNT (see below).

Glevo (A, R): Gloucester (see below).

Gobannio (A, R): Abergavenny MON.

Isca (Pt, A, R): Exeter DEV.

Letoceto (A, R): Lichfield STF (see below).

Longovicio (ND, R): Lanchester DRH.

Luguvalio (A, R): Carlisle CMB.

Mamucio (A, R): Manchester LNC.

Manduessedo (A): Mancetter WAR.

Muriduno (Pt, A): Carmarthen.

Othona (ND): the Roman fort at Bradwell on Sea ESX, called *Ythancæstir* by Bede.

Ritupis (Pt, A, ND, R): Richborough KNT (see below).

Segontio (A, R): Caernarvon (*Caer Segeint* ninth century, *Kaer Seint yn Aruon* fourteenth century).

Sorvioduni (A): Salisbury WLT (see below).

Uriconio (Pt, A, R): Wroxeter SHR (see below).

Venta (Pt, A, ND, R): Winchester HMP.

Venta (A, R): Caerwent MON, also the Welsh kingdom of Gwent.

When a Romano-British settlement-name survives as part of an English name it might appear at first sight that the commonest treatment is the use of the first one or two syllables of the British name as the first part of the Old English compound. When we have Old English (as opposed to post 1066) forms for the English names, however, it can sometimes be seen that both elements of a compound British name were originally used. Thus Dorchester is Old English *Dornwaraceaster*, and Lichfield is Old English *Liccidfeld*, but these names have been shortened to *Dorecestre* and *Lichefelle, Lecefelle* by the time of the Domesday Survey, Other names, such as Brancaster, Corbridge, Lanchester, Manchester, Mancetter and Wroxeter, may have incorporated more of the Romano-British name when they were first coined, but have suffered shortening by the time they are first recorded. There are pre-Conquest spellings for Brancaster, Corbridge and Manchester, but these are from *c.* 960, *c.* 1050 and 923, by which dates shorten-

ing could have occurred. The Old English forms cited above for Dorchester and Lichfield are earlier than this. Short Romano-British names,
such as *Alauna, Dano, Isca, Venta*, were carefully preserved in Alchester
(*Alencestr' c.* 1160), Doncaster, Exeter (Old English *Escanceaster*), and
Winchester (Old English *Wintanceaster*).

In some instances, although there is little doubt that the first element of
an English name is based on a Romano-British name, the phonological
processes do not conform to those which can be shown to have been
normal. The transformation of *Corinium* into the first part of Cirencester
has never been fully explained. Sometimes these phonological irregu-
larities are believed to be due to the substitution of an Old English word
which resembles the British place-name. This explanation is the one
usually put forward for Gloucester and Salisbury. Gloucester is Old
English *Gleawa(n)ceaster*. The first part of the name, *Gleawa-*, cannot be
derived by regular phonological processes from Romano-British *Glev-*, and
it is suggested that the English substituted their own word *glēaw*, 'wise,
prudent', for the unintelligible British name. Later spellings on coins show
that a form *Gleow-* was current before the middle of the eleventh century,
and this gave Middle English *Glow-*, from which the modern form derives.
It may be that the Welsh form of the name, recorded as *Cair Gloiv c.* 800,
influenced Old English *Gleawanceaster* and caused *Gleoweceaster* to be
substituted. The history of the name presents formidable difficulties, but
no one doubts that the first element is based on the Romano-British name.
The relationship of *Searobyrg*, the Old English form of Salisbury, to
Romano-British *Sorvioduni* has been explained as another example of the
substitution of an intelligible Old English word bearing a rough resemblance to the form of the British name. In this instance the substituted
word is believed to be Old English *searu* 'trick'. The final element, *byrig*,
is the normal Old English word for a hill-fort (this is discussed in Chapter
6), and Salisbury appears to be one of the very rare instances of a British
name for a hill-fort surviving in, or at least determining the form of, an
Old English place-name. The interchange of *-l-* and *-r-* is due to later
French influence (see Chapter 1).

Further instances of this rationalizing substitution of Old English words
for British names are Speen and York, discussed below. A more doubtful
instance is Brougham, which has been included in the above list on the
grounds that its first element may bear some relationship to the Romano-
British name *Brocavo*, though orthodox opinion maintains that there is no
philological connection between them. The English name appears to be
from *burh* 'fort' (referring to the remains of the Roman camp (see Chapter
6) and *hām* 'village'. Both these are rare elements in Westmorland, and in

this name *burh* shows the very unusual feature of early metathesis to *bruh*, the earliest spellings being *Bruham* 1130, *Broham* 1176. It is conceivable that *burh* was in this instance a rationalizing substitution for the *Broc-* of the British name, and that a lingering knowledge of the old name caused the metathesis to *Bru-*.

Some comment is required on the derivation of the first elements of Richborough and Rochester from Romano-British *Ritupis* and *Durobrivis*. Richborough is called *Reptacæstir* in Bede's Ecclesiastical History (c. 730), *Raette* in an eleventh-century source, *Ratteburg'* in 1197, *Retesbrough* in the fourteenth century. Bede's spelling shows metathesis of the *t-p* of *Ritupis* to *pt*, and this *pt* was later assimilated to *tt*. Bede refers to the place as 'the city called Rutubi Portus which the English now corruptly call Reptacæstir'; but the subsequent history of the name suggests that the colloquial form known to Bede was **Repta*, and he added *-cæstir* because the name seemed incomplete without it to his learned perception. The names of the other three Saxon Shore forts in Kent (Dover, Lympne and Reculver) have survived without the addition of -chester, and it might have been expected that *Ritupis* would have been in the same category. The addition of -borough to Richborough in the medieval period has not been explained, but the change from *Rat-* or *Ret-* to Rich-, which appears to have taken place *c.* 1500, may have been due to a desire to avoid association with the word *rat*.

The Venerable Bede refers to Rochester as 'the city of Durobrevis which the English call Hrofæscæstræ, after one of their former chiefs whose name was Hrof'. This eighth-century etymology is rejected by Ekwall 1960, in favour of a complicated argument by which *Hrofæs-* is held to be a version of the Romano-British *Durobrivis*. It is suggested that *Durobrivis* became **Rofri* in Old English, that this became **Hrofri* by association with Old English *hrōf* 'roof', the second *-r-* was lost by dissimilation, and *ceaster* was then added to the genitive of the name **Hrofi*. This argument uses more ingenuity than is usually required to equate an Old English name with a Romano-British one, and it is not certain to be correct. On the other hand, there is no independent record of a personal name *Hrof*, and Old English sources do sometimes adduce imaginary chieftains to account for place-names (see the discussion of Portsmouth in Chapter 3). A possibility which does not appear to have been considered is that the first element is actually the word *hrōf* 'roof', the name meaning 'Roman town of the roof' with reference to some building which was in a better-than-average state of preservation in the early Anglo-Saxon period. If this suggestion were taken seriously, Rochester would be removed from the category of Romano-British names which survived in part.

Another problem sometimes posed by the survival of Romano-British names in English ones is that the English name may refer to a settlement at some distance from the Roman one. The development of the first element of Lichfield from *Letoceto*, via Old English *Liccidfeld* does not present any really difficult phonological problems, but what has to be explained in this instance is the apparent transference of the name from Wall on Watling Street to Lichfield, two miles north. One possible explanation is that the Romano-British name survived in its original capacity as a forest-name (the meaning is 'grey wood'), and that this applied to an area of woodland stretching from Wall to Lichfield. Another possibility is that *Letoceto* was already the name of a large estate, perhaps with an as yet undiscovered pre-Roman habitation centre, when the Roman fort was built on Watling Street, and that the fort was always on the edge of the district to which the name belonged. The position of Penkridge in relation to *Pennocrucio* is a parallel phenomenon.

A similar problem arises in connection with Wroxeter. There is no doubt that the first element is Romano-British *Uriconio*; what is open to discussion is the relationship to Wroxeter of the hill-name Wrekin, also derived from the Romano-British name. Ekwall 1960 asserted that the name was transferred from the Roman cantonal capital to the hill. It seems more likely, however, that *Uriconio* was originally the name of the hill, perhaps more specifically of the hill-fort which crowns it, and that the name was transferred to the new tribal capital built by the Romans without ceasing to be the name of the hill. A similar sequence of events is postulated more tentatively for *Ratis*, discussed above.

The third of Mr Hogg's categories, that of Romano-British place-names which survived little altered into the Old English period, is a small but particularly important group comprising the following items:

Anderita (ND, R): the Roman fort at Pevensey ssx, referred to as *Andredesceaster* in the Anglo-Saxon Chronicle. The same source calls The Weald *Andredeslea* 'wood of Andred', which suggests that *Andred* survived as a name without the addition of an English word.

Cataractoni (Pt, A, R): Catterick YON, discussed at the beginning of this chapter.

Dubris (A, ND, R): Dover KNT.

Eburaco (Pt, A, R): York YOE (see below).

Lemanis (A, ND, R): Lympne KNT.

Lindum Colonia (Pt, A, R): Lincoln, discussed at the beginning of this chapter.

Londinio (Pt, A, R): London.

Nido (A): Neath GLA.
Pennocrucio (A): Penkridge STF (see below).
Regulbium (ND): Reculver KNT (see below).
Spinis (A): Speen BRK (see above, and below).

Some comment is required on the manner of survival of three of these eleven names. Speen and York are examples of the process of rationalizing substitution, and Penkridge, like Lichfield, is an example of a Romano-British name which has moved two miles from the Roman settlement.

Speen cannot be derived directly from Latin *Spinis*, as that would have become **Spine*. Speen is from an Old English word **spēne* which means 'place where wood-chippings are left' or 'place where shingles are made'. There is no other place-name derived from this word, though *spōn* 'wood-chipping' is well evidenced. It does not seem likely that coincidence should have produced a unique place-name *Spene* in the vicinity of a Romano-British settlement called *Spinis*; so it is assumed that *Spene* was substituted for the Latin name because it seemed appropriate to the woodland setting of the place.

York is recorded as *Eforwicceaster c*. 893, *Eoforwic c*. 1060. This can be translated 'boar farm', from Old English *eofor* and *wīc*, and it would seem a sensible place-name in its own right; but no one doubts that it is an adaptation of *Evorōg*, which would be the form of the British place-name *Eburaco* known to Germanic mercenaries at the end of the Roman period. It is possible that Germanic mercenaries were accustomed to hearing the civilian settlement outside the military fort referred to as 'the *vicus*', and this influenced the development to -*wic*.

Penkridge is two miles north of Watling Street, on which the Romano-British settlement of *Pennocrucio* was situated. Stenton 1939 pointed to the use of the name *Penchrich* for the River Penk in a tenth-century charter, and concluded that the name was transferred from the Roman settlement to the river, and then became attached to an English settlement further down the stream, which had no connection with the Roman place. He points to the inappropriate nature of a name meaning 'hill-summit' for the modern Penkridge, but as shown above there is nothing on the relevant stretch of Watling Street which merits this description, and the place-name is not more appropriate to the Romano-British site than it is to the modern one. It is possible that there was a large pre-Roman estate here, and that the name applied to the whole area. Stenton's discussion takes no account of the fact that Penkridge (like Lichfield) was a great multiple estate in 1086, and is still one of the largest parishes in Staffordshire. The river-name seems more likely to be derived from the settlement-name (what is technically known as a back-formation) than the other way round, or the river may have been called *Penchrich* because it flowed through a large area known by that name.

The problem of whether place-names like Penkridge and Lichfield bear a direct relationship to the Romano-British settlements whose names they preserve is a very difficult one. It has been said as part of the case against continuity that 'no place-name supplies a certain instance of a British habitation name' (Whitelock 1952, p. 18), and Stenton 1939 draws attention to the 'monotonous succession of (British) names referring to obvious features of the countryside' and to the absence among British names adopted by the English of 'unmistakable habitation names' and of 'names illustrating the possession of land by persons or tribes'. Stenton considered that the absence of these except in the far south-west of England 'is a very serious obstacle to the belief that the place-names which have survived from Roman Britain reflect the continuous life of an organized Romano-British society'. But these observations are based on the assumption that British settlement-names resembled Old English ones, and this is unsound. The analysis of names in the Antonine Itinerary has shown that British settlement-names did not normally contain habitative words, and that personal names and tribe-names occur very rarely. *Pennocrucio* and *Letoceto* are settlement-names as these were understood in Roman Britain. It is not certain that the first settlements they referred to were the stations on Watling Street; these may have used the names in somewhat the same way as some modern railway stations are named from villages several miles away. It is possible that before the Romans came to Britain there were large estates known as *Pennocrucio* and *Letoceto* whose main habitation centres might have lain anywhere in the areas of the great composite estates of Penkridge and Lichfield described in the Domesday Survey in 1086.

The distance between the modern village or town and the Roman station does not disprove the continuous use of the British name for a habitation site. But because of the nature of Romano-British settlement-names it will never be possible to prove that a survival was that of a settlement-name rather than that of the topographical feature which gave rise to it. A devil's advocate can argue that Doncaster means 'Roman ruin on the River Don' rather than 'Roman town called *Dano*', and that Wroxeter means 'Roman ruin near the Wrekin' rather than 'Roman town called *Uriconio*'. Circumstantial evidence for continuity might be accumulated by studying the historical status of estates which preserve Romano-British names, to see how many of them were as important as Penkridge and Lichfield at the time of the Domesday Survey. More is said in Chapter 8 of the recent work aimed at demonstrating the probable continuity of some large estates from prehistoric to Anglo-Saxon times.

Some Romano-British names are represented on Fig. 1 by the symbol o to indicate that their survival is possible but doubtful. These are:

Calleva (Pt, A, R): Ekwall 1960 suggests that the first element of Silchester HMP is based on the British name.

Duroverno (Pt, A, R): the Romano-British name of Canterbury KNT was used until the end of the ninth century by learned Anglo-Saxon authors, but it is not certain that it survived in colloquial use.

Isca (A, R): the Roman fort at Caerleon MON was named from the river, now the Usk, but, although the river-name survived, there seems to be no record of its use for the Roman site after the Roman period.

Leucarum (A): the modern River Loughor GLA is not directly from the Romano-British name.

Nemetostatio (R): *Nymed* appears to have been a district-name in DEV, now surviving in various settlements called Nymet, but more work is needed on the application of this and its possible relationship to the Romano-British settlement-name. The first part of *Nemetostatio* probably means 'sacred wood' and *Nymed* may have survived as the name of a forest.

Olicana (Pt, R): the objections to equating this name with Ilkley YOW are set out in Gelling 1970.

The number of recorded Romano-British settlement-names which remained in use after the Roman period is probably between thirty-five and forty, which is not a very large proportion of the whole, but is by no means a negligible body of material. Mr Hogg pointed out in 1964 that some interest attaches to the distribution pattern of the surviving names, and although some alterations have been made to his map the general pattern which he observed is not seriously affected. Zones in which there seems to be a relatively high incidence of survival are indicated on Fig. 1 by dotted lines.

One point which emerges from the map is that among the known names of Roman Britain the survival rate is at least as good, and probably rather better, in the east than in the west. The most striking group is that which follows the south-east coast and the River Thames, and which includes the

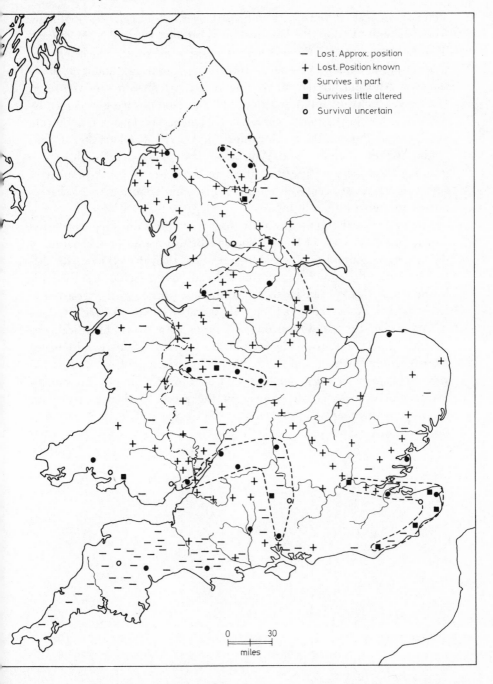

Fig. 1   The survival of Romano-British place-names in southern Britain (from Hogg 1964, lightly amended)

Roman sites at Pevensey, Lympne, Dover, Reculver, Richborough, Rochester and London (Rochester is not as certain a survival as the others). Two more clusters are the one near the north-east coast, which includes Catterick, Lanchester, Chester-le-Street and Corbridge and that along the west Midland stretch of Watling Street, which contains Wroxeter, Penkridge, Lichfield and Mancetter. Two other groups were discerned by Mr Hogg, one in the north, comprising Manchester, Doncaster, Lincoln and York, and one in the south comprising Caerwent, Gloucester, Cirencester, Alchester, Speen and Winchester; but the names in these two groupings are more diffuse than those in the other three. A number of surviving names are relatively isolated, this being a more marked characteristic in the west than in the east.

From this distribution pattern Mr Hogg drew the interesting conclusion that if loss or survival of known Romano-British names be a criterion of disruption or continuity of social organization, then the evidence for disturbance after the end of Roman rule is greater in the Celtic west than it is in the Anglo-Saxon east. He ascribed this disturbance in the west tentatively to the influx of refugees from areas threatened by Germanic invaders.

The evidence may not be strong enough to support firm historical conclusions; but the remarkably high degree of loss of known Romano-British settlement-names in the south-west peninsula, Wales, and north-west England, which was demonstrated for the first time by Mr Hogg's map, deserves note as an element in the puzzle. Other evidence for extensive re-naming of settlements in Wales after the Roman period is discussed in Chapter 4.

Chapter 3

Latin Words in English Place-Names

The sequence of events which accompanied and followed the disintegration of Roman government in Britain in the late fourth and early fifth centuries AD constitutes the obscurest chapter in the history of this country. As we have seen, Roman Britain was a Celtic-speaking country with place-names which, when they are intelligible to the modern scholar, are predominantly Celtic. Two centuries later, by the time of St Augustine's mission to Kent in 597, much of the south and east of Britain was inhabited by Germanic-speaking people using predominantly Germanic place-names. The recorded events of these two centuries have been subjected to much close scrutiny, and have been held to be compatible with widely differing conclusions. Some historians have sought to demonstrate that the population remained mainly Celtic in spite of the change of language, others that only a small remnant of the Celtic population survived the Anglo-Saxon incursion, and these few survivors were reduced to the condition of serfs. On this last interpretation the dense layer of new place-names in Old English would correspond to a new agricultural and administrative geography, at any rate in the south, the east and the north-east.

The arguments for and against continuity of population and institutions during these obscure centuries will continue to be propounded. The present writer has no solutions to offer, but will endeavour in this chapter to present some linguistic evidence which has not always been taken into account, and to consider it against the background of recent archaeological discoveries. The scraps of historical evidence remain the same in spite of recurrent attempts to reshuffle the dates in the chronicles, but the archaeological evidence has changed drastically in recent years, and it is possible to see some of the place-name evidence in a new light by studying its relationship to new archaeological discoveries.

The most important change in the archaeology of the period is the identification of material which indicates that people of distinctive Germanic culture lived and were buried in Britain in the second half of the fourth century, before the disintegration of Roman rule, and that some of them remained here in the first half of the fifth century, in the period between the collapse of Rome and the sequence of events which the chroniclers knew as the foundation of the Anglo-Saxon kingdoms. Dr J. N. L. Myres, in his publication of the finds from the cemetery at Caistor-by-Norwich (Myres and Green 1973) and his book on Anglo-Saxon pottery (Myres 1969), demonstrates the use of Germanic pottery dating from the fourth century (and in a few instances from the late third century) as cremation urns and as grave furniture; and he identifies other types of pottery which he believes to belong to the first half of the fifth century. Historical sources give a date of roughly AD 450 for the *adventus Saxonum*, the beginning of the English settlement, so material dated before 450 relates to Germanic people who were in Britain before the events which seemed to the chroniclers to mark the beginning of the invasions. This and other archaeological material gives rise to Dr Myres's hypothesis of 'The Phase of Overlap and Controlled Settlement' (Myres 1969, Chapter 5).

During this period from about AD 360–410 there is evidence for the presence of Germanic soldiers in the forts of the south-east coast. This coast was known to the Romans as *Litus Saxonicum*, the Saxon Shore, because it had to be defended against Saxon pirates, and the evidence of pottery found in the forts suggests that Germanic soldiers were employed in the garrisons to defend Britain against attacks by their fellow Germans. It has been noted in Chapter 2 that the Romano-British names of these forts, which include *Othona* (Old English *Ythancæstir*), Reculver, Richborough, Dover, Lympne and *Anderita* (Old English *Andredesceaster*) had a relatively high survival rate, and this may be due to the names being known in the late Roman period both to Saxon pirates and to Germanic defenders.

There is good reason to suppose that in the same period Germanic fighting men were employed not only in the Saxon Shore forts but also in some of the walled towns of Roman Britain. There is no doubt that this was so at Caistor-by Norwich, where the pottery in the cemetery indicates a Germanic presence from as early as the third century, which continued throughout the fourth and fifth centuries. In addition to this abundant evidence from Caistor, Dr Myres stresses (1969, pp. 73–4) that 'most of the great cremation cemeteries of eastern England contain some pottery that has its closest parallels among the continental wares of the half-century before 400'; and that even outside this area of eastern England there is some ceramic evidence for the presence of barbarians settled before the end of the Roman occupation. Such evidence comes from Surrey (Mitcham and Ham), Essex (Mucking), and from the Berkshire/ Oxfordshire stretch of the River Thames.

Another type of archaeological evidence relevant to this subject which has been identified in recent years consists of the metal buckles and belt-fittings issued to barbarians employed in the Roman armies in the later years of the Empire. These are highly distinctive; but while they reveal the military status of the original wearer they afford less conclusive proof about his racial origins than is provided by pottery used in burials. On general grounds, however, there is a strong probability that many of the men employed in the late Roman army and issued with this distinctive equipment would be Germanic-speaking. Much of this metal-work comes from Roman towns, forts and villas, but an intriguing problem is raised by the relatively large quantity which has been found in female Anglo-Saxon burials of a considerably later date. Are such belt-fittings relics handed down in the families of men who served in the Roman army, or are they loot taken by marauding Anglo-Saxons, and so irrelevant to the question of an Anglo-Saxon presence in late Roman Britain? (The possibility that objects found in pagan burials are heirlooms must always be borne in mind, but need not apply to burial urns to the same extent as is likely with metal ornaments.)

The bearing of this archaeological material, both ceramic and metal-work, on the history of late Roman Britain is still under assessment, and will probably be so for a long time; but there is little room for doubt that a substantial number of Germanic-speaking people had been settled in Britain under the aegis of the Roman government, and there is a strong probability that communities derived from these settlements were well established in some parts of the country during the first half of the fifth century. Hengist and Horsa did not bring the first Germanic-speaking settlers to Britain.

Those historians who believe that there was very little continuity from Roman Britain to Anglo-Saxon England have as one of their strongest arguments the virtual absence of Celtic influence on the Old English language. Words of Celtic origin which were adopted by the Anglo-Saxons number less than twenty. Professor Jackson (1953, pp. 242–3) does not consider this a serious obstacle to believing that Old English and Brittonic speaking people co-existed for a time; and probably not sufficient study has been made of the effect of one language on another in comparable circumstances for any definite conclusions to be drawn from it, but the fact itself is not open to dispute. Against this lack of British loan-words must be set the adoption by the Anglo-Saxons of a far from negligible number of British place-names, of which some details are given in the next chapter. In this chapter it is proposed to examine some place-name-forming terms of Latin origin. These were formerly considered to have been acquired by the Anglo-Saxons on the Continent but, in view of the new archaeological evidence for a Germanic presence in this country in the late Roman period, they may have been adopted from contact with Latin-speaking people in Britain.

As stated in Chapter 2 it does not seem likely that much Latin was spoken among the farming population of Roman Britain. But the Germanic soldiers and settlers whose pottery and belt-fittings have now been identified may be assumed to have had more dealings with the governing classes than with the population at large, and it is not inconsistent with what has been said about the linguistic situation in Roman Britain to suggest that more Latin than Brittonic words came into the vocabulary of these early settlers. Terms used in place-names which could have entered the Old English language direct from Latin at this date are *camp*, *ceaster*, *port*, *strǣt*, *wīc*. Words ultimately of Latin origin which have hitherto been believed to have been adopted by Anglo-Saxons from British-speaking people, but which may also have been borrowed direct from Latin speakers, are **ecles* and *funta*. These terms enter into a substantial number of English place-names. There are other loan-words from Latin which occur rarely, or only in a single name; these include **fæfer* from Latin *faber* in Faversham KNT, **corte* from Latin *cohors* in Dovercourt ESX, *croh* from Latin *crocus* in Croydon GTL.

If such terms were adopted by soldiers and settlers who served Roman employers in the fourth century or who were employed by 'sub-Roman' rulers in the first half of the fifth century, the words would be adopted with a full understanding of their meaning. The Anglo-Saxon attitude to Roman institutions at this date would be very different from that of the later Anglo-Saxon poets, who wrote marvellous melancholy verses in which crumbling Roman masonry was used to symbolize the transience of earthly power and glory, and deserted Roman towns were anachronistically peopled with revellers from a Germanic mead-hall. This poetic use of the imagery of Roman remains, which makes a deep impression on the student of English literature who encounters it in his undergraduate days, needs to be put aside when we are trying to recover the attitude to Roman things of a hypothetical mercenary soldier of *c.* AD 400. Another approach of the Christian period was the scholarly antiquarian interest in Roman things shown by writers of the age of the Venerable Bede. The anonymous author of the earliest life of St Cuthbert, for instance, in telling how the saint saw by second sight the defeat of the Northumbrian forces at Nechtanesmere in 685, says it was while he and others 'were looking at the wall of the city (Carlisle) and the fountain in it formerly built by the Romans in a wonderful fashion, as Waga, the reeve of the city, who was conducting them, explained'. Neither this antiquarian interest nor the sophisticated literary convention of later centuries is a guide to the outlook of the men whose cremated remains were buried in Germanic urns outside the walls of Caistor-by-Norwich. These proto-Anglo-Saxons were familiar with Roman institutions which were functioning, unromantic and unsymbolic; and if they were indeed the first English speakers to use the words *ceaster* and *wīc* they knew that the settlements they referred to were not the work of giants.

Place-name elements borrowed by the Anglo-Saxons from Latin, either directly or through the medium of British speech, form a field for research which is unevenly covered by modern work. There are recent studies of **ecles* and of *wīchām*, which indicate the potential of this field of study, and Croydon, Dovercourt and some names containing *port* were discussed in Gelling 1970, but no exhaustive study has yet been made of the other words listed above. The method adopted here will be to give in some detail the results of recent work on *wīchām* (Gelling 1967) and **ecles* (Cameron 1968), and to offer some more tentative remarks about the use in place-names of other Latin loan-words.

The word *wīc* became in Old English, as in other Germanic languages, one of many terms for a settlement. The later, diverse, meanings of the word bear little or no relationship to its origin, about which philologists are in agreement: it is a loan from Latin *vicus*. In Gelling 1967 the possibility was explored that before it developed a variety of meanings such as 'salt-working centre' and 'dairy-farm', it might have been used by the earliest English-speaking people in Britain to refer to actual Romano-British settlements, or to Roman administrative units (which was one of the meanings of Latin *vicus*). This study was based on the use of *wīc* with the Old English word *hām* ('village') in the compound appellative *wīchām*, which gives rise to roughly thirty English place-names and field-names, but is not recorded in Old English, except in spellings for some of these names.

The modern spellings of names derived from *wīchām* are Wickham, Wycomb, Wykeham, Wykham, Wyckham; but it is important to note that not every instance of these or similar forms can be derived from *wīchām*. High Wycombe BUC is from a different source, and so is Childs Wickham GLO. Reliable Old English or early Middle English spellings are required before it can be safely assumed that such names are from *wīchām*, and are not different names which have been assimilated to that rather common type. Field-names like Wickham's Close or Field must, if there are no early spellings, be suspected of deriving from a surname.

An attempt was made in the 1967 article to track down all instances, surviving and lost, of place-names from *wīchām*. The corpus has changed slightly since then, but not so as to seriously alter the general pattern. Doubt has been cast on Wickham St Paul's ESX, and until the documentary history of that place has been carefully reviewed this example should be regarded as under suspicion of being derived from *wīcum*, the dative plural of *wīc*, which is the probable source of High Wycombe BUC. This would equate it with Wyken WAR, Wykin LEI, and a number of instances of Wicken, and no special connection with Roman settlements is claimed for these places. Some probable and some possible additional instances of *wīchām* (either accidentally missed or not known in 1967) have been brought forward since the study was made, and more could doubtless be found. Two medieval names which were lurking in the field-name sections of Smith 1964–5 were missed, and these (which make some difference to the distribution-pattern) are discussed below. The most promising of several possible examples in HRT and ESX brought to my attention by Mr W. Rodwell is Wickham Spring in Standon HRT. There is no early documentation for the name, but on other grounds it seems very likely to be a genuine *wīchām*. Before examining the credentials of Wickham Spring HRT it is desirable to state the distinguishing characteristics of the names which make up the group.

The first point which was noted about place-names from *wīchām* was that more than three-quarters of the known instances were situated directly on or not more than a mile from a major Roman road. The known roads of Roman Britain form a widely spaced network (as can be seen from Fig. 2), and it is quite out of the question for this relationship between the roads and the *wīchām* names to be the result of chance. Further investigation revealed that in regard to over half the instances of the place-name a case could be made for them coinciding with or being closely associated with Romano-British habitation-sites. The evidence for this varies a great deal, and cannot be demonstrated simply on a map, as can the evidence for the relationship with roads. One of the clearest instances is the area called Wycomb near Andoversford GLO, where a Roman settlement covering at least twenty acres and classified as a 'small town' has recently been excavated. At the other end of the scale are such sites as Wickham Bushes BRK, where excavation in the nineteenth century revealed 'traces of houses' associated with Roman pottery and coins, and the spot called *wīchām* in Old English charter-boundaries near Wilcote

OXF, where no settlement-site has been located, but where surface finds are sufficient to earn a 'minor settlement' symbol on the Ordnance Survey Map of Roman Britain. Even slighter evidence, not sufficient to cause a settlement to be marked on the Ordnance Survey Map, includes the Romano-British rubbish-pit found in 1887 near East Wickham church in Bexley GTL, and the fragments of Roman pottery found at Wickham in Welford BRK when material was dug out to make a pond near the rectory. All the evidence known at the time for Romano-British habitation at or very near *wīchām* sites was set out in detail in Gelling 1967, and in spite of its uneven nature it has been found convincing by several authorities on Roman Britain. The case has been greatly strengthened since 1967 by the discovery of a Romano-British town, estimated to cover about sixty acres, at Hacheston SFK, adjoining Wickham Market. As regards the direct connection of the place-names with the nearby Roman sites, Wycomb GLO and Wickham Bushes BRK are particularly significant instances, as there is no modern settlement at either spot, so the names refer solely to the Romano-British habitations. The names were preserved, though there must have been a very long period in which nothing was visible and the Roman remains were forgotten.

The statistical probability of *wīchām* names coinciding with known Romano-British habitation sites is considerable, once it has been established that most of the place-names are on Roman roads, because on the whole the settlements follow the road-pattern. In this connection also Wycomb GLO is particularly significant, because this is a rare instance of a small Roman town which is not served by a major road. This suggests that the true connection is between *wīchām* and small towns, rather than between *wīchām* and roads. In other instances the degree of coincidence seems greater than can be ascribed simply to the names and the towns being generally associated with the roads. One of the Oxfordshire examples illustrates this. The stretch of Akeman Street from its crossing with a north-south road at Alchester to its junction with the Foss Way at Cirencester has a length of approximately thirty-six miles. Two settlements are marked on the Ordnance Survey Map of Roman Britain on this stretch of road, leaving aside the towns at either end. The two settlements are about five miles apart, near Asthall and near Wilcote. One *wīchām* place-name is known on this stretch of road, and this coincides with the supposed settlement near Wilcote. (The evidence for this *wīchām* is set out in detail in Chapter 8.) With three points to be arranged on a thirty-six-mile stretch of road, it seems to be more than chance that the single *wīchām* name coincides with one of the settlements.

In a subject where very little can be said to be proved, it seems safe to

claim that there is a probability of a *wīchām* place-name referring to a
Romano-British habitation site. From this arises the suggestion that *wīc* in
wīchām is not simply the common Germanic word used for various types
of settlement, the association of which with the Latin word *vicus* had
probably long been forgotten when most of the Germanic place-names
were coined. In this compound, and perhaps in some other names like
Wickford ESX and Weekley NTP where it occurs as a first element, *wīc* may
have a close connection with *vicus*. Something may be said about the
possible nature of this connection, though here the discussion becomes
very speculative.

Latin *vicus* was the term for the smallest unit of self-government in the
Roman provinces. The places accorded this status varied greatly. The
civitas capitals (like Wroxeter and Leicester) ranked as either single *vici* or
groups of *vici* according to size. The status was accorded to the civil
settlements of traders and retired soldiers which grew up outside Roman
forts. It is known from an inscription that the small town of Durobrivae HNT
(see Chapter 2) was a *vicus*, and this must have been the status of many
other small towns, though positive evidence rarely survives in any particular instance. The small towns are the only category of *vici* to which the
wīchām names could relate, but it is unlikely that we shall ever know how
widespread the status was among the lesser towns of Roman Britain, or
how many of the settlements for which we have evidence at or near
wīchām place-names can be dignified by the term 'small town'. The three
which are certainly small towns are Wycomb near Andoversford GLO, the
new site near Wickham Market SFK, and the town on Wickham Hill near
Braughing HRT, which on air-photographs shows signs of a rectilinear grid,
a feature to which the small towns of Roman Britain seldom aspire. Now
that more information is available about these three sites, it seems possible
that the apparently humble status of many of the Romano-British settlements associated with *wīchām* names which were listed in 1967 may be due
to lack of knowledge, and that some of them could be comparable to the
sites listed above. The situation of a number of the places at important
road junctions is consistent with this supposition.

Two recent papers, Johnson 1975 and Rodwell 1975, contribute new
information bearing on this question of what a *wīchām* may have been.
Rodwell 1975 discusses the *wīchām* names of the Trinovantian area, which
lay north-east of London, and notes the tendency for them to occur near
Roman sites in which the later archaeological levels show no evidence of
early Saxon occupation, and where sub-Roman survival, after the collapse
of Roman government, seems particularly likely. This suggests the
possibility that *wīchām* was an Old English term for a Roman town which

survived without being swamped by Germanic settlers, and was given this name by neighbouring Germanic communities in recognition of its non-Germanic characteristics. Johnson 1975 discusses the changing meanings borne by the word *vicus* and other administrative terms in the four centuries of Roman Britain, and concludes that the administrative sense of *vicus* had been lost by the late Roman period, and that 'By the fourth century we can be fairly certain that "vicus" had come to mean as much or as little as our term "village"'. This rules out the possibility of English-speaking people hearing the term *vicus* used in its early, precise, administrative sense; but if there was continuity from earlier Romano-British times, a term which had once been applied with a specific meaning might have survived as a colloquial way of referring to these small towns.

Another notable characteristic of the *wīchām* place-names is that they systematically avoid the immediate vicinity of the most important Roman towns, such as Caerwent, Bath, Leicester, London, York. The two Berkshire examples, for instance, lie well to the east and west of Silchester. An exception to this general rule is provided by two medieval field-names from *wīchām* which have been noted in the vicinity of Gloucester, one of which was missed when the 1967 article was compiled. As they are lost field-names they cannot be located precisely, but they occur in the parishes of Hempstead, immediately south-west of Gloucester, and Maisemore, about the same distance to the north-west. The Hempstead name, *Wycham*, is recorded in 1263–84, and may refer to the small Roman settlement in the parish recorded in *The Journal of Roman Studies* in 1949. This was noted in Gelling 1967. The Maisemore name, *Wykham*, is recorded in 1316. These two examples are within a two-mile radius of the *colonia* of Glevum. None of the other noted examples of *wīchām* lies closer than ten miles to a major town, though there are examples in Kent very close to the 'lesser walled towns' of Rochester and Canterbury, and East Wickham GTL is quite close to the 'major settlement' of Noviomagus discussed in Chapter 2.

Another Gloucestershire *wīchām*, which was accidentally missed in 1967, may be mentioned here for the sake of completeness. This is *Wikeham* in the parish of Deerhurst, some eight miles north-north-east of Gloucester, recorded in a document of 1424. Excavations at Deerhurst have unearthed finds which suggest Romano-British settlement in the parish, though the exact site has not been located. The addition of these two field-names in their approximate positions to Fig. 2 makes a noteworthy concentration in the region dominated by Gloucester and Cirencester.

Another characteristic of the *wīchām* place-names which occurs so consistently that it cannot reasonably be ascribed to chance is the special relationship they have to the areas of the medieval and modern parishes within which they lie. The antiquity as territorial units of the ecclesiastical parishes of the English countryside is discussed in Chapter 8. In many cases the existing boundaries of these units can be traced back to the period before the Norman Conquest, and there is a growing body of opinion which considers that some of them were in existence during the Roman period and earlier. A consistent pattern in relation to parish boundaries may therefore be regarded as a significant feature in this category of names. Among the *wīchām* names which can be precisely located (i.e. those which have survived to the present day or which occur in Anglo-Saxon charter boundaries) there is in this respect a remarkable dichotomy. With one or two exceptions, they refer on the one hand to the settlement which gives name to a parish or which gave name to an estate at the time of the Domesday Survey, or on the other hand to a place which lies on or very close to the boundary of the parish in which it occurs. In this last category there are several instances in which the parish boundary makes a detour to include them.

More than half of our locateable *wīchām* place-names are modern parishes or are places which were named as distinct units in the Domesday Survey of 1086. This fact alone, had it been noted earlier, might have served to discredit the traditional translation 'homestead with a dairy-farm', since a compound which in a high proportion of instances denotes the central settlement of a parish or an ancient estate should be regarded as referring to a more significant characteristic than the possession of a dairy-farm. The *wīchām* names which are modern parishes are: West Wickham CAM, Wickham Bishops ESX, Wickham HMP, West Wickham GTL, Wickhambreux KNT, East Wykeham LIN, Wickham Skeith SFK, Wickham Market SFK, Wickhambrook SFK, Wykeham YON. (Wickham St Pauls ESX, also a parish, has been omitted from this list because, as stated above, it is under suspicion of not being a true *wīchām* name.) Those which are not modern parishes but which are named as estates in the Domesday Survey are: Wickham in Welford BRK, Wickham Hall in Farnham ESX, Wycomb in Scalford LEI, Wykeham in Nettleton LIN, and Wykham in Banbury OXF.

The *wīchām* names which can be located precisely and which refer to places which are neither modern parishes nor Domesday estates are: Wickham Bushes in Easthampstead BRK (further within its parish than most examples, see *infra*); Wycomb in Whittington GLO (in a projecting corner of Dowdeswell parish which just includes the Roman site discussed above and the adjacent village of Andoversford); Wickham Hill near Braughing HRT (the boundary between Braughing and Standon parishes bisects the hill); East Wickham GTL (in the north-west corner of Bexley parish); Wickham Bushes in Lydden KNT (by a pointed projection on the north boundary of Lydden, and mentioned in an Anglo-Saxon boundary-survey of adjacent Sibertswold); Wickham in Strood KNT (Wickham Reach is the stretch of River Medway between Cuxton and Strood parishes); *Wicham* in Hailey OXF (the position in relation to the parish boundary is shown on Fig. 15); Hurst and Clayton Wickham SSX (on either side of the Hurstpierpoint/Clayton parish boundary); Wyckham Farms in Steyning SSX (near the east boundary of Steyning); Wickham Manor in Icklesham SSX (difficult to evaluate because the medieval town of Winchelsea has been inserted into the old pattern of land-units here); Wickham Green in Urchfont WLT (a tiny hamlet bisected by the Urchfont/Easterton boundary).

This analysis yields the following figures:

wīchām names which are modern parishes: 10.
wīchām names which are Domesday estates but not modern parishes: 5.
wīchām names which are neither parishes nor Domesday estates and which lie on parish boundaries: 10.

Medieval field-names which cannot be located precisely are, of course, not included in this analysis, and Wickham in Icklesham SSX is not classified. Apart from this, the only locateable *wīchām* which does not quite fit into the general pattern is Wickham Bushes in Easthampstead BRK, and even this is only a little more than half a mile from the south boundary of Easthampstead parish. The second and third categories into which the other locateable names have been divided overlap with each other, as some of the 'non-parochial' *wīchām* places mentioned in Domesday Book are also on parish boundaries. Wickham in Welford BRK lies on the boundary between Kintbury and Welford, Wickham Hall in Farnham ESX is on the parish and county boundary, the site of the lost hamlet of Wykeham in Nettleton LIN is a bare quarter of a mile from the south boundary of Nettleton, and Wykham Park in Banbury OXF is on the south boundary of Banbury.

This dichotomy between being centres of ancient land-units and being situated very close indeed to the boundaries of such units may indicate that all the *wīchām* settlements were at one time centres of land-units. The observed pattern could be the result of some of them flourishing and retaining this status, while others failed and were divided between their neighbours. Such a division could leave on a boundary a settlement which had originally been surrounded by its land. No features have been observed in those *wīchām* settlements which became parishes which might suggest that any of them were the centres of multiple estates, of the kind discussed in Chapter 8, but the evidence does suggest that all the places named *wīchām* once stood roughly in the midst of fields and pastures assigned for their support.

The credentials of Wickham Spring in Standon HRT are impressive if measured against the established characteristics of the whole group of place-names. Mr Rodwell informs me that the name refers to a spring which lies at the junction of the parishes of Standon, Much Hadham and Little Hadham, beside the Roman road from Braughing to Harlow, and that it is surrounded by a Romano-British settlement and industrial complex. Two more possible examples brought to my notice by Mr Rodwell are Wickhams in Chigwell ESX, a nineteenth-century field-name in the same parish as a Roman settlement which may be *Durolito* (see Chapter 2), and Wickham Ley, a nineteenth-century field-name in Little Waltham ESX, in a parish where the Roman roads from Dunmow, Braintree and Chelmsford converge, with extensive evidence of Romano-British settlement around the convergence. A possible example in Sussex, sent to me by Mr H. Walden, is Wickham Barn and Lane on the west boundary of Barcombe parish, north of Lewes. The lane crosses the Roman road on which, some seven and thirteen miles further west, Hurst and Clayton Wickham and Wyckham in Steyning are situated. Tempting though such examples are, it must be emphasized that without early spellings they are only to be regarded as possible examples. The modern name Wickham, Wycomb can have other origins, and nineteenth-century field-names, particularly those which have final -s like Wickhams in Chigwell ESX, may be due to a landowner surnamed Wickham.

It is doubtful whether any other category of place-name will be identified in which the examples fit into a pattern quite as neatly as the *wīchām* names do. Conformity is not perfect, but the approach to it is such that one suspects that when there appears to be an irregularity, such as Wickham Green in Urchfont WLT and Wickham Manor in Icklesham SSX being nowhere near Roman roads, this may be because the hypothetical Roman towns shared with Wycomb GLO the peculiarity of being sited away from the road system. The regularity of the characteristics observed in most of the places with *wīchām* names strengthens the possibility that they may all have arisen at much the same date, perhaps in the earliest period of large-scale Germanic settlements. Some other classes of name have a relationship to Roman roads and habitation sites which is less precise than this, but is close enough to be significant. A promising category, of which a full study has not yet been made, consists of names containing the word *camp*.

Old English *camp* is a loan-word from Latin *campus* 'a field'. The word does not occur in all Germanic languages, but it is found in Frisian and Saxon; and by analogy with its use in those languages it is sometimes translated 'an enclosed piece of land'. It is not recorded in Old English except in place-names and charter boundary-marks, so the translation is conjectural as regards the English usage. The Anglo-Saxons were not short of words for fields and enclosures, and it seems possible that some special circumstances governed their occasional use in the south and east of Britain of this loan-word from Latin. They may have been perpetuating in each of the place-names concerned a district-name which they learnt from Latin-speaking people. Until a complete list of place-names and field-names in *camp* has been compiled it is not possible to undertake a '*wīchām*-type' study of the element, but some interesting points emerge from a careful consideration of the distribution of known settlement-names in which it occurs. It is important to distinguish between *camp* as an Old English place-name element and the modern use of the same word, re-introduced from Romance languages and used of a military encampment and hence, in place-names, for a prehistoric earthwork. Hill-forts with names like Caesar's Camp are not relevant here, and field-names like Camp Close should always be suspected of referring to such fortifications. It is not always possible in field-names only recorded in the nineteenth century to distinguish an ancient name in Camp from a modern one; but a field-name containing Comp is probably from the Old English word, as it shows the rounding of *a* before a nasal consonant (*m* or *n*) which happened before the re-introduction of *camp* in the sense 'fort'. As a final element in settlement-names Old English *camp* sometimes becomes modern -combe, and Old or Middle English spellings are essential in order to distinguish it from the much more common *cumb* 'valley'.

The only exhaustive study of the distribution of *camp* in the place-names of any region is that for Berkshire in Gelling 1976 (pp. 803–5). The distribution in Berkshire is probably significant: the five instances (one parish-name and four field-names) occur in those parts of the county where archaeological evidence for Roman habitation is least mixed with that for early Anglo-Saxon occupation, and where the evidence for Celtic linguistic survival is less slight than it is for most of Berkshire. But *camp* is not well represented in Berkshire, and to form an idea of the potential interest of the element it is necessary to study its distribution in areas where it is more common in settlement-names.

First, in this study of settlement-names containing *camp*, three certain and one possible instances in which such names occur in close proximity to names from *wīchām* may be noted. These are:

1. Addiscombe GTL (earlier *Addescompe*), which lies in the parish of Croydon (perhaps another significant name in this connection), and is

between two and three miles west of West Wickham. The map on p. 98 of Rodwell 1975 shows a 'major R.B. settlement' lying between the two.

2. Castle and Shudy Camps CAM, earlier Great and Little Camps, from the plural of *camp*. The use of the same name for two villages which both became parishes indicates either that one is a daughter settlement of the other, or that the name was that of the whole area within which both settlements lie. The two parishes lie south of a Roman road. A 'minor settlement' is shown on the Ordnance Survey Map of Roman Britain, and on Rodwell 1975 (p. 98), on the road at Horseheath, the parish which adjoins Shudy Camps. West Wickham CAM adjoins Horseheath to the north.

3. Campsey Ash SFK, a parish and village immediately east of Wickham Market. The newly discovered Roman town at Hacheston lies between the two.

4. Barcombe SSX (earlier *Bercamp*, *Berecomp*), a parish and village due north of Lewes, lying in the angle made by the junction of two Roman roads. On the west boundary of Barcombe lie Wickham Barn and Lane, for which unfortunately no early spellings have yet been found.

A group of names in *camp* which seems to be related to Romano-British settlement is to be found in Kent, between the valleys of the Darenth and the Medway, both of which abound in Roman villas. Swanscombe adjoins the 'major settlement' of *Vagniacae* (at Springhead), lying between the Roman road on which *Vagniacae* is situated and the River Thames. About six miles south-west of Swanscombe is Maplescombe, on a hill which overlooks Eynsford and Lullingstone in the Darenth valley. About six miles south-east of Maplescombe lie two hamlets called Great and Little Comp, south-east of Wrotham. An outlier from this group of names in *camp* is Balcombe in the parish of Frittenden, south-south-east of Maidstone, near the Roman road which leads south from that town. Although these four examples of *camp* are not very close together, their distribution is a limited and significant one if they are considered in the context of the whole county.

Warningcamp SSX is a parish east of Arundel, immediately across the River Arun, another river valley where Roman settlement is well evidenced. The two instances in Hertfordshire, Epcombs in Hertingfordbury and Sacombe five miles north-east, lie five or six miles east of the 'major settlement' at Welwyn, and Sacombe is on one of the Roman roads which form the road junction at Wickham Hill in Braughing. Hanscombe, the only Bedfordshire name in *camp*, is about three miles north of the Icknield Way, which leads west from the 'major settlement' at Baldock HRT, again a situation on the outer fringe of an area where Roman finds are very common. Campsfield OXF is situated four or five miles east of the famous group of villas which includes Ditchley Park, and about four miles north-west of the Roman settlement at North Oxford. There are Roman buildings in the immediate vicinity, but the name should probably be considered in relation to the areas of dense Roman settlement to the north-west and the south and east. Chipping Campden GLO lies north of the Cotswold villas. Bulcamp SFK lies across the River Blythe from Blythburgh; Roman sites in East Anglia are mostly concentrated inland, to the west of this coastal strip.

Together with Ruscombe BRK, the positions of sixteen names in *camp* have been considered. The total number of surviving place-names containing this element is probably not much greater. Much labour would be required in order to assemble a corpus which would include field-names and points in Anglo-Saxon charter boundaries, but although this field-name and charter material is an unassessed quantity, the sixteen names discussed above are certainly a significant proportion of the whole.

The relationship of *camp* names to known Roman settlements does not seem likely to be the result of chance. It seems possible that these names perpetuate the use of the term *campus* by Latin speakers in the late Roman period for stretches of uncultivated land in certain situations. These would include land on the outskirts of a group of villas, land which lay between two major groups of villas, and a belt of land surrounding a town. Germanic fighting men might learn to refer to such areas as 'the *camp*' in rather the same way as they are here assumed to have formed the habit of referring to 'the *wīc*'. When they or their descendants felt the need for more cultivated land than was available to them they might break in areas on the fringe of the *camp*, and this might lead to the development of a secondary meaning 'enclosure'. As noted above, we have no direct evidence for this meaning in Old English, but some names in *camp* in charter boundaries (in particular *rocgan campæs geatæ* in the bounds of Exton HMP) are thought to imply it, and it would be particularly appropriate to Barcombe which has *bere* 'barley' as first element. The use of the genitive singular as a first element in Campsey ('island of the *camp*') and Campsfield ('open land of the *camp*') is consistent with the suggestion that *camp* may have been an older place-name, and Bulcamp, Swanscombe and Warningcamp ('bulls' or 'bullocks', herdsman's, and stallions' *camp*') have first elements appropriate to the suggested meaning 'open, uncultivated land on the edge of settlements'. The five names (Addiscombe, Epcombs, Hanscombe,

Ruscombe and Sacombe) in which the first element is the genitive of an Old English personal name could be considered appropriate to settlements formed by extending the area of cultivation into the *campus* in late Roman or immediately post-Roman times. The Gloucestershire name Campden (which also occurs as a field-name in Berkshire) means 'valley of the *camps*', and this might refer to an area where such encroachments had been made. The remaining compound names in *camp* have less significant first elements. Balcombe is possibly from *bolla* 'bowl', used in a topographical sense, and Maplescombe is '*camp* of the maple-tree'. All the settlement-names in *camp* discussed in this chapter are marked on Fig. 2.

There is considerable uncertainty about the precise meanings borne by the words *vicus* and *campus* when they were acquired by the earliest Germanic settlers in Britain; it is a relief, therefore, to turn to a Latin word used in English place-names the meaning of which is not open to much discussion. This is *port* 'harbour', a loan from Latin *portus*. There are two other words which give -port in place-names, the most prolific being *port* 'market town' (e.g. in Newport). It is not certain whether this last is a specialized development of *port* 'harbour' or derives from Latin *porta* 'gate', but whatever its origin *port* 'market town' must be discounted for the purpose of the present discussion, as it continued in use as a place-name-forming element very late, and there is no question of names containing it having any reference to Roman institutions. It is easy to distinguish between inland names in -port and the few coastal names (Portsmouth, Portslade, Portland, Portishead, Porlock) which have *port* 'harbour' as first element, and it is only the latter which are relevant in this chapter. The modern word *port* 'town with a harbour' (found in the modern place-name Devonport) is probably not a direct descendant from Old English *port*, but rather a new Middle English borrowing from French.

The reasonable explanation of Portsmouth HMP, and of Portsdown and Portsea (the ridge behind Portsmouth Harbour and the island on which Portsmouth lies), is that the Harbour was known as *Portus* throughout the Roman period and that this name was familiar to Saxon raiders, Germanic mercenaries and everybody in the vicinity in the late fourth and early fifth centuries. The Saxon Shore fort overlooking the harbour, probably the *Portus Adurni* of the Notitia Dignitatum, was called by the Anglo-Saxons *Porteceaster*, modern Portchester. Most place-name experts take the view that *port* in all these is the name of the Harbour (e.g. Smith 1956, Ekwall 1960, Cameron 1961). Sir Frank Stenton was inclined to accept the etymology of Portsmouth implied by the Anglo-Saxon Chronicle in the annal for 501, which says 'Port and his two sons Bieda and Mægla came to Britain with two ships in the place called *Portes mutha* (Stenton 1943,

p. 20), but it is doubtful whether this view has many supporters. The problem of the association in the early annals of the Chronicle between place-names and personal names is discussed in Chapter 7. This is perhaps the most blatant of the instances where a fictitious early chieftain has been inferred from a place-name.

If it be accepted that *port* in Portsmouth is the Latin name for the harbour, then the use of the Old English word *pōl* 'pool' for the next natural harbour to the west, at Poole DOR, may amount to a statement that there had been no Roman development of the harbour there, or at any rate none which compared with that at Portsmouth. (The term *pōl* is not often used of a natural harbour, but there is another instance in Hartlepool DRH.) The next harbour to the west from Poole is Portland DOR, which is referred to simply as *Port* in the Anglo-Saxon Chronicle under the year 837. Continuing to the west, Portlemouth DEV may be Old English **Portwellan mūtha* 'the mouth of the harbour-stream'. Cornish names in *porth* are not relevant here (though the Cornish word is also from Latin *portus*), as *porth* was in use at all periods in the Cornish language, and is used of small coves. Portishead SOM, however, on the Severn estuary, is an Old English name meaning 'headland of the harbour', and this is a place where Roman development is likely enough, though not actually known. Porlock SOM, 'harbour enclosure', is perhaps too far from Roman civilization to refer to a Roman harbour. The only example of *port* 'harbour' which has been noted east of Portsmouth is Portslade SSX, 'crossing place of the harbour'. This seems a likely enough spot for Roman development, though nothing is actually known on this stretch of coast. All these names except Portlemouth and Porlock are shown on Fig. 2.

The words *ceaster* and *strǣt* occur much more frequently in place-names than the terms discussed above (*camp*, *wīc* as a first element, and *port* 'harbour'); and they occur in all parts of the country, which makes it impossible to claim for them the direct relationship with functioning Roman institutions which may be postulated for terms which have a limited distribution. Their significance in English place-names will probably be more appropriately discussed in Chapter 6 than here. It may be noted in passing, however, that no systematic study has yet been made of *ceaster*, and that such an investigation might show that the use of the word in place-names is less casual than it appears at first sight.

Some very rare terms which were adopted from Latin by the Anglo-Saxons are not at all likely to be casual when they occur in place-names. A possible example is the element **corte*, which is found in Dovercourt ESX, a place in which Roman buildings are recorded. The first element is the British river-name discussed in Chapter 2. As regards the second element, it was suggested in 1924 (Ekwall 1924, p. 20) that it might be connected with Latin *cohors*, *cohortem*, which (besides its more familiar meaning of 'multitude') is used by classical authors in an agricultural context to mean 'an enclosed yard'. This last sense must have been current in late Latin, since it is the source of French *court*, from which is derived Modern English *court* (which occurs in numerous place-names of late origin). An Anglo-Saxon borrowing from late Latin seems very much the likeliest explanation of the second element of Dovercourt, though the word did not survive in Old English. Ekwall abandoned his suggestion after 1924, and all subsequent discussions explain Dovercourt differently except that in Gelling 1970, which puts forward the derivation from *cohortem*. This discussion was written under the impression that the etymology was brand new, and only after it was published was the same suggestion noted in Ekwall 1924. There are a few other possible occurrences of this element in English place-names, but the only one which seems safe enough to build on is the boundary-mark *to þære cortan* in an Old English account of part of the boundary between the bishoprics of Canterbury and Rochester. The stretch of boundary described appears to have lain in the vicinity of Goudhurst KNT, south of Maidstone and near the Sussex border.

The single occurrence in Faversham KNT of an element **fæfer*, considered by philologists to be an early Old English loan from Latin *faber*, is either a remarkable coincidence or a reference to the existence at Faversham of a centre of metal-working in the 'phase of overlap and controlled settlement' which preceded the historical coming of the English. Faversham is believed to have had a centre of the finest jewellery production at the end of the pagan period, in the late sixth and early seventh centuries, because the distribution of gold and garnet jewellery in Kentish burials points to it. The word **fæfer* is in the genitive singular, and it may be a personal name, or perhaps more probably a meaningful nickname. A collective use of the singular is not likely, as that is only well evidenced with plant- and animal-names. A meaning 'village of the smith' or 'village of a man known as The Smith' could refer to the existence at Faversham of a notable workshop with a famous master-craftsman, but if this man had been an Anglo-Saxon, with purely Germanic skills, he would surely have been designated by the Germanic word *smith* (which in Old English meant a jeweller as well as a blacksmith). The argument for a late Roman workshop producing fine metal-work at Faversham, a predecessor of the one which produced some of the splendid Kentish brooches and pendants of the late sixth century, is a tenuous one, but worth noting here.

The Old English plant-name *croh* 'saffron' is a loan from Latin *crocus*. This would cause no surprise if the word were only known from learned treatises of the late Old English period, but it is a different matter when such a plant-name appears also in a place-name; and when not only the name but the plant itself is likely to be a Roman introduction to this country the argument for continuity from Roman Britain to Anglo-Saxon times is very strong indeed. Such a case was presented in Gelling 1970 for Croydon GTL. Croydon probably means 'saffron valley', some of the early spellings deriving from a compound of *croh* with *denu*, others from a form which incorporates an adjective meaning 'growing with saffron', either **crogen* or an oblique case of **crogig*. The plant referred to is the Autumnal Crocus, *Crocus sativus*, the stigmas of which yield yellow dye, and it is a native of southern and central Europe, the Levant, and western Asia. Unless we reject the proposed etymology for Croydon it is necessary to inquire how the plant reached this country, and how a name derived from Latin came to be used by the Anglo-Saxon country-people among whom the place-name arose. The dye was in common use among the Romans, and it is obviously possible that they introduced the plant to Britain. A plant grown in the Roman period could have continued to flourish for a while afterwards, and as it has an attractive flower it would naturally be noticed by English settlers. The Latin name *crocus* could have been passed on to them by the British people of the neighbourhood (as they passed on the Celtic name for the hill at Caterham a few miles to the south, and the Celtic name Penge, a few miles north, see Chapter 4), or Germanic mercenaries could have acquired it from Latin-speaking employers. Croydon adjoins Addiscombe and West Wickham, and Anglo-Saxon finds from Croydon now in the Public Library include some late Roman belt-fittings of the type mentioned at the beginning of this chapter.

If the Autumnal Crocus and the word *croh* were in fact to be found in the Surrey countryside before the year 809 (when Croydon is first recorded), both the plant and the word appear to have disappeared at some date after that. The plant is stated in the *Encyclopædia Britannica* to have been reintroduced to western Europe by the Crusaders. The English no longer had the word *croh* for it in the medieval period, but used instead the foreign word *saffron*, which they transferred from the dye to the plant. The modern word *crocus* is a new coinage from the Latin; it was not known to herbalists writing in the sixteenth century.

The plant-name *croh* probably occurs in a few other place-names, but early forms are essential in order to distinguish it from the more common element *cráwe* 'crow'. Crowhurst SSX is *on Croghyrste* in an Old English charter, so may be derived from *croh*, as may Crowle WOR, which is recorded in Old English as *Croglea*, *Crohlea*, and had a *crohwællan* on its boundary. But there is another place-name element **crōh* 'corner, bend', which it is not possible to distinguish from `croh` 'saffron'. Croydon is particularly likely to contain *croh* 'saffron' because early spellings like *Crogedene, Croydene* alternate with those like *Croindene, Croyendene*, and the latter suggest an adjectival formation of a kind particularly well evidenced with plant-names. There was another *Croindene* in High Wycombe BUC, surviving in Crendon Lane.

In the suggestions made so far in this chapter there is a wide range between the more and the less probable. As regards *wīchām* and *camp* a connection with Roman institutions may fairly be claimed as established, but at the other end of the scale the derivation of Croydon from *croh* 'saffron' is not sufficiently definite to carry much weight. It is time to move back on to firmer ground, and this is provided by Professor Cameron's article 'Eccles in English Place-Names' (Cameron 1968). This presents most of the examples of **ecles* in English place-names, with a map which is reproduced here as Fig 5. Since the article was published, information has been brought forward by Mr P. A. Wilson which suggests that Eaglesfield CMB should be added to the list.

The historical significance of the six examples of Eccles, and of the more numerous names which have Eccles- as their first part, is that the term is believed to refer to a Celtic Christian church. Christianity, though not universal, was well established in Britain in the fourth century, but the Anglo-Saxons were pagan at the time of their first contacts with Britain, and if they recognized Christian churches and felt that a reference to them was appropriate in naming settlements they would be likely to borrow a Latin or Welsh word. The word in question is Latin *ecclesia*, from which is derived Modern Welsh *eglwys*. Professor Jackson (1953, p. 412) states that the Primitive Welsh form of this word, **eglēs*, was adopted by the English in the form **eclēs*, and (p. 557) that -*c*- was substituted for -*g*- because Old English did not have -*g*- in this position. Professor Cameron (pp. 87–8) points out that a shift of stress from the second to the first syllable must have occurred to account for the modern name Eccles. Neither authority envisages the possibility of Latin *ecclesia* being borrowed into Old English without the intermediary of British speech. In view of the distribution pattern shown on Fig. 5, which has a strong bias towards the north-west Midlands, **ecles* should in most instances be regarded as a loan from Welsh, and most of the names in which it occurs belong in the category discussed in Chapter 5. But the three examples of Eccles which have been noted in south-east England are widely separated from all the others, and it is worth considering the possibility that these three represent a very early borrowing, direct from Latin. The word could have been borrowed twice by English speakers, from Latin in the south-east, and again, at a considerably later date, from Welsh in the north and west. If it had entered English at the likely date (before AD 500) of the south-eastern names, and remained in the language till *c.* 600, the likely date of the north-western names, it might have been expected to appear in place-names in the central part of England, where it is not, in fact, evidenced. An early borrowing from Latin which was used in a few place-names in the south-east probably dropped out of the language after a very short period of use.

Eccles KNT is five miles south-south-west of Rochester, a mile west of the Roman road which leads south from that town. This part of Kent, comprising the valleys of the Darent and the Medway with their rich concentrations of Roman remains, has already been noted as having something of a concentration of the types of place-name examined in this chapter. Roman buildings have been identified immediately to the north and north-east of Eccles, and it is possible that a centre of Christian worship was associated with these. Eccles near Attleborough NFK lies at a junction of Roman roads in an area where Roman settlement is well attested. Eccles near Hickling NFK was instanced in Cameron 1968 as one of the few Eccles names which is not near a Roman road, but it is actually on the line of the east-west route which has been traced to Smallburgh five miles west of Hickling, and which the Ordnance Survey Map of Roman Britain marks conjecturally as turning south-east near Hickling. These three names are marked on Fig. 2.

The final word to be considered in this survey of English place-name elements which are borrowings from Latin is the word **funta*, 'spring, fountain', only recorded in place-name spellings, which occurs in some fifteen settlement-names. This has hitherto been considered to be an Old English loan from Primitive Welsh **funtǭn*, which is itself from Latin *fontāna*, but it seems possible that it may have come into Old English direct from Latin. The distribution of names which contain it supports this suggestion. Smith (1956, Part 1, p. 189) characterized the distribution of **funta* as 'chiefly in the South Country from Essex to Warwickshire and south, especially in Hampshire, Wiltshire'. The relatively small class of names is, however, very unevenly distributed within that broad area, and the exact siting of the individual items shown on Fig. 3 suggests that names in **funta* have close associations with the other types of place-name discussed in this chapter.

It is not always obvious from the modern spelling that a name contains **funta*, partly because, as a rare element, it is particularly liable to reduction and distortion, and partly because owing to a regular interchange of *f-* and *h-* it becomes -hunt in a number of examples. Here again, early spellings are essential before a name can be identified as containing *funta*. It is usually the second, or defined, element in a compound name, and it is not used by itself in settlement-names.

One striking feature of the limited distribution of names in *funta* is that five of the six names in the Home Counties are arranged in a rough circle round London. These are: Bedfont MDX, on the Roman road which crosses the Thames at Staines; Chalfont BUC; Bedmond HRT (the same name as Bedfont, see below), which lies three miles south-west of *Verulamium*; Cheshunt HRT, which lies by Ermine Street and probably has *ceaster* as first element; and Wansunt in Bexley GTL. The sixth Home Counties example is Tolleshunt ESX, which lies near the course of the Roman road which led south-west from Colchester. Only a short stretch of this has been traced, but this short stretch is heading for Tolleshunt.

Apart from these six examples, there are clusters of settlement-names containing *funta* in Hampshire and Wiltshire. Of the four names in Hampshire two, Boarhunt and Funtley, lie close together between Portchester and the parish of Wickham. A third name, Havant (Old English *Hamanfunta*), lies between six and seven miles east of Boarhunt, on a Roman road and in an area of dense villa remains. The fourth Hampshire name is Mottisfont, which lies inland to the north-west of this area, on the River Test and two miles south of the Roman road which connects Winchester and Salisbury.

The three Wiltshire names in *funta* are Fovant (Old English *Fobbanfuntan*), Teffont and Urchfont. Fovant and Teffont are adjacent parishes lying between the Roman roads which lead north-west and south-west from Salisbury. The etymology of Fonthill, a few miles west of Teffont, has not been completely worked out, but the name is in some way a derivative of *funta*. The remaining Wiltshire example, Urchfont, is the parish on the boundary of which Wickham Green is situated, and since this is the only *wīchām* name in the county the conjunction may fairly be considered significant.

Two more names in *funta* are listed in Smith 1956. One is Bedford Well in Eastbourne SSX (*Bedefonte* 1486, the same name as Bedfont and Bedmond, see below), which only survives as a street-name. The other is Chadshunt WAR. All these names are marked on Fig. 2. As with *camp*, the number of field-names and charter-boundary names which may contain *funta* is an unassessed quantity. There is, however, little doubt that settlement-names containing this element have a striking relationship to Roman remains, and that the two main groups, round London and east of Southampton, are in areas where we have already found evidence suggesting contact between English speakers and Latin speakers at the end of the

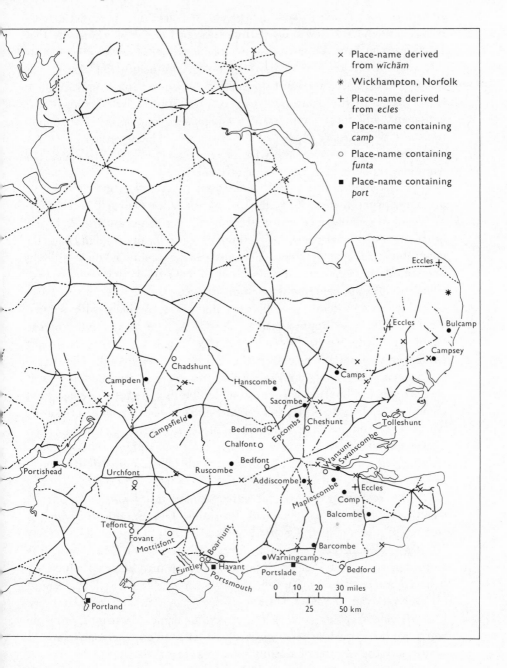

Fig. 2   English place-names containing loan-words from Latin (from *Anglo-Saxon England* 6, by permission of Cambridge University Press)

Roman period. When looked at in detail, the distribution of settlement-names containing **funta* suggests that the word may have come into Old English direct from Latin, in the manner postulated for the other words discussed in this chapter. This is phonologically possible; Jackson 1953 (p. 273) says that early Latin loan-words borrowed into English had *u* substituted for *o* in certain circumstances, which include *ŏ* plus nasal plus consonant, and these circumstances are present in *fontāna*. Two points remain to be considered: what sort of object would be described by a loan-word from Latin *fontana*, and what are the first elements with which the word is compounded in English place-names.

It is unlikely that the Anglo-Saxons used a word of Latin origin for an ordinary spring. Bedfont MDX adjoins a parish called Stanwell, and the use of **funta* in one instance and of the normal Germanic word *wella* in the other suggests that there was something of a specifically Roman character about the spring at Bedfont. The obvious possibility is that building operations had been performed in order to make the spring easier to use. Stone troughs are common enough on Romano-British sites, and a fairly elaborate arrangement for collecting the water, perhaps with spouts, would be likely to impress barbarian settlers. One is reminded of the 'fountain' made by the Romans at Carlisle. Such a construction might survive and continue to be used in the vicinity of a derelict villa. The triple occurrence of the compound which has become Bedfont, Bedmond and Bedford (in Eastbourne) is interesting, as the first element is considered (Smith 1956, Part 1, p. 72) to be Old English *byden*, 'vessel, tub, butt', which is also compounded with *wella* in place-names. In other names, such as Beedon BRK, *byden* is used in a transferred topographical sense to mean 'steep-sided valley', but when combined with **funta* and *wella* it is likely to refer literally to a trough for collecting water from a spring.

Of the remaining twelve settlement-names in **funta*, four have a significant word as first element. Boarhunt, Old English *Byrhfunt*, is 'spring of the manor', Chalfont is 'calf spring', Cheshunt probably 'spring by a Roman town', and Teffont 'boundary spring'. In Funtley the word is used as first element. This leaves seven names, six of which are believed to contain Old English personal names. These are: Chadshunt (**Ceadel*), Fovant (**Fobba*), Havant (*Hama*), Tolleshunt (**Toll*), Urchfont (**Eohrīc*) and Wansunt (*Wont*). The remaining name, Mottisfont, probably contains Old English *mōtere* 'speaker', either used as a personal name or referring to the holding of assemblies at this spring.

Chapter 4

The Celtic Survival

The preceding chapter examined in some detail a relatively small class of English place-names, those which contain words borrowed from Latin, and which may bear a direct relationship to Romano-British institutions. These were discussed at length because this is the first work in which they have been presented as a single class of English names, and because the historical context suggested here for some of them—the period between *c.* AD 370 and the mid fifth century—has not been put forward in any earlier book. The much larger class of place-names to be discussed in this chapter will be dealt with in less detail, not because it is of less historical importance, but because its vital bearing on Dark Age history has been recognized for a long time. This class comprises the bulk of the names which are believed to have been acquired by English settlers from the Welsh-speaking people of the countryside. The survival of some recorded Romano-British names has been discussed in Chapter 2. Here we are concerned mainly with names which are not actually on record from the Romano-British period but which are believed to have been in use then because they are in the Primitive Welsh language. It is convenient to consider in this chapter also place-names in the English language which contain references to people of Welsh nationality.

When the study of place-names became an academic discipline it became apparent that there were enough pre-English names still in use to render untenable some of the more extreme views of nineteenth-century historians concerning the virtual disappearance of the Celtic stock from the south and east of England. Volume I of the English Place-Name Society's publications, *Introduction to the Survey of English Place-Names*, published in 1924, has for its second chapter an essay on 'The Celtic Element' by Eilert Ekwall. Here he says, 'A study of British place-names will have among its chief aims the establishment of the extent to which a British population survived after the Anglo-Saxon conquest, the relation between Britons and Saxons after that event, and similar problems. The view often held that the British population was exterminated or swept away, seems to have lost ground of late years. The numerous British place-names in England tell strongly against it.' All subsequent writers must echo that statement. The survival of pre-English place-names, either so as to be recorded in medieval writings, or so as to be still in use today, proves that there was a period of co-existence by Welsh and English speakers. Probably no one today would wish to assert the converse, that the absence of such names from an area proves that there was no such co-existence. There are other ways in which the likelihood of continuity may be demonstrated, and one of these is discussed in Chapter 8. The positive statement—that most surviving pre-English names must have become familiar to the English as a result of peaceful intercourse with the descendants of Romano-British people—is, however, the one which concerns us in this chapter.

The identification of Celtic and pre-Celtic place-names is one of the most important tasks of English place-name studies, but it is also one of the most difficult. The scholars to whom the work of the English Place-Name Survey is entrusted are necessarily specialists in Old English and Old Norse, the languages of the vast majority of our place-names. This means that they are not well equipped to identify or interpret Celtic names.

The study was placed on a new footing in 1953 by the publication of Kenneth Jackson's *Language and History in Early Britain*, which discusses a large number of place- and personal names which are certain or virtually certain to be Celtic. Place-names included in Professor Jackson's book are awarded a sort of certificate of authenticity; but there are a great many names which were outside the scope of his inquiry, and concerning which a final decision is difficult or impossible. Professor Jackson is now vetting the English Place-Name Society's county volumes, so that recent and forthcoming surveys should be sound in their lists of names likely to be of pre-English origin. The pre-war volumes, on the other hand, are very unreliable in this respect; and even Professor Eilert Ekwall, whose enlightened attitude to this material has been quoted above, and whose magnificent pioneer work in *English River-Names* (1928) and *The Oxford Dictionary of English Place-Names* (first ed. 1935) cannot be too highly praised, must be regarded as a not wholly reliable guide.

In spite of these difficulties and dangers, it is highly desirable that attempts should be made to identify pre-English names in all areas, and to draw maps which make it possible to study their distribution and their relationship to other types of place-name and to archaeological remains from the Roman and early Anglo-Saxon periods. Professor Jackson provided only one distribution map (reproduced here as Fig. 3), showing rivers which have British names. This class of evidence is much more

——— Certainly or probably Celtic
············· Possibly Celtic

AREA 3

AREA 2

AREA 4

AREA 3

AREA 1

AREA 3

AREA 4

0   30
miles

Fig. 3   British river-names (from Jackson 1953, by permission of Edinburgh University Press)

common in the west than in the east, and Professor Jackson divided the country from east to west into Areas I–IV, most of England falling into Areas I and II, where the survival of such river-names is very much the exception.

This division of the country into zones on the basis of the proportion of pre-English river-names has provided a useful framework for most discussions of the material since 1953. But the importance of our stock of pre-English place-names is such that it merits more detailed mapping than this. One of Professor A. H. Smith's maps (Smith 1956) shows a great deal of relevant material in addition to the British river-names. This is one of the most interesting place-name distribution maps ever to have been printed, but the scale is so tiny and the printing so poor that the student is liable to give up in despair after trying to decide which names are represented by the symbols. This map does, however, show up more clearly than most previous ones the tendency of Celtic place-names to occur in clusters, an aspect of the distribution pattern which deserves more attention than it has hitherto received. Even when they are at their scarcest, as in Berkshire, Oxfordshire and Warwickshire, names which may fairly be taken as indicating the presence of Welsh speakers in an Anglo-Saxon context often occur in small groups rather than being dotted about evenly.

Two general principles about Celtic or pre-Celtic names may be taken as established. First, they are most likely to be the names of the greatest rivers (e.g. Thames, Tame, Teme, Avon, Severn, probably Tees), larger hills (e.g. Malvern WOR, The Chevin YOW, probably Pennines, Cheviots and Quantocks), and more extensive forests (e.g. Arden WAR, Wyre WOR), since these were known to a great many people and this gave them a greater chance of survival than the names of the smaller features of the countryside. Second, despite important exceptions (such as a cluster of names near Penge SUR and a large blank area in central Shropshire), there is a general increase in the number of surviving Celtic names as one goes further north and west in England.

Little further progress can be made in the detailed evaluation of the historical significance of Celtic place-names in England until more detailed distribution maps are available. The map here reproduced as Fig. 4 was compiled in 1960 as part of a study of the Birmingham region. It serves as an illustration of the dangers and rewards of this type of mapping. The dangers lie in the large area of uncertainty as to which names should be included. The pre-English status of a large proportion of them is beyond question, but there are a considerable number for which a final decision is difficult or impossible, and if the map had been compiled a few years earlier or later a different decision might have been made about

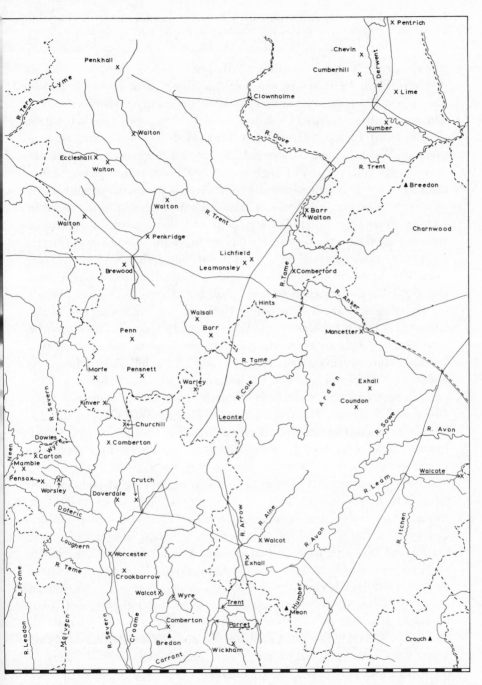

Fig. 4   The Birmingham region, showing place-names which may indicate the presence of Welsh-speaking people after the English settlement

some of the names for reasons which have little scientific basis. For this reason it is important that each item shown on such a map should be named in full, not represented by a symbol. This map may provide a useful starting point for further study, but a person using it may well disagree about the status of some names shown, and may wish to add names which have been omitted. Names previously considered Celtic which have been omitted include Cannock STF (for reasons set out in Gelling 1970), Lizard STF (for which Old English spellings in *Lus-* seem to preclude Welsh *llys* as first element), Ercall and Ewdness SHR (which are more easily explained as Old English than as Welsh), Ismere WOR (the first element of which is a river-name, Ouse, which is of obscure origin), and a number of WAR names—Brailes, Cosford, Dassett, Dosthill—discussed in Gelling 1974b (pp. 74-5). Arden WAR is included against the current of recent opinion, and the reasons for this are given in Gelling 1974b (p. 74).

The names shown on Fig. 4 include not only fully Celtic names, like Penn, Barr and Malvern, but also hybrid compounds with one English and one Welsh element. Bredon WOR and Breedon LEI, which consist of Welsh *bre* and English *dūn*, both meaning 'hill', are typical specimens of the tautological hybrids discussed in Jackson 1953 (p. 245). It looks as if the local British people spoke of 'the hill', and the English, not realizing that *bre* was a common noun, took it for the name of the hill. A later failure to understand the meaning of Old English *dūn* has caused the Leicestershire name to become Breedon on the Hill. Similar tautological compounds elsewhere include Pendle Hill LNC ('hill called *Pen*' to which modern *Hill* has been added), Cheadle CHE ('wood called *Cēd*') and Cheetwood LNC. Other hybrid compounds, not of this special type, shown on Fig. 4 include Coundon WAR, much corrupted from earlier forms such as *Condelme*, *Cundelma*, which show it to refer to the source (Old English *āewielm*) of a river with the pre-English name Cound; Doverdale WOR, in which Old English *dæl* 'valley' has been added to the Celtic river-name Dover; Crookbarrow and Churchill WOR, which are discussed in Chapter 6; and Charnwood LEI, which has as first element Welsh *carn* 'rock'. Lichfield and Mancetter are hybrids of the sort discussed in Chapter 2, in which an English word has been added to a Romano-British town-name. Worcester has a pre-English first element, apparently identical with the name of Wyre Forest, but this was probably not the name of the Romano-British town at Worcester. Penkridge, which looks superficially as if it might be a hybrid, is actually the Romano-British name *Pennocrucium* with both elements of the British name preserved (see Chapter 2).

In addition to the British names, and the hybrid British/English names shown on Fig. 4, there are two categories of names in the English language which have been included because they are thought to refer to people of British nationality and to British institutions. The first category consists of the names in Wal- and Cumber- or Comber-, the second comprises the three names, Eccleshall and two instances of Exhall, which are thought to refer to Celtic Christian churches. Both categories deserve to be discussed in some detail.

The names shown on Fig. 4 which may refer to people of wholly or partly British descent fall into two groups. One group includes Walton (four in Staffordshire, one in Derbyshire), Walcot (one in Worcestershire, two in Warwickshire) and Walsall STF, all probably containing Old English *walh* used either as a noun or as a personal name; and the other includes Cumberhill DRB, Comberford STF and the two Worcestershire examples of Comberton, containing Old English *Cumbre*, which may also be used either as a noun or as a personal name.

There is a division of opinion concerning the significance of *walh* (plural *walas*, genitive singular *wales*, genitive plural *wala*) in place-names. In written Old English the word has two meanings, 'Welshman' and 'serf'. It is the former meaning which has survived in modern English, Wales being the plural, and Welsh the derivative adjective. The plural, *walas*, is also the second element in the name Cornwall. This word *walh* is a Germanic formation from Latin *Volcae*, the name of a Celtic tribe. It was applied in Germanic languages to the speakers of Latin, as well as to the speakers of Celtic languages, and Professor Tolkien (1963, p. 26) suggested that this was due not only to the fact that Latin eventually became the language of most areas of Celtic speech known to Germanic peoples, but also to the ability of the Germans to recognize similarities between Latin and Gallo-Brittonic speech. As regards the Old English use of *walh* to mean 'slave', Professor Tolkien considered that this was not a total generalization of the national name (as *slave* is from *Slav*), but that it must often have involved a recognition that particular serfs were Welsh speaking.

A recent discussion of the problem, Faull 1975, provides a careful analysis of all the linguistic evidence relating to the use of *walh* (and the West Saxon form, *wealh*) in legal codes, literature, personal names and place-names in the Anglo-Saxon period. This establishes that *walh* meant 'a Celt' when the English entered Britain during the course of the fourth, fifth and sixth centuries. It is likely that in the earliest settlement period the majority of slaves would be British, being either the descendants of people who had that status during the Roman period, or people reduced to it during the wars which led to the establishment of the Anglo-Saxon kingdoms, so it was natural that the secondary sense 'slave' should develop. The racial meaning persisted, however, and Miss Faull demon-

strates that the sense 'Briton' is clearly apparent in the laws of King Ine
of Wessex (dating from AD 688–94), which provide for free *wealas*, who
may or may not be owners of land, to have a lower social status (measured
by their *wergild*, the compensation paid for killing them) than Englishmen
in equivalent positions. When these laws use the term *wealh* of a slave, it is
clear that they refer to a Welsh slave as opposed to an English one. The
date at which the two senses became separate, so that a slave referred to as
a *walh* need not be Welsh, is not ascertainable on account of the shortage
of eighth-century evidence, but the separation appears to have occurred by
the second half of the ninth century. At the end of the ninth century there
is some evidence that *Wealas* could still be used of Britons living within the
English territories, but by the eleventh century *Wealas* as a racial term
could only be applied to the Celts of Wales and Cornwall. Miss Faull
considers that *walh* 'slave' was not very widely adopted in Old English, the
alternative term, *thēow*, being usually preferred. This excellent article
provides the sober documentation for Professor Tolkien's inspired
rhetoric. As regards the use of *walh* in place-names and personal names,
Miss Faull's views coincide very closely with my own, and no attempt is
made in the following paragraphs to distinguish between her ideas and
mine. She is rather more definite than I feel able to be about the likelihood
of *walh* meaning 'Welshman' in some examples of the place-names
Walcot and Walton.

The occasional use of *walh* to mean 'serf' in Old English means that the
Waltons and Walcots marked on Fig. 4 are ambiguous. If they were coined
in the first years of the use of English speech in the area they may well
mean 'farm and cottages of the Britons', but if they are of later origin they
need mean no more than 'farm or cottages where there are serfs'. There is
some reason to think that place-names which refer to owners or inhabitants
of a particular social class, such as priests, *ceorls*, 'knights', were coined at
a rather late stage of English name-giving (this point is discussed in
Chapter 5), and Walcot and Walton could be considered to belong to this
category, and so to have arisen at a date when the meaning 'Briton' is not
certain to be the operative one for *walh*. In addition to this doubt about the
historical significance, there is some difficulty in deciding whether or not a
modern Walton or Walcot certainly contains this word. There are several
other Old English compounds which yield these modern forms, and a
Walton may be a farm near a forest (Old English *wald*), a farm near a wall
(e.g. Walton CMB) or, in the Mercian dialect area, a farm near a spring. It is
generally assumed that names which have a majority of Middle English
spellings with *Wale-*, as opposed to *Wal(l)-*, contain the word which means
'Briton' or 'serf'.

The meaning of *walh* may be less ambiguous when it occurs in the genitive singular in a place-name than it is when it occurs in the genitive plural. The only name of this type marked on Fig. 4 is Walsall STF, but there are a few others in the country, such as Walshford YOW and Walls-worth GLO. Walsall STF means 'sheltered place belonging to a man named *Walh*'. Both *Walh* and *Welisc* are on record as names of people in the Old English period. A priest named *Welisc* is one of the witnesses to the charter issued *c.* 685 by King Ceadwalla of Wessex (who himself had a British name) granting land for the foundation of a monastery at Farnham SUR. The theme *W(e)alh*, besides occurring several times as an uncompounded personal name, is the first element of a number of compound names, such as *Wealhheard*, *Wealhhere*, *Wealhhūn*, and occurs as the final element in the names of two seventh-century kings of Sussex and Wessex, *Æthelwalh* and *Cēnwalh*, and in the names of several members of the royal house of Mercia. It is unlikely that it was used as a personal-name theme without any reference to its meaning. It cannot be assumed that all Old English personal names were bestowed on account of the meaning of the elements (this point is discussed in Chapter 7), but it seems most unlikely that a word primarily understood to mean 'serf' would have been used in the naming of a male child, and unthinkable that such a meaning would enter into the names of Saxon princes. The word *thēow*, also meaning 'serf' is used in personal names, but this is associated with the verbs *thēowan*, *thēowian*, which are used of the most dignified forms of service as well as the servile ones. Probably the Saxon royal families in which the *-walh* theme occurs were acknowledging a Celtic strain in their ancestry. In the names of non-royal persons it seems possible that *W(e)alh* and *Welisc* are nicknames, corresponding to modern Taffy. The Old English word *wealhstōd* 'interpreter' is used as a personal name, one of the bearers being the first known Bishop of Hereford. This may well have been a name acquired in adult life by a man who spoke Welsh and English. The first known king of the Magonsæte, whose territory was north Herefordshire and south Shropshire, was named *Merewalh*, literally 'famous Welshman', and it is possible that an English prince adopted this name as a matter of political expediency.

No ambiguity attaches to the Old English term *Cumbre*, which enters into a number of names shown on Fig. 4. This is an English borrowing from the Primitive Welsh form of Modern Welsh *Cymro*, 'Welshman'. It is the first element of Cumberland, 'land of the Welsh', and enters into names in Cheshire (Comberbatch, Comber Mere), Lancashire (Comberhalgh), Herefordshire (Comberton), Wiltshire (Cumberwell), Gloucestershire (Cumberwood), and the West Riding (Cumberworth), as well as into the Staffordshire, Derbyshire and Worcestershire names shown on Fig. 4. A personal name *Cumbra* is on record, and here again it probably refers to the ancestry of the bearer. Whether it is in the genitive plural, as probably in Comber Mere and Comberford, or used as a personal name, as probably in the two instances of Comberton in Worcestershire, there is little reason to doubt that the place-name element refers to people of British descent.

Cumbre was perhaps a politer term for a Welshman than *walh* when English speech became current in the west Midlands, by which time the servile connotation of *walh* may have been stronger than it was when English kingdoms were established in the south and east. But although *Cumbre* appears to be best represented in the west Midlands and the north-west, it does enter into some names in eastern England, such as Cumberlow in Rushden HRT, Cumberton in Great Chishall ESX, Comberton CAM, Cumberworth LIN. A complete distribution map of names containing *Cumbre* and *walh* would probably be interesting. Professor Smith's map referred to above uses the same symbol for names in *walas*, *Brettas* and *Cumbran*. The element *Brettas* is not relevant here, as it is not certainly evidenced in place-names until the time of the Scandinavian settlements in the ninth century, which are discussed in Chapter 9.

Eccleshall and the two instances of Exhall marked on Fig. 4 contain Old English **ecles*, which (with the possible exception of three instances discussed in Chapter 3) is a borrowing from the Primitive Welsh ancestor of Modern Welsh *eglwys* 'church'. Most of the names known to contain this word were listed in Cameron 1968, and Professor Cameron's map is reproduced here as Fig. 5. Another probable instance, Eaglesfield CMB, has been brought forward by Mr P. A. Wilson since this map was compiled. This is one of our most evocative place-name elements, as it suggests that Celtic Christian churches continued to function in the post-Roman period in some areas, and that they were recognized and respected by the pagan Anglo-Saxon settlers.

The corpus of **ecles* names is not certain, but the six examples of Eccles seem absolutely safe, and those compounds which are repeated seem reasonably so. This is a word which appears in place-names either by itself or as the first element of compound names with a limited range of second elements. The fact that it is not used as a second element means that the Anglo-Saxons never felt moved to bestow a distinguishing name on one of these churches, but they sometimes used the church as a defining feature when naming something else. The compound of **ecles* with Old English *tūn* is found in Lancashire (three examples, one west of St Helens, another west of Chorley, and Great and Little Eccleston near Poulton) and in Cheshire (Eccleston south of Chester). The compound with *halh*, the meaning of which is discussed below, is found in the West Riding (Eccleshall south-west of Sheffield), Staffordshire (Eccleshall south-west of Stone), and Warwickshire (two examples of Exhall, one near Alcester and the other north of Coventry). A compound with *feld* gives Ecclesfield north of Sheffield YOW and probably Eaglesfield south-west of Cockermouth CMB, and a compound with *hyll* gives Eccleshill near Darwen LNC and Eccleshill north-west of Bradford YOW. The repetition of these compounds makes it less likely that the first element is a rare Old English personal name *Eccel*, which would be a derivative of the recorded *Ecca*, and which may enter into some boundary-marks in Anglo-Saxon charters. There appears to be only one example of each of the following compounds: with *clif* 'bank', in Egglescliffe south-west of Stockton DRH; with *lēah* 'clearing', in Exley south of Bradford YOW; and with *wælle* 'spring', in Eccleswall south-east of Ross HRE. In these a stronger case could be made for the first element being the genitive of a personal name *Eccel*.

It is surprising that there are four examples of the compound of *ecles* with *halh*, and that three of the four should lie in the area shown on Fig. 4. Old English *halh* is usually a topographical term. It is very common in English place-names in the sense 'sheltered place', often with reference to situation in a small valley or a hollow. Eccleshall near Sheffield lies in broken country, where this sense would be appropriate, and it seems reasonably suitable for Eccleshall STF, which occupies a shallow curve in the contours of the gently rising ground south of the River Sow. It is not, however, obviously appropriate to the situations of the two places in Warwickshire called Exhall. Exhall near Alcester and Exhall near Coventry both lie on low, flat shelves of land. Another of the senses of *halh* evidenced in place-names is 'land in the projecting corner of an administrative unit'. This use is discussed in Gelling 1973a (p. 116), under the Berkshire name Bracknell. Although this is probably a relatively late meaning of *halh* it may not be totally irrelevant to the two Warwickshire names. A sense 'land not included in the general administrative arrangements of an area' might be conjectured as one of the earlier meanings of *halh*, preceding the well-evidenced sense 'land in an angle of a parish or county', and this might be appropriate to an area surrounding a Celtic Christian centre. This is highly conjectural, however.

The possibility of *ecles* referring to churches which had ecclesiastical jurisdiction over a wide area has recently been explored by Professor G. W. S. Barrow (Barrow 1973, pp. 26ff.) After discussing the districts in the north called 'shires' (for which see Chapter 8) he says:

Hallamshire with its hall at Sheffield and its mother church at Ecclesfield prompts us to look at the 'Eccles' names of Lancashire. They were surely not scattered about the county at random. From the twelfth to the nineteenth century South Lancashire was divided among five hundreds, Salford, West Derby, Leyland, Blackburnshire and Amounderness. Eccles is in Salford Hundred, just west of Salford. Eccleston in West Derby Hundred lies only a few miles east of West Derby, the hundred capital, but in 1086 it formed part of the small hundred of Warrington, afterwards merged with that of West Derby. Eccleston in Leyland Hundred is immediately southwest of Leyland. It was, indeed, the site of the three-weekly hundred or wapentake court in the thirteenth century. Eccleshill in Blackburnshire is not only in Blackburn parish but was immemorially linked to the Celtic-named township of Mellor which occupies a hill on the opposite edge of Blackburn. As for Amounderness Hundred, it has twin Ecclestons, Great and Little, adjacent but in different parishes, the ancient parishes respectively of St Michael on Wyre and Kirkham. The survival of 'Eccles' names in each of the hundreds of medieval Lancashire is paralleled, most interestingly, in Kent, where Eccles is and was in Aylesford parish, while Aylesford itself was the capital of one of the older lathes of Kent, the *locus* of a court by 961 and no doubt from much earlier, and still royal demesne in 1086. Other English evidence seems equally suggestive. Eccleston in Cheshire, for example, is two miles south of Chester itself and was in Chester Hundred. The Staffordshire manor of Eccleshall, though it does not seem to have been in any sense the 'capital' of Pirehill Hundred, was nevertheless the centre of an exceptionally large estate with twenty berewicks. It was part of the endowment (probably the early endowment) of the seventh-century church of Saint Chad at Lichfield.

In this discussion Professor Barrow is mainly concerned to establish that the Scottish place-names in Eccles- have a similar significance to the English ones, and that previous authors have been over-cautious in emphasizing that some of the Scottish names could be relatively late Gaelic formations, rather than Primitive Welsh ones.

Before leaving the subject of *ecles* it is necessary to utter the usual caveat about the danger of mistaking other place-name types for this one. Ekwall 1960 (p. 159) considered that Ecchinswell HMP (*Eccleswelle* 1086), Ashford MDX (Old English *Ecelesford*, *Echelesford*) and the River Ecclesbourne DRB contained a river-name *Ecel*. It is certainly necessary to regard Ecchinswell and Ashford as distinct from the *ecles* 'church' names, as their development shows that they had palatal *c*, but this does not apply to Ecclesbourne DRB, which could reasonably be ascribed to *ecles* 'church'. Professor Cameron pointed out that one of the most marked features of the *ecles* names was proximity to water, and the River Ecclesbourne may have been named from a lost settlement called *Eccles*. Ekwall's suggestion that some names in Eccles- contain an Old English personal name has already been mentioned. Caution is required when dealing with field-names on the line of Roman roads known as Icknield or Ryknield Street, or on the line of the Icknield Way, as these sometimes have spellings suggestive of *ecles though they actually contain a corrupt form of the road-name.

A name of particular historical significance on Fig. 4 is Pensax WOR. This Welsh name means 'hill of the Saxons', and it must have been coined at a time when English settlers were in the minority in north-west Worcestershire. Moreover, this situation must have lasted long enough for the name to obtain general currency, so that it survived the eventual change of language from Welsh to English. Names of this kind are very rare in England—Nansawsen CNW, 'valley of the English', is the only example to hand—but there are similar ones in southern Scotland. such as Pennersax and Glensaxon DMF, and Glensax PEB. Welsh speakers did not retain the *x* of *Saxon* for very long (cf. Modern Welsh *Sais*, 'Englishman'), so Pensax must have been coined in the early years of the contact between Welsh and English. The hill in question is probably the massif now called Clows Top. Another village on the side of Clows Top is Mamble WOR, and it is likely that this derives from the ancient Celtic name of the hill, the base being British *mammā* 'breast', which is found also in Manchester (see Chapter 2). This may have been displaced by the name Pensax at a time when the main distinguishing feature of the hill appeared to be the presence in its vicinity of some English settlers. At a later stage both hill-names, one certainly and the other possibly unintelligible to the English, were understood as referring to ancient settlements near the hill, and the massif itself acquired its modern name Clows Top from a settlement higher up on its slope called *clūs*, 'the enclosure'.

The order of elements in Pensax—noun first and qualifying element second—provides a useful contrast to that in Malvern, also near the south-west edge of Fig. 4. In Malvern ('bare hill') the adjective comes first and the noun second. The change in the Welsh manner of making names is believed to have occurred in the sixth century AD, so the order of the elements would disqualify Pensax from being an ancient British name, even if it did not refer explicitly to English settlers. If the map showing Celtic names were continued to the west, however, a number of Hereford-shire names would be brought within its scope, and some of these exhibit the modern Welsh word-order without the reason for it being so obvious. Dinmore north of Hereford is an example. This must be 'great fort', Welsh *din mawr*, but it is not clear why the later type of compound should be evidenced here when an ancient British name, becoming something like

Morthine, would have seemed most appropriate. It can only be noted that many names in Wales itself exhibit this 'late' order of elements, as if there had been extensive re-naming after the Roman period. The phenomenon has not been observed in any ancient name in Shropshire (where British names are surprisingly rare), and it appears to be evidenced in Worcestershire only in the special instance of Pensax. The modern Welsh word-order in place-names is a characteristic of areas where the Welsh language survived.

Pensax can be assigned a relative chronological position with regard to other British and Primitive Welsh names by three criteria—the order of the elements, the explicit reference to English settlers, and the preservation of the *x* of *Saxon*. It is likely that a number of Celtic place-names in England could be assigned relative dates on phonological criteria, but most English place-name students are not sufficiently skilled in the details of Celtic phonology to attempt this exercise. A few such points have been raised by Celtic experts about names on Fig. 4, and these deserve mention here.

Lichfield STF (see Chapter 2) appears in the two earliest manuscripts of Bede's Ecclesiastical History as *Lyccidfelth*, *Lyccitfeld-*, and *Licidfelth*, *Liccitfeld-*. The possible significance of the use of *-y-*, *-i-* to represent the first vowel in the Primitive Welsh name *$L\bar{e}tg\bar{e}d$* is discussed in Jackson 1953 (pp. 332–4). The symbols $\bar{e}$ and $\bar{e}$ used in this spelling are Professor Jackson's representation of two distinct vowels. The first is a long *e* of the sort called 'close' by philologists, the second is a long 'open' *e*. These symbols are explained in Jackson 1953 (p. 7). If the Old English form really was *Lyccid* for this name (as it certainly was for Lytchett DOR which has Middle English spellings *Lechet* 1269, *Luchet* 1291), it seems likely that this was borrowed from Primitive Welsh *$Luitg\bar{e}d$*, a form which shows the development of Welsh $\bar{e}$ to *ui* which Jackson dates about AD 675. This chronology offers little difficulty in the case of Lytchett DOR, as English speech may only just have been gaining ascendancy in the south-west at this date; but the development of $\bar{e}$ to *ui* in the first part of Lichfield can only be postulated on the assumption that an enclave of Welsh speech persisted in this part of Staffordshire long after the first coming of the English to the surrounding areas. In fact, if the Welsh sound-development had really occurred before the name was taken over by the English speakers, the hybrid name Lichfield was probably coined by English people at the time of St Chad's appointment to the Mercian bishopric in 669, when he selected the place as his seat. The possible reasons for St Chad's choice of Lichfield are discussed in Chapter 6.

West of Lichfield, on the extreme edge of Fig. 4, is the name Neen, a river-name preserved by the two settlements of Neen Savage and Neen

Sollers SHR, though the river itself has been re-named Rea. The British river-name had the same vowel as the first part of *Lētgēd*, but the early spellings for Neen make it clear that the name was adopted by English speakers before the development to *ui* occurred. This appears to mean that Welsh speech persisted longer round Lichfield than it did round Pensax, which is not impossible, but implies that we should be thinking in terms of enclaves of Welsh speakers rather than a steady east to west progression of English speech. I am indebted to Mr Victor Watts for pointing out to me the potential historical significance of the different treatment of Primitive Welsh *ē* in Lichfield and Neen; his observations are now published in Watts 1976 (pp. 213–14).

Another name on Fig. 4 which is relevant to the possible late survival of Welsh speech in the Lichfield area is Hints STF, which lies on Watling Street. This was included on the map on the assumption that it derives from the Welsh word *hynt* 'a road', which is from British **sento-*. The vowel development would be regular in this case, but the initial H- requires comment. If the derivation from **sento-* be correct, the name must have been used by Welsh speakers up to the completion of the change of *S-* to *H-* which is seen in *Hafren*, the Welsh form of the river-name Severn. This change is dated by Jackson 1953 (p. 521) to the middle or second half of the sixth century, so the assumption that it occurred in Hints does not require us to postulate anything like so late a Welsh survival as may be implied by the earliest spellings of Lichfield, but it is a scrap of evidence pointing in somewhat the same direction. There were English-speaking people in the valley of the Warwickshire Avon a good deal earlier than this, certainly from the beginning of the sixth century, when the pagan Anglo-Saxon cemeteries at such sites as Baginton, Stratford and Bidford were in use, and these are only about thirty miles south of Hints. There is another Hints in Shropshire, about three miles west of the name Neen on Fig. 4, and this may have the same derivation as the Staffordshire name; it is difficult to think of any alternative etymology. The preservation of S- in Severn is doubtless due to the name of this great river being familiar to many people in Europe during the Roman period.

The possibility of determining the approximate date at which a Welsh name was adopted by English speakers by studying the stage of development which the vowels or consonants of the Welsh name had reached when the English encountered it is one which deserves attention by philologists. The subject cannot be thoroughly explored in the present study because it is a field for the Celtic rather than the Old English specialist; but one more instance may be cited here of a west Midland name which presents special phonological problems as regards the date of

transfer from Welsh to English speakers. This is Maund HRE, a name borne
by two small settlements, Maund Bryan and Rosemaund, lying some six
miles north-east of Hereford. Maund is stated in some reference books to
be the source of the name *Magonsǣte*, borne by the small sub-kingdom of
Mercia which lay between the Welsh district of Archenfield and the River
Severn, comprising an area which is now the northern half of Herefordshire and the southern half of Shropshire. On this assumption, *Magonsǣte*
would mean 'dwellers by Maund'. This type of group-name is well
evidenced in the west Midlands, other examples being *Wreocensǣte*
'dwellers near the Wrekin' and *Tomsǣte* 'dwellers near the River Tame'.
There is a noteworthy line of such names running along Offa's Dyke from
Oswestry SHR, which was in the Hundred of *Mersete*, to the River Wye,
where there was a Hundred of *Stepelset*. Usually it is easy to identify the
pre-English place-name (such as Wrekin, Tame) which is the basis of these
group-names, or to point to an Old English topographical term (such as
gemǣre 'boundary', *stēpel* 'steep place') from which they are formed, but
Magonsǣte is more difficult to explain than most names of this type.

Some authorities (e.g. Williams 1949, p. 39) have considered that the
Magonsǣte derived their name from *Magnis*, the Romano-British town at
Kenchester HRE (see Chapter 2). *Magnis* is probably a British name
meaning 'the rocks', perhaps originally the name of the fort at Credenhill.
This was subsequently rejected as the source of *Magonsǣte* on the grounds
that the British name would not have had -*g*- when the English reached
that part of the country in the second half of the seventh century. Much
earlier than this, in the second half of the sixth century, the -*gn*- of *Magnis*
would have reached the stage of development which Professor Jackson
spells *in*, as the word from which it derives was on its way to becoming
Modern Welsh *maen* 'stone, rock'. More recently, perhaps because of this
objection, the alternative suggestion has been preferred which gives
Maund as the source of *Magon*- (e.g. Smith 1956, Part 2, p. 94). It seems to
have escaped notice that as the only etymology so far suggested for Maund
is that it is derived from the same word meaning 'rock, stone' as *Magnis*
(Ekwall 1960, p. 318), exactly the same objection applies to derivation of
Magonsǣte from Maund as to the old derivation from *Magnis*.

Early spellings for Maund HRE are *Mage*, *Magene* 1086, *Magena* 1161,
Magene 1187. If this were an Old English name, as opposed to a British
name adopted by English speakers, the preservation of -*g*- until the Middle
English period would offer no difficulties. In English the consonant -*g*- was
vocalized in this position after the Norman Conquest. Because of this
vocalization in Middle English we have Modern English *draw*, *haw*, *own*,
bow from Old English *dragan*, *haga*, *āgen*, *boga*; but the -*g*- of these and of

similar words and names would be preserved throughout the Old English period. In Maund, to judge by spellings *Mawene* 1240, *Maune* 1337, the vocalization seems to have taken place late in the Middle English period. If Maund were an English name coined in the seventh century its development would offer no serious phonological problems, but there is still the etymological problem of finding an Old English word which is a possible source. The only English word known which could give the spellings noted above is *maga* 'stomach', modern *maw*. On strictly formal grounds, the name could derive from the dative of this word, *magan*, giving a meaning 'at the stomach'. Place-names from the dative of an uncompounded element are more often in the plural, however, which in this instance would be *magum*. This last could be spelt *magan* in late Old English, and would probably have given *Magen* in post-Conquest spellings. The final *-e* of most of the Middle English spellings for Maund could be explained as an inorganic letter added because most place-names have a final *e* in Middle English. The addition of *-d* is a modern development which is of no importance for the etymology.

The questions arising from this are, first, is 'at the stomach(s)' a credible place-name etymology, and second, is the superficial resemblance between Maund, *Magonsǣte*, and the Romano-British *Magnis* to be dismissed as a coincidence? The answer to the first question is probably in the negative. Old English terms for items of human and animal anatomy are frequent in place-names, including such words as *bæc*, *bile*, *brægen*, *brǣw*, *brū*, *ceole*, *clā*, *cneo*, *ears*, *flǣre*, *fōt*, *hals*, *hēafod*, *horn*, *hraca*, *mūtha*, *steort*, *swēora*, *tægl*, *tunge*, *wrōt*. These are all external features of the body, however, the only possible exception in the list being *brægen* 'brain', which probably means 'crown of the head' in place-names. The word *maga* refers to an internal organ, and if Old English speakers were coining a place-name referring to a physical feature which reminded them of that region of the body they would have been more likely to use the word *belg*, modern *belly*, which also meant 'bag, sack, bellows', and which occurs in a few place-names, such as Ballidon DRB, Belluton SOM. The topographical use of *maga* is unlikely, and it has not been noted in any other place-name. On the other hand, if the name Maund could be understood as referring originally to the flood-plain of the River Lugg, on the eastern edge of which the settlements lie, and which is the sort of geographical feature likely to be mentioned in a *-sǣte* name, a meaning 'at the stomach(s)' is perhaps not quite outside the range of credibility. A verdict of 'unlikely, but not totally impossible' may be given on the suggestion that Maund and *Magonsǣte* derive from an Old English topographical term.

What of the other possibility, which is that Maund and *Magonsǣte*

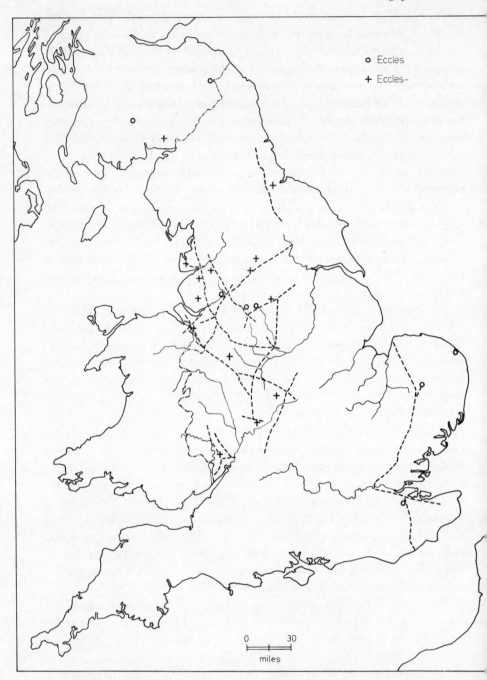

Fig. 5 Eccles in English place-names (from Cameron 1968, by permission of Leices
University Press)

derive from a British term? If this is postulated, then there is no need to
separate these names from *Magnis*. The British name could be seen as that
of a district, referring (if it means 'the rocks') either to Credenhill camp or
to all the hilly ground which lies north of Kenchester, but being liable to
appear in settlement-names on the other side of the River Lugg because
the district extended that far to the east. This is in many ways a more
attractive solution. But it is only possible phonologically if it be assumed
that *Magnis* became known to English speakers before AD 550, and that
their knowledge of the name was preserved without influence from British
speakers after that date. Probably the only way to explain this would be to
assume that *Magnis* was known to federate Germans who were in the west
Midlands at the end of the Roman period. The types of decorated metal-
work which may indicate such a presence (see Chapter 3) are well represented at Caerwent MON and Cirencester GLO, and occur sporadically at
sites further north in Gloucestershire. These places are well to the south of
Kenchester, but it is likely that troops stationed at Caerwent or Cirencester
would know the name *Magnis*. If they and their descendants remembered
it as the name of a district on the rivers Wye and Lugg, it is perhaps not
inconceivable that it was used again as a district-name in the seventh
century when English-speaking people became the rulers of the district,
and that it was then used in its archaic form, without the development to
*Main which would have taken place if it had been preserved by Welsh
speakers.

These are alternative desperate solutions to difficult problems, and the
reader may well reject both on the grounds that they outrage common
sense. The main task of the philologist is to clarify the problems, and in the
case of Maund-*Magnis*-*Magonsǣte* philologists may fairly be accused of
failing to do this. It was not a sound solution to bring forward Maund as an
alternative to *Magnis* as the first element of *Magonsǣte*, unless some
suggestion was made to account for the preservation of -*g*- in Maund until
it became incorporated in the name of the kingdom. Similar points have
probably been overlooked in other instances owing to the lack of detailed
understanding of Celtic phonology which characterizes most of us who
study English place-names.

Chapter 5

The Chronology of English Place-Names

The most dramatic development in English place-name studies since 1960 has been the rejection of the assumptions made by the first generation of specialists in this field about the nature of the earliest names in the English language. These were considered to be:

1. Those in which the suffixes *-ingas* and *-ingahām* were added to a man's name, giving place-names like Reading, Hastings, Gillingham, Wokingham. These compounds, which mean 'the followers of Rēad (or Hæsta)' and 'the homestead of the followers of Gylla (or Wocca)' were supposed to represent, in the case of the *-ingas* names the first land-takings of bands of immigrant Anglo-Saxons, in the case of the *-ingahām* names the immediate second stage of the settlement.

2. Those which refer to the sites of pagan religious worship (like Harrow GTL, Wye KNT) or to Germanic gods (like Wednesdbury STF, Thundersley ESX).

3. Those containing personal names or words which there is evidence for considering 'archaic', i.e. only current in the Old English language during the earliest years of the Anglo-Saxon presence in this country. For instance, the use of a small number of archaic words was put forward in the Cambridgeshire place-name survey (Reaney 1943, p. xviii) as compensation for the scarcity of *-ingas*, *-ingahām* names in the county, and some surprisingly concrete assertions were made on the basis of supposed lines of place-names containing related archaic personal names: in the Buckinghamshire Survey (Mawer and Stenton 1925, pp. xiv–xv) it was suggested that the occurrence of *Hygerēd* in Harlington MDX and *Hycga* (which may be a short form of *Hygerēd*) in Hitcham, Hedgerley and Hughenden BUC showed that

there was an original connection between the two regions, and that 'the southern slopes of the Chilterns were colonized from the early settlements on the Thames bank, of which Hitcham, OE *Hycgan hām*, is one'.

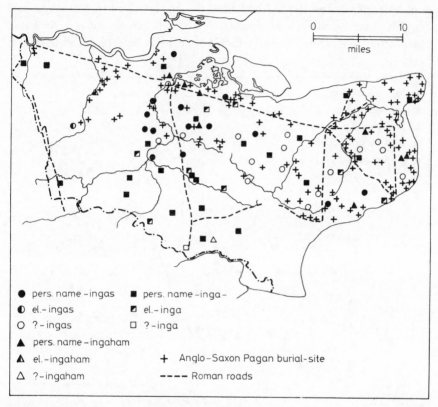

Fig. 6 Kent, showing English place-names in *-ingas*, *-inga-* and Anglo-Saxon burial sites (from Dodgson 1966, by permission of the Society for Medieval Archaeology)

In addition to these three articles of faith there was also, at least as late as 1965, a belief that the 'habitative' type of settlement-name (defined below) was likely to be earlier than the 'topographical' type. None of these assumptions about the earliest types of English place-names has emerged unscathed from the critical scrutiny of the last fifteen years, and the main tasks to be attempted in this chapter are to summarize the objections which have been brought against them and to look for alternative criteria for distinguishing between 'early' and 'late' English place-names.

The hypothesis that the *-ingas*, *-ingahām* place-names represent the

earliest settlements of English-speaking people in this country, and that
they may be related to the bands in which the immigrants migrated from
the Continent, goes back at least to 1849, when it appeared in J. M.
Kemble, *The Saxons in England*. The theory was developed and refined by
a number of scholars in the first half of the present century, but its general
validity was regarded as sacrosanct, and it was not seriously questioned
until after 1960. The doubts which began to be expressed at that date

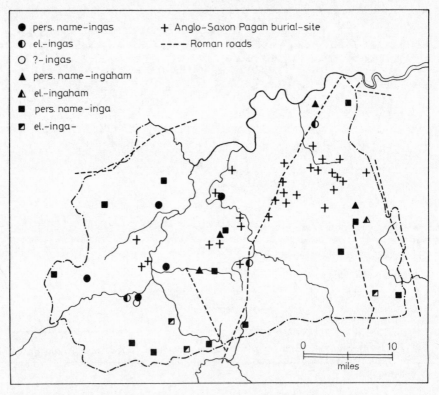

Fig. 7   Surrey, showing English place-names in *-ingas*, *-inga-* and Anglo-Saxon
burial sites (from Dodgson 1966, by permission of the Society for Medieval
Archaeology)

culminated in a major attack by J. McN. Dodgson (Dodgson 1966). The
theory has since been abandoned by most specialists, but it is proving
difficult to dislodge from the consciousness of authors and lecturers who
are not specialists.

The main objection to it is that *-ingas* and *-ingahām* place-names
coincide with early Anglo-Saxon archaeological remains about as little as
is possible, given that both occur in substantial numbers in the same

southern and eastern portion of England. The maps which have been compiled of both types of evidence suggest that, if we must regard them as contemporary, there was a law in operation from AD 400 to AD 600 which said that people of English descent might either have a pagan burial or live in a place with an -*ingas* name, but were to be strongly discouraged from doing both. The point is, of course, that we are not obliged to regard the -*ingas* names as contemporary with the early burials. The theory which asserted that names of the Hastings type must go back to the first land-takings of the English invaders was never more than a hypothesis, based on the feeling that a name meaning 'the followers or dependants of Hǣsta' was appropriate to a migratory group, and the fact that this type of name is well-represented on the Continent. It was a reasonable hypothesis, but (apart from a few instances in which sound-changes can be closely dated) place-names do not have a scientific chronology in the way that Anglo-Saxon grave-goods do; the study is scientific only from the point of view of etymology. If a hypothesis concerning the chronology of place-name types is conspicuously unsatisfactory in the light of archaeological evidence, there is no reason why it should not be abandoned.

John Dodgson's detailed maps showing the burials and the -*ingas*, -*ingahām*, -*inga*- place-names in the counties of Kent, Sussex, Surrey, Hertfordshire, Middlesex and Essex (of which two are reproduced here as Figs. 6 and 7) have the significant characteristic of clarity, owing to the symbols for burials seldom coinciding with those for place-names. If the theory of the early date of the settlements with -*ingas* names had been satisfactory, it would have been much more difficult to show the names on the same maps as the burials. Mr Dodgson's suggestion that these place-names represent a secondary colonization, from centres more or less corresponding to the location of the early burials, has met with general acceptance.

The study of the -*ingas* place-names is complicated by a considerable area of uncertainty about which names really belong in this category. There is another important place-name category which is particularly liable to confusion with the -*ingas* one. The plural suffix -*ingas* is related to the singular -*ing* which was added to a man's name in the Anglo-Saxon royal genealogies to give a meaning 'son of' in such a sequence as *Cerdic Elesing, Elesa Esling, Esla Giwising.* . . . In place-names, however, the plural -*ingas* seems to have meant 'people of' rather than 'sons of'. It is added not only to personal names (though that is the commonest use), but also to river-names (e.g. Avening GLO, Blything SFK) or topographical terms (e.g. Nazeing ESX, 'the people of the spur of land'). Potential confusion arises from the fact that the singular suffix -*ing* could also, in the

Germanic languages, be used to form place-names, and in these formations there is no connotation of filial relationship. A typical specimen of this type of formation is Clavering ESX, in which *-ing* is added to Old English *clæfre* 'clover' to give a meaning 'place where clover grows'. It is obvious that this is a totally different phenomenon from the Hastings, Reading names, but the two types of formation are sometimes difficult to distinguish if only Middle English spellings are available. In the earlier volumes of the English Place-Name Survey, compiled when no one questioned the significance of *-ingas* names, and when the singular *-ing* names were not considered of special historical importance, insufficient attention was paid to the problems of sorting them into the correct categories. Fresh studies of both types of name suggest that the Clavering type may have a better claim to be 'early' than the Reading type, and the care now being taken to ascertain the relationship of *-ingas* names to archaeological remains makes it vitally important to avoid classifying the singular names as plural. More is said of this below.

A similar objection to that raised against the *-ingas*, *-ingahām* names has been brought against the view that place-names which denote sites of pagan Germanic worship are likely to date from the first stages of the English settlement. Here, also, it has been noted that most of the specimens are not situated in areas which would on other grounds be considered to be those of the earliest English penetration (Gelling 1961, 1973). Something will be said in Chapter 6 of the significance recently suggested for names like Harrow, Weedon and Wednesbury.

As regards the argument that 'archaic' words in place-names are a guide to early settlement, this looks less convincing as the place-name survey continues, since almost every county of which a detailed survey is made produces additions to the known vocabulary of Old English, and it appears less likely that such terms were only incorporated in place-names coined in the fifth century. Allowance should probably be made for the use of a more conservative vocabulary in the countryside than in the centres from which our written records come. This is a widespread phenomenon today, in spite of the powerful modern factors which encourage standardization of language. If such otherwise unknown Old English words could be shown to be markedly more numerous in one area than in others, a sound historical argument might be based on this, but it is doubtful whether a good case has yet been made. The examples cited in Reaney 1943 (p. xviii)—**dung* 'underground chamber' in Wilsmere Down (earlier *Wlmaresdung*), **ēan* 'lamb' in Yen Hall, and a possible derivative of a Germanic root meaning 'mud' in a river-name *Must*—are insufficient to support his contention that 'the place-names of Cambridgeshire . . . fully agree with the indications of an early settlement provided by the archaeological materials discovered within the county'. The etymology of Wilsmere Down (a farm in Barrington) looks far from certain to the critical eye. The name is not recorded until the thirteenth century; most of the spellings are fourteenth century or later, and from 1324 and 1461 respectively we have the forms *Wulmarsdunghel* and *Wylfmeredunghyll*, which suggests the possibility that the name is really 'Wulfmǣr's dung-hill'. Such an etymology is reasonable for a minor name; another Old English term for a midden, *mixen*, enters into minor names like Mixon STF, and even occasionally into major names, like Mixbury OXF. It is not appropriate here to enter into detailed argument about individual 'archaic' terms which have been postulated to explain difficult English place-names; but it should be noted that some of them are highly speculative, and it seems surprising that concrete assertions about the early date of some place-names, and consequently of the English settlement, should have been put forward on such numerically slender and linguistically uncertain bases as these three names in Cambridgeshire.

As regards the argument from 'archaic' personal names, this is only valid if the personal names compounded in place-names are assumed to be those of very early settlers, so that Hygerēd and Hycga can be taken as the founding fathers of the villages of Harlington and Hitcham, or at least the Saxon leaders who took them from the British. The whole question of the significance of personal names in place-names is discussed in Chapter 7. This is one of a number of topics which might profitably have been given greater consideration in the early years of scientific place-name study. One of Sir Frank Stenton's chapters in the *Introduction to the Survey of English Place-Names* was entitled 'Personal Names in Place-Names' (Stenton 1924), but this is a brilliant essay on the personal names themselves rather than a critical assessment of their significance in place-names. If, as is suggested in Chapter 7, they are at least as likely to denote manorial estate owners as to belong to the original settlers, the historical information they offer is very different from that deduced from them in the Introductions to many of the English Place-Name Society's volumes.

Most of the names which fall into the categories listed above are relatively early. The pagan names were probably coined between AD 600 and AD 700; Dodgson 1966 (p. 19) suggests that 'the *-ingas* place-name seems to be the result of a social development contemporary with a colonizing process later than, but soon after, the immigration-settlement that is recorded in the early pagan burials'; and a king's thegn with an archaic personal name is more likely to be an estate owner of the sixth or seventh century than of the later Anglo-Saxon period. But there is no reason to believe that any of the place-names in these categories are the best guides to the process by which the English first made their homes in any area.

Two recent studies of English place-name chronology in the east Midlands—Cox 1973 and Kuurman 1974—have been devoted to the three types of name which end in *-hām* ('village'), *-ingahām* ('village of x's followers') and *-ingas* ('x's followers'); and from these studies it emerges that this order, *-hām, -ingahām, -ingas*, seems likely to be the chronological sequence in which such names arose. Kuurman is more concerned with the evidence that *-ingahām* is earlier than *-ingas*, Cox with the reasons for considering names in *-hām* to be earlier than either of the other types. The conclusions of both authors are based on detailed distributional studies of all three name-types, and on their relationship to Roman roads, pagan Anglo-Saxon cemeteries and major rivers. It is noteworthy that similar conclusions were reached by two scholars working independently on this material. The conclusions are, of course, in direct contradiction to the long-held view that *-ingas* names belonged to the earliest, and *-ingahām* names to the second stage of the settlement.

The Cox and Kuurman articles are important contributions to the problems of place-name chronology; but two major problems beset the use of names in *hām* as a guide to some of the first English settlements. One is the difficulty of distinguishing *hām* 'village' from another place-name element *hamm*, which is of totally different origin and significance. The other is the absence or rarity of names in *hām* in some areas where the archaeological evidence demonstrates a very early English presence.

The difficulty of distinguishing between *hām* and *hamm* as final place-name elements is one of the major snares which the use of place-name evidence contains for unwary historians and archaeologists. Even those non-specialists who are aware that two separate words exist sometimes forget to check which is the likelier in a particular name, the result usually being that a claim is made for the special historical and administrative significance of some name like Farnham SUR or Eynsham OXF by authors or lecturers who have failed to notice that these are more likely to contain *hamm* than *hām*. The uncompounded name Ham offers no problems, as it always derives from the topographical term *hamm*, which has been considered to mean 'land in a river-bend, promontory, dry ground in a marsh, river-meadow, cultivated plot in marginal land', perhaps also 'a piece of valley-bottom land hemmed in by higher ground'. This word may be used on its own, as in East and West Ham GTL, or as a first element, as in some instances of Hampton, but it occurs most frequently as a final element. The habitative term *hām* 'village, estate', is not used as a simplex place-name, and only occurs as a first element if the name derives from a compound appellative like *hāmtūn, hāmsteall, hāmstede*. In some parts of the country it is relatively frequent as the final element of compound names like Amersham and Burnham BUC, 'Ealhmund's village' and 'village by the stream', and it is names like these which are now being considered as possible indications of very early English settlement.

In place-names for which the Middle English and modern spellings end in -*ham* it is often difficult to be certain whether the topographical or the habitative word is involved. It is far from certain that a clear distinction was maintained between them in Old English, and in many names the best that can be done is to try to assess the combined evidence of spellings and topography. As regards the spelling evidence, the reasons for preferring *hamm* to *hām* in a compound name include the occurrence of Old English or Middle English forms with -*mm*-, like *Buccingahamme* 918 for Buckingham, *Burnhamm c.* 880 for Burnham SOM, *Wodehamme* 1370 for Woodham BUC. Old or Middle English spellings with -*o*-, like *Ihomme* 1205 for Iham SSX and *Hynehom* 1248, *Hynehome* 1282 for Highnam GLO, are also considered to indicate *hamm*. The non-specialist may feel that this second criterion, of -*hom* rather than -*ham*, is unreasonable, as the habitative word *hām* is the ancestor of Modern English *home*. The development of *hām* to *home* in Standard English is due to the change of *ā* to *ō* which happened in the dialects of the Midlands and the South in the early Middle English period. No account is taken of this when place-names in -*hām* are under consideration because it is believed that the word ceased to be used for place-name formation centuries before the Norman Conquest, and that in place-names it would have become fossilized as -*ham* long before this sound-change occurred. The topographical term *hamm* remained an active name-forming element into modern times, at any rate in its sense 'river-meadow', so the forms it took in place-names are much more likely to be related to the sound changes of the Middle English period. As explained in the discussion of *camp* (Chapter 3), short *a* (a different sound from the long *a* of *hām*) often became *o* before *n* or *m*, and it is this development which is considered to give some -*hom*, -*homm*, -*home*, -*homme* forms for names containing *hamm*. The final -*e* of forms like *Wodehamme*, *Ihomme* is another indication of *hamm*, as it derives from the dative ending -*e*, and would not be appropriate to Old English *hām*, which has the same form in the dative as in the nominative.

Probably no place-name specialist would claim that the spelling criteria detailed above always provide a certain indication that a name derives from *hamm* rather than *hām*, but when such forms occur in Old English texts, or when they are particularly frequent in relation to -*ham* spellings in the Middle English period, they may fairly be taken as establishing a probability that the name is topographical rather than habitative. More difficult is the problem presented by many names for which there are no Old English spellings, and for which all the Middle English spellings have -*ham*. The absence of Middle English spellings in -*hamm* or -*homm* does not preclude derivation from *hamm* (Buckingham is *Buccingahamme* in the Anglo-Saxon Chronicle, but has only -*ham* forms elsewhere), and most toponymists base their decision about such names on topographical considerations and on the status of the place concerned. Cox 1973 (p. 19) says 'Unless spellings in -*hamme*, -*homme* or -*hom* survive, the only way to recognize the presence of *hamm* is by a study of the topography', and a pioneer study of *hamm* by the present author (Gelling 1960) asserted that some names in bends of the Bedfordshire Ouse (Blunham, Biddenham, Bromham, Pavenham, Felmersham BDF, Haversham, Tyringham BUC) and in loops of the Wye and Lugg (Ballingham, Baysham, Lulham HRE) should be considered as containing *hamm* because of their situation, though the spellings give no hint of this. A more recent attack on the problem in south-east England by John McN. Dodgson says (Dodgson 1973, p. 7):

> My method has been first to isolate the names in -*ham* which demonstrate distinctive spellings from -*hamm*. My second step (very arbitrary, but nonetheless effective in prospecting a mass of material) has been to assume that any name which exhibits only -*ham* spellings and never -*hamm*, -*homm*, etc., is from *hām*, provided that (1) the place is an ancient manor or an ancient parish or is otherwise historically distinguished as an important centre of settlement, (2) it is on record before, say, 1300–50 as something more than a field-name or boundary-point and (3) the site does not have a topography which might be that of a *hamm*.

This last quotation may be taken as a fair indication of the difficulties. No certainty will ever be possible as to the origin of many names in -ham.

Since the first draft of this chapter was written an article has appeared in which a Swedish scholar, Karl Inge Sandred, takes issue with the suggestions made in Gelling 1960 and followed (with some refinements) in Dodgson 1973 concerning the meaning of *hamm* in English place-names. This article (Sandred 1976) puts forward the view that *hamm* means 'enclosure' with no reference to topographical features, and that the situation of a high proportion of the major names in which it occurs (like Buckingham BUC and Evesham WOR) in sharp river-bends, or (like Eynsham OXF and Farnham SUR) in particularly well-watered land by rivers, should not be considered as evidence that the word had a special topographical significance. I find this unconvincing. The use of the term in English place-names is quite different from that of other words, such as *worth*, which refer to man-made enclosures, and the topographical evidence still seems to me to support much of what was said in Gelling 1960. Possibly the best translation of *hamm* is 'place hemmed in by some feature of the topography, often by water or marsh'; but the matter should be regarded as under discussion for the time being.

The distribution within the country of the terms *hām* and *hamm* is probably different, and this is another factor of which account should be taken. Both terms must be reckoned with in south-east England and the south-east Midlands, but it seems probable that *hamm* occurs further west than *hām*, and *hām* occurs further north than *hamm*. In Gelling 1960 an attempt was made to demonstrate that the use of *hamm* in the formation of major place-names (i.e. those of modern parishes or Domesday manors) was limited to the area of England south of a line from Presteigne RAD through Droitwich WOR to Coventry WAR, south to Buckingham, north to Huntingdon, then east to Ely CAM, and south to the Crouch estuary; and it was suggested that this geographical limitation showed the term to have been a Saxon as opposed to an Anglian one. It is possible that this line was drawn too far south, as there are two names on the River Severn in Shropshire, Coleham in Shrewsbury and a lost *Fordesham* in Ford, which contain *hamm*. These may be classified as minor names, and the likelihood of *hamm* being used in minor names and field-names in a much wider area was envisaged in the 1960 article; but neither of the Shropshire names seems likely to be post-Conquest in origin, and once the possibility has been admitted of early names in *hamm* occurring this far north, the topography of some major names, like Atcham SHR and Birmingham WAR begins to look disturbingly appropriate to *hamm*. More detailed studies of the topography of *hām* (?*hamm*) names in the northern half of the country may enable a decision to be taken as to whether *hamm* really observes the geographical limit suggested in Gelling 1960.

There is little doubt that *hām* is well represented in north-east England, in Yorkshire and in Northumberland and Durham, even if subsequent study reclassifies some of the many -ham names of these counties as ?*hamm*. It is less common in the north-west, but certainly represented there. Dodgson 1973 gives a distribution map of *hām* names in Cheshire which shows fifteen examples. There is thus no northern limit for *hām*, but in the southern half of the country there may be a western limit. In Gelling 1976b it is demonstrated that there are two distinct zones in Berkshire, separated by a belt of territory running west and south of Reading, and that the use of *hām* in major place-names is common to the east of this, but rare to the west of it. In the Midlands it is clear that *hām* is very rare—possibly non-existent except in Newnham 'new village'—in Warwickshire, Worcestershire and Herefordshire. We are not yet in a position to be dogmatic about the distribution of either element, however, and can only ask non-specialists to note that both words exist and that great care must be taken before assuming that any place-name certainly contains *hām* 'village'. The *-inga-* formula, which has given rise to many names in *-ingahām*, is well evidenced also with *hamm*. Buckingham BUC and Birlingham WOR contain *-ingahamm*.

The second reason why *hām* is of limited usefulness as a guide to early English settlement is that it is not used in all parts of the country where early settlement is attested by archaeology. The area of the Midlands and the south in which *hām* is a common element in major place-names has a western limit which excludes the valley of the Warwickshire Avon and the valley of the River Ock in Berkshire. The distribution of names in *hām* in the Midlands can be seen from Dr Cox's map, here reproduced as Fig. 8. The only certain examples in Warwickshire are three instances of Newnham, 'new village', a compound which may have continued in use after *hām* had otherwise ceased to be a living place-name element. In Berkshire, the division is not so clearly marked as in the Midlands, but of the ten names in the county which seem reasonably certain to contain *hām*, only one, Wytham, is in the north-west of the county. In south-west Berkshire and the adjacent portion of Wiltshire the element only occurs in minor place-names, and there is a contrast with the forest area of east Berkshire and the adjacent part of Surrey, where *hām* is a serious factor in the major place-names. The absence or scarcity of *hām* as a major place-name element in two areas, the Oxford-Abingdon-Dorchester stretch of the Thames and the valley of the Warwickshire Avon, in both of which there are important concentrations of early English archaeological remains, must be set against the evidence for *hām* being a guide to early settlement in East Anglia and the east Midlands.

A more profitable approach to the question of the earliest English place-names might have been to study the areas of the pagan burials and to see what the place-names are which actually occur there. There are only a few detailed studies of this kind available yet, and it would be helpful if local historians would undertake others. The exercise is not as simple as it sounds, as the assembling of evidence for pagan Anglo-Saxon burials, and the sifting of the better evidence from the type of record which says 'skeleton with pot' or the like, is a laborious task, and the identification of the find-spots with sufficient accuracy for the compilation of large-scale maps is often difficult. This kind of study would be useful for Cambridgeshire, Kent and Sussex. Something of the kind has been attempted for Berkshire (Gelling 1976b), for the Mucking area of Essex (Gelling 1976a) and for south Warwickshire (Ford 1976); and some account will be given here of the results of these investigations, without implying that the

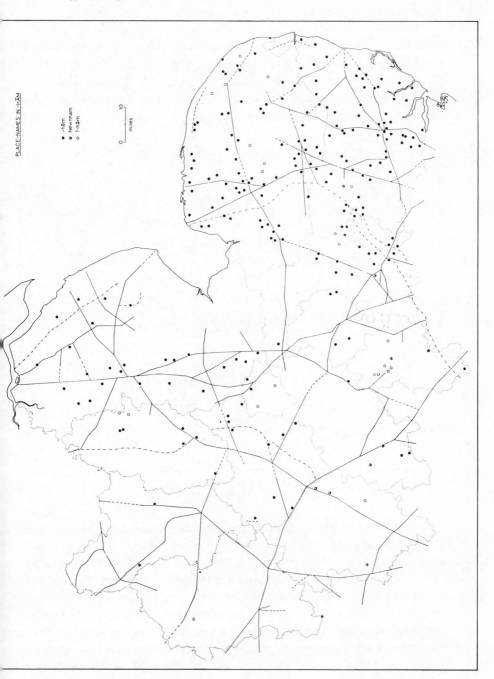

Fig. 8   Place-names in *hām* in the Midlands and East Anglia (from Cox 1973, by permission of the English Place-Name Society)

findings are certain to be applicable to other areas.

The answer in Berkshire seems to be that certain categories of topographical settlement-names are especially characteristic of the north-west
portion of the county, which lies between the Downs and the River
Thames. The archaeological evidence for very early English settlement
here is concentrated in a smaller area between Frilford BRK and Dorchester
OXF, but this evidence, which is continuous for the century AD 400–500,

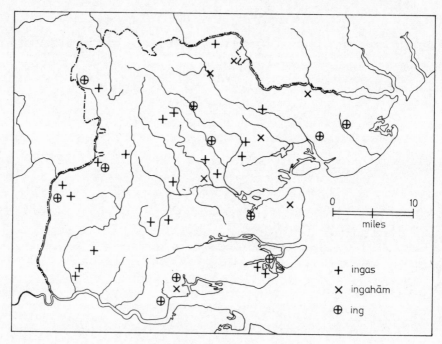

Fig. 9   Essex, showing place-names in *-ingas*, *-ingahām* and *-ing*

probably implies the agricultural use of the whole Ock Valley. The
'topographical' settlement-name is the type which describes the physical
setting of a place without mentioning buildings, in obvious contrast to the
'habitative' type which incorporates a word for a settlement. Throughout
the history of place-name studies there has been a general assumption that
habitative names are likely to be earlier and more important than topographical ones, and that little historical information can be deduced from
the latter; but recent studies make it doubtful whether this assumption is
tenable, and it seems badly at variance with the evidence in north-west
Berkshire. Here, the topographical settlement-names, which heavily out-
number the habitative ones, show a marked unity of theme. The emphasis

is on the drainage—water-supply, water-control, crossing-places, and dry sites for villages. The names of very small streams are used as village-names in Balking, Ginge, Lockinge, Wantage, Hendred and Hagbourne. Some of these streams had been canalized or had their courses altered in the tenth century, the evidence for this being contained in charter-boundaries, some of which are discussed in Chapter 8. Small as the streams are, the control exercised over them by the local farmers was clearly of great importance to the management of the land. Crossing-places are referred to by names in -ford, such as Garford, Lyford, Shellingford, Wallingford, Stanford, Hatford, Frilford, Appleford, Moulsford. Dry sites for villages give rise to modern names in -ey (from Old English *īeg* 'island, dry ground in a marsh'), such as Charney, Goosey, Mackney, Tubney, Pusey, Hanney, Cholsey. Water-supply is referred to in Brightwell, Coxwell, Sotwell and Harwell, in all of which Old English *wielle* refers to a spring. There are four names ending in *hamm*, which usually means 'river-meadow' in this area, as in Shrivenham, Marcham, Fernham, but may mean 'land in a river-bend' in Wittenham. There are habitative names in the area, but they are less numerous, and there is evidence to suggest that some of them have replaced earlier English names, and that others belong to settlements which had a dependent relationship to places with topographical names. This question of the relationship between the two main types of settlement-name is discussed later in this chapter. As mentioned above, there is only one *hām* name in this area, this being Wytham, north-west of Oxford.

There are no names in *-ingas* in this part of the county, the only examples in Berkshire being Reading and Sonning, which lie close together further down the Thames, not beyond the range of the early Saxon burials, but peripheral to the main area. Most of these Berkshire names are shown on Fig. 16.

South-central Essex, where the village of Mucking is situated, is another area which has been studied in an attempt to correlate types of settlement-name with archaeological evidence for an early English presence (Gelling 1976a). The archaeological importance of Mucking is a relatively new discovery, not a long-known factor in Dark Age studies, like that of the Oxford region. The Mucking site was little known at the time of the publication of John Dodgson's demonstration that place-names in *-ingas* could not satisfactorily be equated with the earliest English land-takings (Dodgson 1966). The subsequent discoveries of very early Saxon material there, and the demonstration that one of the largest known Saxon villages lay in the parish together with two Saxon cemeteries, seemed ironic, as Mucking and the neighbouring Fobbing are given in place-name reference books as *-ingas* names meaning 'the followers of Mucca' and 'the followers of Fobba'. It seemed at first sight as if the new archaeological discoveries would have fitted better with the old place-name hypothesis. A fresh look at the early spellings for Mucking and Fobbing suggests, however, that they are by no means certain to belong to the *-ingas* category. Here it becomes necessary to discuss in some detail the singular place-name suffix *-ing* which is difficult to distinguish from *-ingas* in names for which there are no pre-Conquest spellings.

Clavering ESX and Docking NFK are good examples of the *-ing* type of name. The singular suffix has here been added to Old English *clǽfre* 'clover' and *docce* 'dock', to give names meaning 'place where clover (or dock) grows'. In other examples, like Bocking ESX, the suffix is believed to be added to a personal name, to give a meaning 'place associated with Bocca'. In stream-names, like Lockinge BRK, the suffix is sometimes added to the stem of a verb, in this instance *lācan* 'to play'. Names of this type are a good deal less common than the *-ingas* type, though allowance should be made for some of them having been mistakenly classified with the latter. Their distribution is patchy, and it is generally considered that they are most numerous in Kent, south Hampshire and Berkshire. The Berkshire examples have recently been studied in detail in Gelling 1976b. In that county the examples constitute a group of seven names, all originally stream-names, and all but one lying in the area of north-west Berkshire which is discussed above. It is possible to make firm statements about the nature of the Berkshire *-ing* names because five of them are recorded in charter-boundaries (see Chapter 8) as the names of small streams. If the charter-boundaries had not survived, the names would either have been lost or would have been known only from later sources as the names of settlements, so that their original application would have been open to doubt. There is no comparable body of charter-boundaries for Essex, so the likelihood of *-ing* names there being originally stream- or creek-names depends on analogy with the known use of the type elsewhere.

The question is, can Mucking and Fobbing be singular *-ing* names referring originally to the creeks which the settlements adjoin? It is only possible to make absolutely categorical statements about the plural or singular nature of names like Mucking when there are reliable Old English spellings, and these do not exist for either Mucking or Fobbing. After the Norman Conquest, the spellings for singular names regularly include some *-s* forms, and those for plural names regularly include some without *-s*. If there are only post-Conquest spellings the best that can be done is to balance the quantity of spellings with and without *-s*, and to see which type is best evidenced among the earlier ones. For Fobbing (*Fobbing, Fobbinge*

1068 in a copy of 1309, *Phobinge* 1086, *Fobinges* 1125, *Fobinghe* 1212) the spellings are definitely in favour of its being a singular name in *-ing*. For Mucking (*Mucinga* 1086, *Mocking* 1178, *Mokinga* 1182, *Muckinges* 1199, *Mucchinges* 1200, *Mucking* 1219) the evidence is less conclusive, but seems more consistent with *-ing* than with *-ingas*. There is certainly no philological justification for regarding either as a proven *-ingas* name.

Other names in Essex which are, on the evidence of the available spellings, likely to be singular names in *-ing*, are Frating, Matching and Tendring, all of which could have been originally the names of small streams. These have been assigned to the *-ingas* category by previous authors, as have Mucking and Fobbing. Essex names which have been assigned to the *-ing* category by previous authors, and which are much more likely than not to belong there, are Bocking, Clavering, Cobbins Brook, Cressing, Lawling and Potton (earlier *Potting*). There are twenty Essex names which are certainly or probably from *-ingas*, so the *-ingas* category is more numerous in the county, but if all the eleven possible *-ing* names be accepted, Essex should be listed among the counties in which the singular type is particularly well evidenced. If it be accepted that Mucking and Fobbing are likely to be singular names in *-ing* referring originally to creeks, this will fit well with the situation in north-west Berkshire, where a striking group of such stream-names is associated with archaeological evidence for very early Anglo-Saxon settlement.

Fig. 9 shows the distribution of all the Essex names which are here considered to fall into the three categories of *-ing*, *-ingas* and *-ingahām*. This shows Fobbing and Mucking at the centre of a wide area in which there are no certain *-ingas* names and only one *-ingahām*, this last being Corringham which lies between the two. As explained above, the present tendency is to regard *-ingahām* names as rather earlier than *-ingas*, so the single *-ingahām* name is not so incongruous here as two certain *-ingas* names would have been. John Dodgson's view of the *-ingas* names as 'the result of a social development contemporary with a colonizing process later than, but soon after, the immigration-settlement that is recorded in the early burials' accords well with the occurrence of a cluster of three *-ingas* names (Barking, Seven Kings and Havering) some fifteen miles west of Mucking, and of two examples (Barling and Wakering) about the same distance to the east.

If Mucking and Fobbing can be regarded as singular *-ing* names their presence in this part of Essex accords very well with the situation observed in north-west Berkshire. The place-names of the two areas have a number of characteristics in common in addition to this. Topographical settlement-names are even more characteristic of the Mucking area than they are of north-west Berkshire, and this has the ironic effect of causing the region to appear blank on most of the distribution maps supplied with the English Place-Name Society's Essex volume (Reaney 1935). The main habitative terms were mapped here, but there were no topographical ones except those which were considered to indicate the presence of woodland. This system, which was the usual one until the recent attempt to break new ground in the maps supplied with Gelling 1974c, has probably resulted in the earliest names not being mapped at all.

The parish-names for the area round Mucking are: Basildon, Benfleet, Bowers, Bulphan, Canvey, Chadwell, Corringham, Dunton, Fobbing, Horndon, Horndon-on-the-Hill, Laindon, Laindon Hills, Lee, Mucking, Nevendon, Ockendon, Orsett, Pitsea, Stanford, Stifford, Thurrock, Tilbury, Vange, Wickford. Only four of these twenty-five names could possibly be considered habitative, and only one, Dunton, which lies on the northern edge of the area studied, is what might be termed an 'ordinary' habitative name. It means 'hill farm', the second element being *tūn*, which is by far the commonest word for a settlement in English place-names, though less common in Essex than in most counties. Bowers is a rare habitative term, which occurs also in Bower in Somerset, in Bures which straddles the Suffolk/Essex border, and in some minor names in Essex and Kent. The final *s* of Bowers and Bures does not mean that the names were necessarily plural; both are *Bura* in Domesday Book, and short names often acquire an inorganic -*s* in Middle English. In literary Old English the most distinctive use of *būr* is for an inner chamber in a house, but it sometimes means no more than 'dwelling', and as a place-name element it is usually translated 'cottage'. The usual place-name term for a cottage is, however, *cot* (in numerous Cotes and Cotons), and it is possible that *būr* denoted a more specific type of building, perhaps a grander type of dwelling than the sunken huts in which most people were living at the settlement a few miles away in the parish of Mucking. One of the other habitative names in the area is Corringham, which has already been discussed. The other possible one is Tilbury, a difficult name in which *byrig*, dative of *burh* 'fortified place', may refer to an ancient fort rather than to a manor house, in which case the name would not be habitative.

The topographical parish-names in this group include six which have as final element *dūn* 'hill', an important element in major names in Essex. These are Basildon, Horndon, Horndon-on-the-Hill, Laindon, Laindon Hills and Ockendon. The two Horndons and the two Laindons are different names, though the modern forms have been assimilated. Horndon-on-the-Hill is probably 'hill called *Horning*', referring to the horn-like shape made by the 100 foot contour, and illustrating another use of the

-ing suffix. Nevendon has *denu* 'valley' as second element, but association with this notable group of names in *-dūn* has caused the ending to become *-don* instead of *-den*. Stanford, Stifford and Wickford end in *-ford*, and Canvey and Pitsea in *-ēg* 'island', though only Pitsea shows the use of this word to mean 'raised ground in a marsh', Canvey being an island in the modern sense. Benfleet means 'tree-trunk creek', perhaps referring to a bridge. Bulphan (much corrupted by Norman French pronunciation) is 'fen by a fortification'. Chadwell means 'cold spring'. Lee probably means 'wood' in this instance, since it is an isolated example (this point is discussed later in this chapter). Orsett, like Bowers, is a rare type of name. There are two Old English spellings, *orseathan* 957 and *Orseathun*, *Orseathum c.* 1000. These show that the second element is the dative plural of *sēath* 'pit'. This is a rare second element in settlement-names, the only other certain example being Roxeth in Harrow GTL. Orsett probably means 'at the ore pits', referring to excavations for bog iron.

The remaining parish names in the group, Thurrock and Vange, are both highly distinctive. Thurrock is from Old English *thurruc*, which is believed to have meant 'the bilge of a ship'. It is a good name for a stretch of marsh, but the term has not been noted in any other place-name. Vange is a compound of *fenn* 'marsh' (the second element of Bulphan) and *gē* 'district', a word believed to have become obsolete at an early date in Old English, and found only in a few names (Eastry, Lyminge, Sturrey, Denge KNT, Ely CAM, and the county-name Surrey).

The groups of names in north-west Berkshire and in south Essex to which attention is here directed would have been dismissed as 'unremarkable' or 'neutral' by place-name scholars until very recently; but the possibility of this type of settlement-name being commonly used by our earliest English-speaking colonists deserves serious consideration. It has already been noted (Chapter 2) that the evidence from Roman times suggests that Celtic settlement-names in Britain were nearly all of the topographical type, and it may be that in Welsh and in English the widespread use of habitative names is a comparatively late development, which does not become a common practice until after the earliest period of the English settlement.

Another feature of the topographical settlement-names which deserves notice is that in some areas they are regularly used for the main settlement in large conglomerate estates, within which there may be a number of less important settlements with habitative names. This phenomenon is very well evidenced in Berkshire, three striking examples being Lambourn, Blewbury and Faringdon.

At Lambourn there was a great royal estate which features in King

Alfred's will, drawn up between AD 873 and 888, as a bequest to his wife. By the time of the Domesday Survey, in 1086, there were five estates there, which the Survey treats as separate units. Four of the five are surveyed under the name Lambourn, the other is called Bockhampton, a habitative name in which *hāmtūn* may have the sense 'dependent farm in a great manor'. Other habitative names in the area are recorded later. Eastbury (i.e. the manor to the east of Bockhampton) is recorded *c.* 1090. East Garston is a corruption of *Esgareston* ('Esgar's estate') first recorded in 1180; and this is a particularly significant name, as the land-unit can be equated with the thirty-hide estate, one of those surveyed under the name Lambourn, which Domesday Book tells us belonged before the Norman Conquest to a man named Esgar who was an official of Edward the Confessor. Clearly *Esgarestūn* arose in local usage in the mid eleventh century, but did not become the official name of the estate until after 1086. A comparable process has been observed in Wiltshire, where it has been demonstrated (Bonney 1969) that an estate given in AD 933 to a king's thegn named Wulfgar, which is described in the charter as 'at Colling-bourne', can be firmly identified with the tithing of Aughton in Colling-bourne Kingston. Aughton means 'Æffe's estate', and Æffe was Wulfgar's widow. Wulfgar's will begins 'Ic Wulfgar an thæs landes æt Collinga-burnan ofer minne dæg Æffan hiere dæg' ('I, Wulfgar, grant the estate at Collingbourne after my death to Æffe for her lifetime'), and it is clear that although the name Aughton is not recorded till much later it must have arisen in popular use while the widow held the estate. The great con-glomerate estate here was called Collingbourne by the English. The two settlements of Collingbourne Kingston and Ducis lie by the River Colling-bourne, and this is an exact parallel to Lambourn, where a number of settlements in a great estate took their name from the river.

The great pre-Conquest estate at Blewbury BRK is the subject of a land-grant dated AD 944, which is discussed in Chapter 8. The survey attached to this grant makes it clear that the estate comprised the five modern parishes of Blewbury, Aston Upthorpe, Aston Tirrold and North and South Moreton. Blewbury means 'hill-fort with variegated soil' and was originally the name given by the English to the large prehistoric hill-fort whose position in the estate can be seen from Fig. 12. Aston (in this instance 'estate east of Blewbury') and Moreton ('estate in marshy land') are habitative names for places which clearly at one time had a subsidiary relationship to the village called Blewbury.

Great Faringdon BRK ('fern down') appears at one time to have been the centre of a large territorial unit extending on both sides of the Thames. Little Faringdon OXF, about six miles north-west, lies on flat ground by the

River Leach, so the name cannot have arisen with reference to the northern part of the estate, but must be due to the use of the name of the main settlement, the Berkshire town, for the whole unit. Land in this part of Oxfordshire was accounted to be in Berkshire until *c.* 1831, and there is reason to believe that the composite estate of the early Anglo-Saxon period included land in the adjacent portion of Wiltshire also (Gelling 1974c, p. 366).

This tendency for the place which is central to a great composite estate to have a topographical name has been observed elsewhere; examples in south Warwickshire and north Oxfordshire are cited in Ford 1976 (pp. 283–6). Watts 1976 (p. 217) cites a number of instances in Durham of topographically named settlements which occupy particularly desireable sites in areas where there are no names in *tūn*.

Some categories of habitative names must be of relatively late coinage because they refer to social and administrative arrangements which cannot go back to the first coming of the English. Kingston ('royal manor'), Bishton ('episcopal manor'), Knighton ('estate of the young retainers'), Preston ('estate of the priests'), Chilton ('estate of the young noblemen') refer to manorial arrangements which belong to a relatively late stage of social organization, not to the conditions of the migration period. With these may be classed some other names like Buckland ('estate granted by charter') and Fyfield (earlier *Fifhyde* 'estate assessed at five hides'), both of which occur in north-west Berkshire among the topographical settlement-names to which attention has been drawn. These, like Kingston and Knighton, cannot go back to the time of the first English settlements, and they may be supposed to have replaced earlier names in the English language. On the other hand, some of the topographical settlement-names of north-west Berkshire, such as Wantage which refers to a tiny stream, would hardly be applied to a village at a late stage of the English settlement, and these are most probably the first English names the villages had.

The importance of topographical settlement-names in some areas of early English settlement is emphasized here because they have hitherto been neglected when the historical significance of place-names has been under discussion. But it cannot, of course, be asserted that all topographical settlement-names are a guide to early English colonization or infiltration. This heterogeneous category cannot be offered as a replacement for the dethroned *-ingas*, *-ingahām* names. In fact there is some reason to believe that topographical names are also characteristic of regions of exceptionally late settlement. This seems to emerge from a recent study of the Birmingham region (Gelling 1974b), where attention is drawn to the group of topographical names which include Solihull, Sheldon, Elmdon, Knowle,

Dorridge, Berkswell and Meriden, lying south and east of Birmingham in territory where colonization of forest and waste is believed to have been still taking place after the Norman Conquest, and where population seems to have been very sparse at the time of the Domesday Survey. Ford 1976 (pp. 280–2) brings out the special character of this area, through which ran the ancient boundary of the kingdom of the Hwicce, and within which many settlements in the valley of the Worcestershire/Warwickshire Avon and in the Feldon of Warwickshire held outlying woodland pasture, some-times over twenty miles distant from their village. Most such areas of late colonization are known to local historians, and there is little danger of anyone being misled by what has been said above about topographical settlement-names being specially characteristic of areas of early English settlement. One of the factors contributing to this use of a varied topo-graphical vocabulary for coining names in an area such as the Forest of Arden may have been that the most widespread habitative place-name element, *tūn*, was felt to mean 'estate' rather than 'farm' when this late colonization occurred, and that others, such as *worth* and *wīc*, were either obsolete or restricted to specialized senses like 'dairy farm'. Colonization in the Birmingham region at an even later date than that postulated for the Arden area is marked by the use of Heath, End and Green in names of farms and hamlets.

From the limited regional studies so far completed it looks as if a group of topographical settlement-names may be characteristic either of an area of exceptionally early or of one of exceptionally late English settlement; but such names should always be considered as potentially the earliest English ones in any region, and they should not be dismissed as having nothing to contribute to historical studies.

Two important topographical terms which may repay careful study in any region are those which give -ley and -field in modern names. The most detailed regional study yet undertaken of names in -ley is contained in the article referred to above, dealing with the Birmingham region. The only detailed examination of a group of major names in -field concerns the part of Berkshire which lies west and south of Reading (Gelling 1976b, pp. 835–836). Both terms are usually related to woodland, though *feld* also bears a relationship to heath which may not always be close to woodland, and in some late Old English names like Butterley DRB and HRE and Butterleigh DEV the word *lēah* refers to pasture.

The findings suggested by the study of *lēah* in relation to *tūn* in the Birmingham region (Fig. 10) were that both elements were probably in very common use for a long period which excluded both the earliest and the latest periods of formation of major place-names, that *lēah* was the

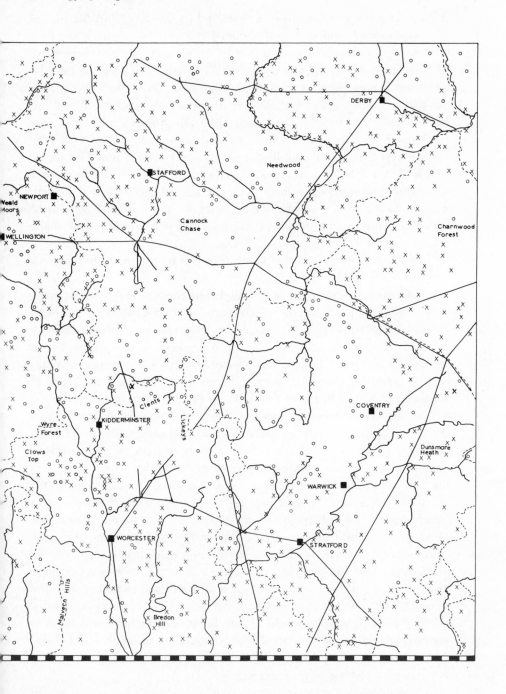

Fig. 10   The Birmingham region, showing place-names in *tūn* and *lēah*. (x = tūn; o = lēah).

regular term for a settlement in a woodland environment and *tūn* for one
in open country, and that *lēah* should be translated 'clearing' when it
occurs in a cluster of names, but 'wood' or 'meadow' when it is isolated.
The mapping of settlement-names in *feld* in Berkshire suggested that the
eight contiguous parishes (Bradfield, Englefield, Burghfield, Wokefield,
Stratfield, Swallowfield, Shinfield, Arborfield) which lie west and south of
Reading (see Fig. 16) may have constituted a belt of open heath-land on the
outskirts of Windsor Forest which was used as common pasture for a time
by the West Saxons and Middle Saxons before it was reclaimed for use as
farmland. Such belts or clusters of names in *feld* occur elsewhere, and
while the exact significance may differ in each case, it is clear that there
was something special about the circumstances of the English settlement
which caused this word to be used in preference to habitative terms or the
more usual variety of topographical ones.

New place-name distribution maps are a welcome addition to materials
for place-name study, and if more local historians engaged in this activity
new patterns would certainly be revealed. The correlation of types of name
with drift geology and soil (of which more is said in Chapter 9), and with
the known Roman and post-Roman archaeology of an area offers promising
fields for research. Useful work can also be done on the precise use of
topographical terms which the dictionaries define as if they were synonyms,
such as *cumb, dæl, denu, hop, slæd*, all terms for a valley, and the group of
words which can all be translated 'hill'. In Berkshire, for instance, there is
a clear distinction between *cumb* and *denu*, the former being applied to a
short, straight valley, and the latter to a twisting, elongated one. The sort
of results which can be obtained from a study of topographical words in
relation to the terrain and to the history of the settlements named from
them is exemplified by a study of *mōr* and *mersc* in the valley of the
Warwickshire Avon (Maynard 1974). Mrs Maynard shows that in this area
(where *mōr* is used of low-lying marsh as well as of barren upland like
Dunsmore Heath), there is a clear distinction between the type of marshy
land described by the two words, *mersc* being consistently employed for
much more desirable land than *mōr*. Such a finding cannot be regarded as
proved for the whole country. The use of *cumb* and *denu* and *mōr* and
mersc may be different in other areas, but it is probable that a substantial
number of such studies would enable broad geographical and chronological patterns to be discerned which would be of great interest and
value. It is probable that insufficient allowance has been made for regional
differences in the use of place-name elements.

Following this last statement, a warning should be given against
mechanically transferring any methods of place-name analysis from one

area to another. The vocabulary used differs in different parts of England for reasons which are not simply chronological ones. For instance, there are some counties in the south-east Midlands—Surrey, east Berkshire, Bedfordshire, Huntingdonshire, Hertfordshire and Essex—where *tūn* is less common than in most parts of the country. Before embarking on regional studies or maps of the kind shown in Fig. 10, the student should study the place-names of the region in conjunction with those of the surrounding regions, and try to ascertain what is the norm for his area. A scarcity of names in *tūn* is not a very significant feature if the region is part of a larger area where *tūn* is relatively scarce. On the other hand, a region of the west Midlands where there are few names in *tūn* is atypical, and the reasons for this will certainly be worth inquiry.

Chapter 6

Place-Names and the Archaeologist

In most of England the density of the layer of post-Roman place-names in the English language is such that it enables us to see the countryside through the eyes of peasant settlers of the fifth to ninth centuries—the fifth century being the period of the first large-scale English settlements in the east, and the ninth century that of their penetration into the extreme south-west. At the time of the English settlements all our prehistoric and Roman remains existed as part of the landscape, and the terms by which the Anglo-Saxons referred to them, besides having a considerable imaginative appeal, may be of practical interest to the archaeologist.

It is evident from the manner in which English place-names refer to prehistoric remains that there has been a break in the historical sequence, and that the monuments are viewed as relics of other cultures erected in forgotten circumstances. There is a marked contrast with the situation in some Celtic-speaking areas such as Ireland and Cornwall, where there is a continuous linguistic tradition from Iron Age times. In Ireland, it has been observed that such words as *ráth, dún, daingean, caiseal, cathair*, which are all used of fortified dwelling-sites, are not employed indiscriminately in place-names, but have a fairly consistent relationship to the type of fort. Thus *ráth* is used of a site surrounded by a ditch and bank, *dún* and *daingean* are applied to more strongly-built structures, usually having stone or stone-faced ramparts, *caiseal* and *cathair* to structures built entirely of stone (O'Kelly 1970). In Cornwall there is a distinction between *car* or *ker* (plural *kerrow*) and *dynas*, the latter normally referring to a larger fortification than the former (Pool 1973). The Anglo-Saxon perception of prehistoric sites in England involved a classification according to the assumed functions of burial or defence, with little or no interest in relative chronology, and no attempt to classify monuments according to size or to the methods and materials of construction. It is only in regard to late Roman institutions and to their own structures of the pagan period that the Anglo-Saxon vocabulary is at all precise.

Since no continuous tradition can lie behind references in English place-names to prehistoric forts and burial mounds, the modern archaeologist may feel inclined to doubt whether these early farmers were really capable of recognizing such features. Most modern observers require training and professional experience in order to distinguish man-made bumps in the ground from those of geological origin, and this may lead them to doubt the validity of the untrained Anglo-Saxon judgment in such matters. It is necessary to remember, however, that peasant farmers have by nature some of the abilities which modern people, particularly those of urban background, only acquire by training; and the ability of the early medieval peasant to distinguish and to some extent to classify man-made disturbances of the land surface, like his power of visualizing a landscape as we can only see it with the aid of a map, was part of his natural equipment. If a place-name can be shown to refer to something which the Anglo-Saxons thought to be artificial the site will certainly be worthy of modern archaeological investigation. A knowledge of the specialized terms which the new settlers used when referring to monuments of earlier cultures is not only interesting for its own sake; it is also of practical value when the monument referred to in a place-name has been reduced by time and events to a shadow of its appearance in the fifth or sixth century, or has disappeared entirely at ground level.

This chapter will endeavour to set out the terms used in English place-names for (*a*) burial-mounds, (*b*) prehistoric fortifications, (*c*) some Roman remains, and (*d*) some Anglo-Saxon structures of the pagan period.

(a) *Prehistoric Burial-Places*

The two words most frequently used by the Anglo-Saxons for a tumulus were *beorg*, which is our modern *barrow*, and *hlāw*, which becomes Low in place-names. The usual Old Norse word was *haugr*, and this is used of burial-mounds in the place-names of the Danelaw. Also to be considered are the word *crūc*, borrowed into Old English from Welsh, and the three related words *byrgen*, *burgæsn* and *byrgels*.

None of the words considered in this section is a fool-proof guide to the existence of a tumulus. The three main words, *beorg*, *hlāw* and *haugr*, were all used of natural hills as well as of artificial ones. The frequent siting of tumuli on commanding natural eminences adds to the uncertainty; but there are so many clear instances in which these words refer to burial-mounds that place-names containing any of them merit consideration from the archaeologist, and obviously they deserve very serious attention if they are found in a spot where there is no natural hill. There are a number of other Old English and Old Norse words for a hill which do not appear to be used of tumuli, so *beorg*, *hlāw* and *haugr* may be regarded as partially specialized terms.

(i) *Old English beorg, modern barrow.* The adoption of this word by modern archaeologists as a technical term for a tumulus was due to its survival in that sense in the dialect speech of Wessex and the south-west, an area which attracted much early archaeological attention. The *New English Dictionary* gives quotations which illustrate this survival, e.g. from 1576 'These hillocks, in the West Countrie . . . are called Barowes . . . which signifieth Sepulchres', and from 1656 'Those round hills, which in the Plains of Wiltshire are . . . by the Inhabitants termed Barrowes, like as in the Midland part of England they call them Lowes'. In the Old English period, *beorg* and *hlāw* were both used in place-names in southern England, so the distinction between the south and the Midlands referred to in the second quotation was of later date.

In place-names *beorg* is certainly used of a tumulus in numerous examples of the name Barrow Hill. It was used of a Neolithic long barrow in *Wodnesbeorg*, the Old English name of Adam's Grave in Alton Priors WLT. Old-English *langan beorge*, Middle English *langeberge*, the exact equivalent of the modern term 'long barrow', is known to refer in place-names to this type of monument. This has become Lambrough in Lambrough Banks in Bibury GLO, where the long barrow survives, and the village-name Longborough, south-west of Moreton-in-the-Marsh in the same county, refers to a long barrow which stands above the village.

Some names containing *beorg* appear to refer to early treasure hunting. There was a tumulus (no longer there, but marked on old maps) at a spot called Idel Barrow in Upton St Leonards GLO, and a Berkshire tumulus south of White Horse Hill has the modern name Idlebush Barrow. These names contain Old English *īdel* 'empty, vacant, useless'. Brokenborough WLT derives from Old English *brocenan beorge* 'broken barrow', and this and other instances of the same name in field-names may refer to barrows with the familiar robbers' hollow in the top.

Barrows were often chosen in the pre-Conquest and post-Conquest periods as the markers for the open-air assembly-places of the 'hundreds', the ancient administrative divisions which were the basis of regional government (see Chapter 8). The hundreds were often named from their meeting-places. In Dorset, a number of hundred-names contain *beorg* in the sense 'tumulus'. These include Modbury (Old English *gemōtbeorge* 'moot barrow'), which was the name of a tumulus on the hill north-east of Cattistock, Hundredsbarrow, a tumulus at the bottom of a cottage garden a mile south of Bere Regis, and Loosebarrow, the old name of a tumulus near the west end of Charborough Down. In Gloucestershire there is the hundred of Brightwellsbarrow, which met near a large barrow about a mile south-east of Hatherop, and in Wiltshire the hundred of Swanborough, which met near a barrow which was called Swanborough Tump *c.* 1880, two miles west of Pewsey.

Many names which can be shown by the early spellings to contain *beorg* probably referred originally to tumuli, but the mounds in question have either disappeared or not been looked for. No systematic investigation has ever been made in order to discover the comparative frequency with which the word refers to tumuli and to natural hills. There seems little doubt that the reference is often to a natural hill, as probably in Grandborough BUC ('green hill') and Farnborough HMP, KNT, WAR and BRK ('fern hill(s)'). This means that the term is not automatically of interest to the field archaeologist, and he should perhaps only devote serious attention to it when it occurs in the name of a hundred meeting-place, or when a name containing it refers to relatively flat ground. Grandborough WAR, for instance, which has the same etymology as Grandborough BUC is on very flat ground, and this name may have referred originally to an artificial hill.

The archaeologist with no philological expertise may require expert help in distinguishing *beorg* from *burh* and its dative *byrig*, which are discussed in the next section. These elements were confused in Middle English. Had they been consistently differentiated, *beorge* (the dative of *beorg*) would give -berrow or -barrow in modern names, *burh* would mostly give -borough, and *byrig* -bury. But it can be seen from the small number of examples cited here that names which now have -bury or -borough can often be traced back by means of early spellings to an Old English compound containing *beorge*. As *beorg* and *burh* are both of interest to the archaeologist the confusion does not diminish the number of names he will wish to consider. But an archaeologist who has evidence of a field-monument associated with a name ending in -barrow, -berrow, -borough or -bury may need an opinion from a philologist about the likeliest derivation.

Coverage of England by detailed place-name surveys is as yet uneven, and this makes it difficult to be sure of the northern limit to the use of *beorg* in the sense 'tumulus'. It is certainly much less common in the north than in the south. As a place-name element *beorg* is common in the West Riding, but it refers in many instances to glacial drumlins. It is rare in the East and North Ridings in any sense. It is common in Westmorland, but not apparently with reference to tumuli. It occurs occasionally in Nottingham-shire. It is rare in Derbyshire; one of the few examples, Wigber Low in Kniveton, certainly refers to a tumulus, but it is significant that -low was added to this name, as if in this region *beorg* was not sufficient identification for a tumulus. Probably *beorg* is not much in evidence as a term of archaeological significance north of Birmingham.

(ii) *Old English hlāw, hlǣw, modern -low, -lew.* This word was used of burial-mounds over a wide area, from the south coast to the West Riding, and possibly further north than that; but when one reaches Northumberland, where it is one of the commonest terms for a natural hill, archaeological significance becomes very difficult to isolate.

The meaning 'burial-mound' occurs in literary references, the most famous being *Beowulf* 2802–5 'Bid them make a *hlǣw* . . . on *Hronesnæsse*'. (In lines 2806–7 the dying king adds that the *hlǣw* shall be called *Biowulfes biorh*.) The form used here is *hlǣw*, which is only found in place-names in the south country and the south Midlands. A good example is Lew OXF, where the one-inch map marks a tumulus a quarter of a mile west of the village. Another instance, this time in the plural, is Lewes SSX, which refers to the tumuli which dot the hills east and west of the town. The other form of the word, *hlāw*, is found e.g. in The Low in Bushbury STF, two miles north of Wolverhampton, which refers to a large tumulus described by a seventeenth-century writer, and in Bartlow CAM, which refers to the great tumuli which dominate the village. Groups of barrows are sometimes referred to, in such names as Twemlow CHE and Tomlow in Napton on the Hill WAR '(place by) the two tumuli', or Rumbelow in Wednesfield STF '(place by) the three tumuli'.

Place-names sometimes comment on the unusual shape of a tumulus. One instance is Ploughley Hill, south of Souldern OXF, earlier *Pokedelawe* 'baggy tumulus'. This is no longer visible, but it is described in William Stukeley's *Itinerarium Curiosum*, 1776, as 'a curious barrow, neatly turned like a bell, small and high'. Copley Hill in Babraham CAM, earlier *Coppelawe*, is considered to mean 'rounded tumulus'. *Le Coppedelowe* 'the peaked tumulus', occurs as a medieval field-name in Derbyshire, and Sharplow in Tissington DRB means 'pointed tumulus'.

A particularly interesting class of names containing *hlāw* is that in which the first element is the genitive of an Old English personal name. These names are discussed under (*d*) below.

Hundred-names often contain *hlāw* for the reason given above, and this function of being a marker for a meeting-place is referred to in the name Mutlow ('moot tumulus') which occurs in Cambridgeshire and Essex. In the hundred-names of the southern counties *hlāw* is not as well represented as *beorg*, but it becomes more common in those of the south Midlands. Ploughley OXF (discussed above) was a hundred meeting-place. In Warwickshire four of the hundred-names contain this element: these are Knightlow Hill in Ryton on Dunsmore ('tumulus of the young men'), Brinklow (probably 'tumulus on the brink of a hill'), *Tremelawe*, a lost place probably in Lighthorne ('at the three tumuli'), and Pathlow in Aston Cantlow ('tumulus by the path'). The word tumulus has been used loosely in the last sentence. It has not been established that all the mounds mentioned in the Warwickshire hundred-names are sepulchral, but it is probable that, whether sepulchral or not, all were either man-made or had something artificial in their outline.

One use of *hlāw* in place-names is for a hill which has been scarped. This is illustrated by Harlow ESX, where the name refers to the small hill by the railway station, formerly surmounted by a Roman temple. The hill was surrounded by a ditch and one end of it had been artificially scarped, and it was probably recognition of this artificial outline which led the Anglo-Saxons to use the word *hlāw* in naming it.

The exact status of some mounds in this type of place-name baffles archaeologists. The shire-moot of Berkshire met at a spot now called Scutchamer Knob by The Ridgeway. Scutchamer is Old English *Cwicelmeshlǣwe*, and it has sometimes been supposed that this steep conical mound was the burial-place of one of the two men called Cwichelm who occur in the West Saxon royal family, one of whom died in 593, the other in 636. This does not appear to be possible, however, as excavation in 1934 led to the conclusion that the mound was not sepulchral, and here again the use of the word *hlǣw* may only signify that the Anglo-Saxons recognized that it was not entirely of geological origin.

It is difficult to say how often, in the southern half of England, the words *hlāw* and *hlǣw* were used of natural hills. My own estimate is that in the south this use is very rare, possibly not to be reckoned with at all. But there are many names for which the evidence may have been lost. One such is Mucklows Hill, west of Birmingham. This is the name of a particularly steep part of the edge of the Birmingham plateau, and as Mucklow derives from Old English *miclan hlāwe*, which can be translated 'great hill', the meaning might seem obvious enough. But *hlāw* is not usually applied to an escarpment, and it seems possible that the name referred to a great burial-mound at the top of the hill, about where the offices of the Midland Electricity Board now stand. This can never be more than a conjecture. Muckley Corner, three miles south-west of Lichfield STF, was earlier *Mucklow*, and may be another example of the same name.

A similar name for which there is fortunately some evidence is Ludlow SHR. This means 'mound by the torrent', and as Ludlow Castle occupies a great hill surrounded by the River Teme it could reasonably be argued that the name requires no further elucidation. The word *hlāw* is not normally used in Herefordshire or Shropshire of this type of hill, however, and it might have been suspected that the name referred to an artificial hill nearer to the town, even if there had been no evidence for the existence of such a feature. Fortunately this suspicion was entertained by a nineteenth-century writer, and the discussion in the first volume of T. Wright's *The History of Ludlow and its Neighbourhood*, published in 1841, deserves quotation. Wright says:

> [Ludlow] . . . signifies *the hill of the people*. But the Anglo-Saxon *hlæw* was generally applied not to a natural hill like that on which the town of Ludlow stands, but to an artificial burial-mound, a tumulus or barrow, like the Bart*low* Hills in Cambridgeshire. . . . These *lows* were intimately connected with the mythology and superstitions of our early forefathers, and in their minds were wrapped up with the notions of primeval giants and dragons which kept a jealous watch over their hidden treasures. In old times we find them frequently the scenes of popular ceremonies and meetings. I was long doubtful as to the cause of this name being assigned to the town, till I accidentally discovered a document which clears up the difficulty in the most satisfactory manner. It appears that up to the end of the twelfth century, the site of the present churchyard of Ludlow, the most elevated part of the hill, was occupied by a very large tumulus, or barrow. In the year 1199, the townsmen found it necessary to enlarge their church . . . and for this purpose they were obliged to clear away the mound. In doing this they discovered in the interior . . . *three* sepulchral deposits, which were probably included in square chests as at Bartlow, and the narrator perhaps exaggerates a little in calling them 'mausolea of stone'. . . . The clergy of Ludlow . . . determined . . . that the bones . . . were the relics of three Irish saints, the father, mother, and uncle, of the famous St Brandan, and they buried them devoutly in their church.

While there is no detailed study of the place-names containing this element which would enable one to be dogmatic about its use, it seems likely that at least as far north as the west Midland section of Watling Street the archaeologist should pay very close attention to place-names containing *hlāw*. The archaeological sense is probably to be reckoned with well to the north of Watling Street in Shropshire: there are two places called The Lowe, near Worfield and near Wem respectively, in the north of the county, both of which seem unlikely to be named from natural hills. There is also Longslow north-west of Market Drayton SHR, one of the names discussed in (*d*) which may refer to pagan Anglo-Saxon burial places.

North of this vague line the word *hlāw* is less exclusively used of an artificial mound. The frequent occurrence of this element is one of the distinguishing features of the place-names of Derbyshire, and here one can do no better than quote Professor Cameron's summary of the evidence in his survey of that county (Cameron 1959, p. 705):

> *hlāw* is very common, though most of the examples are confined to High Peak and Wirksworth hundreds. The lack of modern archaeological research in Anglo-Saxon Db, and the great difficulties encountered, both in identifying the burial-mounds investigated by the Batemans and others during the nineteenth century, and in interpreting the evidence presented, makes it almost impossible to determine how many of these are names of tumuli. Out of over seventy examples for which reasonably early forms are available, some thirty are certainly burial-mounds, and it is likely enough that with additional field-research this number will be much higher. In point of fact a large number of the examples for which only late forms have been found are known to be tumuli. It is perhaps significant that almost one-sixth of the early names in *hlāw* have an OE monothematic personal name as first element.

In Nottinghamshire, where *hlāw* is rare in contrast to Derbyshire, it can refer to a tumulus, as in Blyth Law Hill. In north country place-names, where the element may appear as -law instead of -low, the sense varies widely from 'tumulus' to 'mountain', examples of the latter being the Lancashire names Horelaw, Pike Law, Brownlow. The word is not common in Cumberland, Westmorland or Yorkshire. It is much in evidence in Northumberland and Durham, but most of the examples probably refer to hills or mountains.

(iii) *Old Norse haugr.* The Danish speakers who settled in north-eastern England after the Danish wars which began in AD 865 used the word *haugr* in a manner similar to the Anglo-Saxon use of *beorg* in southern England. It is frequently applied to a tumulus, but it can refer to a natural hill. In the North Riding of Yorkshire, where *haugr* is a common place-name element, A. H. Smith commented 'in many cases the tumulus to which the name refers is still extant' (Smith 1928, p. 320). In the East Riding *haugr* is less common, and here the same author commented 'like *beorg* it seems to have been used both of hills and burial-mounds' (Smith 1937, p. 313). It is certainly used of a tumulus in Spell Howe in Folkton, Hawold in Huggate, Howe Hill in Kirkburn, Aldro in Birdsall. In the West Riding, where the element is again common, as it is in the North Riding, *haugr* is used of both tumuli and hills. It is not possible to give a complete assessment of the use of *haugr* in some other counties where there was dense Danish settlement, as there are as yet no detailed place-name surveys for Leicestershire, Lincolnshire, Norfolk and Suffolk. It is not common in Derbyshire, but one notable example in that county is the parish-name Hoon. This place, which lies two miles north of Tutbury, derives its name from the dative plural *haugum*, referring to a group of barrows, one of which is now called Hoon Mount.

In the areas of the north-west, where Norwegians settled at a somewhat later date, the word *haugr* is probably more likely to refer to a natural hill, or occasionally to a mountain. In this last sense it is the final element of Skiddaw. The people of this region may have been less inclined to use *haugr* of a burial-mound because the word *burgæsn*, discussed below, was fulfilling this role in their vocabulary.

It will be seen from the examples of names in -*haugr* quoted above that the form of the word is often much reduced in modern place-names, and that it can be shortened to -o or -a at the end of a compound name. The most likely development, however, is to Howe, and a field or minor name containing Howe in the Danelaw may indicate a tumulus if there is no obvious natural feature to which it could refer.

This is a suitable place to insert a cautionary word about place-names containing Hoo in eastern England. Old English *hōh* 'heel, spur of land' is especially common in Bedfordshire and Northamptonshire, and fairly common in Hertfordshire, Essex, Suffolk, Durham and Northumberland. Perhaps because of its resemblance to *haugr*, and perhaps because of its occurrence in Sutton Hoo, this element has sometimes been stated to be of special archaeological significance. There does not seem to be any foundation for this, and it is, in fact, a purely topographical term. It can refer to a great hill spur, but one of its senses is 'a low projecting piece of land in the bend of a river or in more level ground'. Such a spot in a low-lying area may often be the site of archaeological remains, but the use of Hoo in such a name as Sutton Hoo refers to the slightly raised ground, not to the archaeological mounds situated on it.

It is not always possible to distinguish *hōh* from *haugr*, but as a rough guide Hoo is more likely to derive from *hōh*, and Howe from the Old Norse word.

(iv) *Welsh crug.* The Primitive Welsh ancestor of this word is the source of the place-names Creech DOR, SOM, Crich DRB, Crook DEV, DOR, Crutch WOR, Crouch OXF. It is the second element of Evercreech SOM, Penkridge STF, Pentridge DOR, and the first element of Cruckton and Crickheath SHR,

Cruchfield BRK. In these and other names it refers to natural hills, which are often small and abrupt in shape, like the one at Crouch OXF, but which are sometimes part of a considerable massif, like Creech Hill near Evercreech SOM, or low flat-topped hills, as in Cruchfield BRK. The Anglo-Saxons are assumed to have adopted the names of these hills from Celtic-speaking people.

The interest of this word for the archaeologist lies mainly in the recurrent compound of *crūc* (the form which the word took in Old English) and *hyll* 'hill'. This has usually become Churchill, and is therefore indistinguishable in its modern form from the compound of Old English *cirice* and *hyll*, which simply means 'hill near a church'. There are two instances of the name Churchill in Worcestershire. The one which lies four miles east of Worcester has an ancient church on a hill, and so presents no difficulty. The other Worcestershire Churchill lies east of Kidderminster, and the village and the church are in a valley, not obviously to be associated with any of the surrounding hills. The English Place-Name Society's Worcestershire volume in discussing these two names put forward the suggestion that in instances where the church is not on or near a hill the first element might be *crūc*, later associated with the commoner word *cirice*. This discussion was written in 1927, and the arguments put forward there are in need of reassessment and supplementation from the fuller material now available. It is particularly unfortunate that this discussion should have been printed as a commentary on the Churchill which lies east of Worcester, where the church of St Michael crowns the low hill on which the village is situated, and no special explanation of the name is required. But although the 1927 discussion cannot be recommended wholly, it still seems probable that Church- in some place-names is an adaptation of *crūc*. There is also some reason to think that when it was adopted into English, the Welsh word acquired a more specialized meaning than it had previously had, and was more likely to be used of a tumulus.

One of the villages called Churchill is in Oxfordshire. Here the old church is on the slope of a long ridge; the tip of the ridge, immediately west of the village, is crowned by a tumulus called The Mount, and the name seems more likely to refer to that than to the church. This is perhaps the most convincing instance among major names, but it is noteworthy that the Ordnance Survey maps sometimes mark Church Hill on an eminence which is not in a village and which seems a most unlikely spot for a church. One such is to be found north of Clows Top WOR, at GR SO 710730. Others are Church Hill Wood near Pontesbury SHR, GR SJ 416041, and Church Hill east of Leintwardine HRE, GR SO 410739. It is possible that there were tumuli or earthworks on these hills, though none are shown on modern maps.

Crookbarrow Hill in Whittington WOR was *Cruchulle* in 1182, *Crok-berewe c.* 1225. There seems little doubt that the correct etymology of the 1182 form is 'barrow hill', and that *beorge* was later substituted for *hyll* because it seemed particularly appropriate to the great mound, which may be a prehistoric tumulus. An excellent view of this ancient monument can be obtained from the M5 motorway.

This postulated specialized use of *crūc* to mean 'tumulus' is mainly to be looked for in the south-west and the west Midlands, but there is a name in Northumberland, Kirkley north of Ponteland, which presents similar problems. Kirkley was earlier *Crikelawe*. The scattered hamlets with this name lie on flat ground by the River Pont, and neither element of the name seems likely to refer to a natural hill. It is possible that this is a similar formation to Crookbarrow WOR, with *hlāw* instead of *beorg* as second element, and that *crūc* has here been assimilated to Kirk, instead of to Church as in some southern English names.

(v) *Other terms for tumuli.* The Anglo-Saxons had three words derived from the same stem as the verb 'bury' which they occasionally used in place-names to denote tumuli. These are *byrgen, byrgels, burgæsn.* Burnhill in Stone BUC, which has *byrgen* as first element, is a hill marked by a barrow. Hebburn DUR means 'high tumulus', but there is little hope of locating the ancient monument here. Kinsbourne HRT consists of *byrgen* with an Old English personal name. As can be seen from these three examples, the modern spellings of names containing *byrgen* may be identical with those from the much more common element *burna* 'stream', and only Middle English spellings or conclusive topographical evidence can enable this word to be identified.

Either *byrgen* or *burgæsn* (probably the former) is found in two minor names in Oxfordshire, Berring's Wood in Glympton and Berins Hill in Ipsden. There are early spellings for both these names, and the derivation is certain in the first instance and probable in the second. This etymology was put forward for both names in Gelling 1953, superseding a long-standing antiquarian association of Berins Hill in Ipsden with St Birinus, the apostle of the West Saxons, who was the first Bishop of Dorchester on Thames. There was an unexpected sequel to this when, by the sort of ghastly coincidence which place-name students must always look out for, an important pagan Anglo-Saxon cemetery recently came to light at a spot now called Berinsfield north of Dorchester OXF. This discovery led to immediate speculation about the derivation of Berinsfield from *byrgen*, which would have proved continuity of tradition about the cemetery from early pagan times. The caution prompted by the failure of the name Berinsfield to appear in any of the sources consulted for the place-name survey of Oxfordshire proved justified, however, and inquiries revealed that Berinsfield had been invented by a local historian for the benefit of the airfield situated there, and that he intended it to commemorate Bishop Birinus. Although the false derivation from *byrgen* had a short life, it managed to appear in at least one Ph.D. thesis, and the incident makes a salutary cautionary tale. However convincing a modern name looks, no conclusions should be based on it unless it can be shown to have some history, that is to go back at least to the first edition one-inch map, or the Tithe Award, or the Enclosure Award, and not much weight should be placed on any name which is not recorded at least as early as the sixteenth century. It is worth noting the circumstances in which this name, although of quite recent invention by a very well-known local historian, took root and appeared genuine to a team of archaeologists who knew the area intimately. The sequence of events appears to have been: (1) the anti- quarian association of Berins Hill near Ipsden with St Birinus of Dor- chester; (2) the invention of the name Berinsfield for an airport near Dorchester, presumably on the model of Berins Hill; (3) the alternative derivation of Berins Hill from *byrgen* in Gelling 1953; (4) the discovery of the cemetery at Berinsfield by archaeologists who knew that Berins- could be from *byrgen*.

The word *byrgels* is important because of its occurrence in the phrase *hæðenan byrgels* 'heathen burial' which is common in Anglo-Saxon charter-boundaries. This is discussed in Section (*d*). The word *burgæsn* is found in place-names in the north-west. Sewborwens in Newton Reigny CMB means 'seven burial-mounds'. Burwains in Whalley LNC is from *burgæsn*, and so is Bornesses in Croft YON. The element is very common in the place-names of Westmorland, but is not used with great precision, and appears to refer to undated stone cairns and even to Roman camps as well as to prehistoric tumuli. In the north-west a field-name Borran(s), Bor- wan(s) may indicate a tumulus, but may refer to a stone cairn of uncertain origin.

(vi) *Dragons and treasure.* One of the images embedded in the Anglo- Saxon poetic imagination was that of a tumulus containing treasure, guarded by a dragon. This situation is the basis of the second half of the epic poem *Beowulf*, and it is referred to in the Gnomic verses—'draca sceal on hlæwe, frod, frætwum wlanc' ('the dragon shall be in the tumulus, old, rich in treasures'). From place-name evidence we can infer that this image was not only to be found in sophisticated poetry, but was also known to the farming people in the countryside. The place-names Drakelow BDF, DRB, WOR, and Dragley in Ulverston LNC, mean 'dragon tumulus', with first element *draca* and second element *hlāw*. *Drechowe*, a medieval field-name in the North Riding of Yorkshire, is a similar compound with Old Norse *haugr*, as is *Drakehowe* in Maltby YOW, thought to refer to a tumulus on the first edition one-inch map. The Anglo-Saxons used *wyrm* for a dragon, as well as *draca*. Wormwood Hill in Stapleford CAM was earlier *Wyrmelawe*, and this indicates that the tumulus here was considered to have a resident dragon. Worm- in place-names is not as safe a guide to superstitious beliefs of this kind as Drake-, however. Another Wormelow in Herefordshire, south of Hereford at GR SO 492302, is a compound of *hlāw* with the name of Worm Brook, and the latter is a Celtic river-name from the adjective which has become Modern Welsh *gwrm* 'dusky, dun'. Wormelow Tump was a hundred meeting-place, and the *hlāw* was probably an artificial mound, but there is no reference to dragons in this instance. Some other names in Worm- contain personal names *Wyrm* and *Wyrma*, and the minor name Wormstall refers to a shelter for cattle into which they would retire to escape parasitic flies whose eggs would hatch into grubs called *worms*. Place-names and field-names in Worm- should not be taken too seriously by the archaeologist, but Drakelow is more likely than not to refer to a tumulus, and any field or minor name in Drake- may be of interest. If not flying through the air, a dragon was most likely to be in a barrow.

The word *hord* 'hoard' occurs in place-names, and is believed to refer to finds of coins or other metal objects. In Hurdlow Town in Hartington DRB this element is combined with *hlāw*. At Hordley SHR (second element *lēah* 'wood, clearing') a Roman coin-hoard was found in 1950, and it is possible that the *hord* of the place-name refers to earlier finds of this kind. A compound of *hord* and *draca*, as in Drake North in Damerham WLT (earlier *drakenhorde*) clearly refers to the dragon-guarded treasure familiar from the poetry. This compound has been noted in medieval field-names; it occurs, for instance, in thirteenth-century sources for Garsington OXF, along with the name *Brokenebereue*, discussed above. Place-names containing *hord* will mostly indicate that the treasure was found and removed in pre-Conquest times, but they may sometimes be a clue to burial-mounds, even if these have been robbed. The compound *gold-hord* occurs occasionally as a place-name, as in Goldsworth in Woking SUR, Goldhard in Godstone SUR, Gollard in Amport HMP, Goldsworth in Stoke CHE, Gaulter in Steeple DOR, and this compound is also found in field-names. The word *gold* without *hord* is not a reliable indication of ancient treasure, as it may refer to golden flowers or yellowish soil.

(b) *Prehistoric Fortifications*

Hill-forts were probably the most impressive prehistoric monuments which the Anglo-Saxons saw in this country. Many still survive, and these would have outlines in the fifth and sixth centuries similar to those visible today, but others which were visible then have since been much reduced or totally obliterated by farming or building. A knowledge of the terms by which such monuments are referred to in place-names is valuable to the field archaeologist.

The standard Old English term for a hill-fort was *burh*, dative *byrig*. Other well-evidenced terms are *weard-setl* and *tōt-ærn*, both meaning 'look-out building'. The term *eorth-burh* sometimes refers to a prehistoric earthwork.

(i) *Old English burh, byrig, modern borough, -bury.* Old English *burh* means 'a defended place'. It is one of the commonest elements in English place-names, where it has a wide variety of meanings of which 'hill-fort' is only one. Others are 'defended manor-house', and, in late Old English, 'town'. 'Manor-house' is the likeliest meaning in numerous settlement-names ending in -bury. 'Town' is found in the names of several places which grew up at the gates of tenth-century monasteries, such as Peterborough NTP and Bury St Edmunds SFK; and this sense persisted into the post-Conquest period, being found, for example, in Newbury BRK, where the trading centre was probably founded immediately after the Norman Conquest. The sense 'manor house' may have persisted into Middle English also, a possible instance being Nobury in Inkberrow WOR, which has 'new' as first element and appears to refer to a new manor-house built in 1235. It will be apparent from this that many names containing *burh*, *byrig* are not of special interest to the prehistorian, but it is not too difficult, in practice, to decide whether such a name refers to a hill-fort.

If a name in -borough or -bury refers not to a settlement but to a hill, it is virtually certain to contain the element in its archaeological sense; and it usually does so if the name is that of a village at the foot of a defended hill. Further guidance can be derived from the first elements of compound names in *burh*, as some compounds recur regularly in the names of hill-forts. As regards the form of the element, the nominative, *burh*, is most likely to become Borough or Brough in modern names, but in the west Midlands the variants Burf and Berth should be noted. The dative, *byrig*, normally becomes Bury. There are many examples of defended hills called Borough Hill or Bury Hill, and the existence of such a name for a hill with no

visible ramparts almost certainly indicates that fortifications were formerly
to be seen there.

In the country as a whole, the dative, Bury, is probably more common
than the nominative, Borough, Burgh, or Brough (ocasionally Burrow),
but the use of the nominative is specially common in the west Midlands,
and this gives rise to some distinctive names which are of interest to the
archaeologist. Old English final -*h* could develop into modern -*f* (as in the
pronunciation, though not the spelling, of such words as *laugh, tough*), and
this development has led to *burh* becoming Burf instead of Borough in such
names as Abdon Burf and Clee Burf SHR and Burfa Banks RAD, which are
all hill-forts. In areas where the form Burf was common, the confusion of
-*f* with -*th* (found in some modern dialects) led to some of the hill-forts
being called Berth. Two striking examples are the great fort called The
Berth near Baschurch SHR, and a Staffordshire fort of the same name near
Maer. The one-inch map shows several instances of places called Berth
where forts are apparently not known, such as Berth Hill on the WOR/GLO
border, GR SO 810306, and Berth House, south of Shelve SHR, GR SO
335974. Both these names appear on the first edition one-inch map.

A number of prehistoric forts, or settlements situated by such forts,
have the name Oldbury. These include the villages of Oldbury on Severn
GLO and Oldbury WAR, and the fort called Oldbury Castle in Cherhill WLT.
It is sometimes tempting to postulate a lost fort to explain the name, as in
the case of Oldbury west of Birmingham, where Bury Hill would have been
a likely site for such a structure. It must be remembered, however, that in
this compound -bury can have the alternative meanings 'manor house' or
'town', and Oldbury is sometimes the counterpart of Newbury, in which
case it refers either to the more ancient part of a town (as perhaps in
Oldbury Road in Tewkesbury GLO) or to an old or abandoned manor-
house. The part of Tewkesbury called Oldbury appears from recent
excavations to have been the nucleus of the Roman settlement.

Compounds in which -bury is preceded by an animal or bird-name
sometimes refer to hill-forts. An interesting example is Ramsbury, which
derives from Old English *hræfnesbyrig*, 'raven's fort'. This compound
occurs in a Wiltshire village-name and in three minor names in Berkshire,
and three of the four examples refer to hill-forts or to something which the
Anglo-Saxons took for one. Two of the Berkshire instances occur in Old
English boundaries; one of these refers to some cultivation terraces on the
slope of Weathercock Hill near Ashbury, which look somewhat like
ramparts, and the other to the fort on Rams Hill near the Ridgeway, the
modern name of which preserves the first part of Old English *hræfnesbyrig*.
The third Berkshire example is Ramsbury Corner and Wood in Buckle-

bury, GR SU 525696, where a hill-fort was discovered by means of an air photograph in 1948. There is another place-name reference to this last fort in the field-name Totterdown which occurs in the Bucklebury Tithe Award, and this name is discussed below. No prehistoric fort has yet been found at Ramsbury WLT, but the evidence is probably sufficient to justify a search for a hill-fort wherever the name occurs in Berkshire, Wiltshire and perhaps north Hampshire. The name 'raven's fort' may be of mocking significance, like Rat's Castle and Owl's Castle applied at a later date to ruined fortifications, or it may refer obliquely to the god Woden. To judge by Old Norse accounts of Othin, the raven would have been a familiar creature of Woden, and Woden was certainly associated with earthworks in the Anglo-Saxon imagination (see below). It cannot be assumed that Old English *hræfnes-*, modern Rams- or Ravens-, will have this significance in all the names in which it occurs, and not all names in Rams- are derived from *hræfn*, as can be ascertained from a glance at Ekwall 1960 (p. 380).

Both *burh* and *byrig* are fairly common as the first element of place-names, in such compounds as Bourton, Burton, Berrington, Burgham, Burham, Burghill, Burley. The meanings of these compounds have not been established in every case. The ones most likely to be of interest to the archaeologist are probably Burghill and Burley, which appear in some instances to mean 'hill with a fort' and 'wood by a fort'. Burlton SHR (GR SJ 458260) is from *burh-hyll-tūn*, 'settlement by a hill with a fort', and an air photograph has recently shown a large multivallate enclosure just west of the village. Near Berghill in Whittington SHR there are crop-marks at GR SJ 353312 showing a settlement with enclosures. Burghill north-west of Hereford lies between two hills neither of which has earthworks marked on the Ordnance Survey map, but it is a reasonable supposition that such features were formerly visible in the vicinity. Burley HMP is probably named from the fort on Castle Hill.

Burton and Bourton sometimes refer to prehistoric fortifications, as in Burton CHE, which is named from a promontory fort on Burton Point, and Bourton on the Water GLO named from the hill-fort called Salmonsbury; but there was an Old English appellative *burhtūn*, which denoted a type of Anglo-Saxon settlement, and Burton, Bourton and Berrington are seldom to be considered of special archaeological interest. In many cases they derive from the compound appellative *burhtūn*, or they describe a settlement by an ancient town or manor known as 'the *burh*' or 'the *byrig*'. It is just worth noting, however, that if a place-name with *burh* or *byrig* as first element occurs in an area where there is no nearby Anglo-Saxon settlement likely to have been known as 'the manor' or 'the town', it is possible that the name refers to a prehistoric fort.

In the northern half of England, *burh* is sometimes used of Roman forts, as in Brougham and Brough WML, Aldborough YOW. This usage is certainly rare, possibly not known, in the south, and Burgh Castle near Yarmouth SFK, which refers to the Roman fort of *Gariannonum*, may be the most southerly instance.

(ii) *Old English weard-setl.* Old English *weard-setl*, which means 'guard-house', does not occur as a major place-name, but is found occasionally in minor names and in Old English charter-boundaries. It seems probable that it was a specific term for an ancient fort. One of the instances in boundaries occurs in a survey of a large estate at Bromley GTL, dating from AD 862. This *weard-setl* is said to be on the boundary between Keston and Farnborough, and it is almost certainly to be identified with the hill-fort now called Caesar's Camp. Another instance occurs in the bounds of Highclere HMP, attached to a charter dated 749, and this has been identified with Beacon Hill, which is crowned by a large hill-fort.

As a surviving minor name *weard-setl* is best evidenced in north Worcestershire, where there are three examples, all of which have early spellings. Warshill Top Farm near Kidderminster stands on a hill where there is an earthwork (GR SO 794776), and Wassell Wood, another development of the name, lies on the opposite side of the hill. Wassel Grove in Hagley is overlooked by the great hill-fort of Wychbury. Wast Hills in the north of Alvechurch parish, GR SP 039762, lies on a long ridge where no ancient monument has yet been located.

It may be felt that four instances—two in charter-boundaries in Greater London and Hampshire and two in minor names in Worcestershire—in which *weard-setl* certainly refers to a hill-fort do not constitute a sufficient body of evidence to justify its being treated as a specific archaeological term. It is worth noting as a possibility, however, and as it is in any case a term of rare occurrence, the number of red herrings will not be a serious matter. Minor names which probably incorporate *weard-setl* are to be found on one-inch maps. These include Wassell north of Leintwardine HRE, GR SO 415753, which is a hill spur. Another possible example is Wassells Dale, which is shown on the Tithe Award for Smethcott SHR at GR SO 452992.

(iii) *Old English tōt-ærn.* This compound, from *tōt* 'look-out place' and *ærn* 'house', is perhaps the most reliable place-name guide to a hill-fort. It is necessary to remember, however, that *tōt* by itself does not imply fortifications, and most instances of Toothill, Tuthill, Tuttle denote nothing more than an eminence with a view. Similarly, *weard* by itself does not refer to a fortified site, the crucial element being *setl*, which, like *ærn*, means 'house'. The element *ærn* is preserved intact in Totternhoe BDF, 'hill-spur near the look-out house', and the spur may have been named from the hill-fort called Maiden Bower, west of Dunstable. The preservation of -n- in Tottern- is unusual, and the element *ærn* usually reveals itself in modern forms by the syllable -er-, giving minor names like Totterhill and Totterdown, which are very likely to refer to forts. Totterdown occurs as a Tithe Award field-name in Bucklebury BRK, near Ramsbury Corner where a camp was spotted on an air photograph in 1948, and there are several more instances in Berkshire, one being Totterdown in Chieveley, near Bussock hill-fort. There is a Totters Bank at Chesterton near Worfield SHR, where there is a large fort now called The Walls. The nearby Tuters Hill on the outskirts of Pattingham STF may refer to another fort which is no longer visible on the ground. Totterton Hall near Lydbury North SHR is overlooked by a hill-fort called Billings Ring. Old and New Totterdown north-west of Marlborough WLT lie at the southern end of a ridge which appears to have every kind of ancient monument on its crest. Tatteredge Hill south-east of Leintwardine HRE (Totteredge Hill on the first edition one-inch map) is a very likely place for a fort, though none is marked on the map.

(iv) *Old English eorth-burh.* This compound, which means 'earth fort', can become Arbury, Harbury, Harborough, Yarborough in modern names, but the group has to be approached with extreme caution as these modern forms sometimes have other origins. Market Harborough LEI, and the parish-names Harborough and Harbury WAR are from three different compounds, none of them from *eorth-burh*. Arbury LNC and WAR and Harborough Banks WAR certainly derive from *eorth-burh*, however, and Arbury CAM and HRT probably do. Yarborough and Yarburgh LIN certainly have this origin. There are known prehistoric forts at some of these places (e.g. Harborough Banks in Lapworth WAR, which certainly refers to the earthwork as there is no village, and for which there is the conclusive spelling *Erdbyr'* 1220), and the type of name is worth noting as a possible guide to prehistoric remains, though even greater caution than usual needs to be exercised in dealing with it.

A further complication arises from the use of Arbour in comparatively modern names, like Robin Hood's Arbour in Maidenhead BRK, in which ancient enclosures are linked with folk-lore. Arbour may sometimes represent earlier *eorth-burh*, but it may equally well be the modern word *arbour*, which came into Middle English from French.

Yet another source of confusion is the word *harbour*, from Old English *here-beorg*, which may give modern forms resembling those from *eorth-burh*, and which may also sometimes refer to an ancient building or encampment.

(c) *Linear Earthworks : Grim and the Devil*

The other main type of prehistoric earthwork recognized by the Anglo-Saxons was the linear earthwork, the date and historical context of which is often difficult for the archaeologist to determine. With the notable exception of Offa's Dyke, place-names do not help with the problem of dating these works. But they may give help with the plotting of long ditches visible in only part of their original length. There are a number of instances, the most notable being Offa's Dyke and the two stretches of Wansdyke, which demonstrate the ability of the Anglo-Saxons to appreciate a very long ditch as a unity, and not to give it different names in different stretches. In view of this, a mention of an earthwork with a distinctive name in a field-name or minor place-name could give valuable guidance about its exact course in a stretch where the bank and ditch had been destroyed. Distinctive names for linear earthworks include Wansdyke ('dyke of the god Woden') and Fleam Dyke CAM ('dyke of the fugitives'). The common term Grim's Dyke is discussed below.

An example of the consistent use of a dyke-name over a long distance is set out in a recent article (Owen 1975), which shows that a line of sea banks between the Humber and the Wash, probably built in the eleventh century, can be traced for thirty miles by means of such names as *le Hafdik*, *Hafdic*, *Hauedich* in medieval documents; these are derived from Old Norse *hafdík* 'sea-dyke'.

The usual word employed for linear earthworks is *dīc*, the ancestor of the modern word *ditch*. The alternative term *dike* is probably due to influence from the corresponding Old Norse word. The majority of ditches mentioned in place-names, however, are neither defensive nor prehistoric. Innumerable ditches were dug both in prehistoric and in Anglo-Saxon times for drainage and for boundary demarcation, and *dīc* in a settlement-name or a field-name is not automatically of interest to the archaeologist.

A curious feature of place-names referring to prehistoric ditches is the persistent Anglo-Saxon association of such works with the god Woden, implied by the widespread Grimsditch, Grim's Dyke names. The only explicit reference to Woden in connection with a ditch occurs in Wansdyke. This is not a prehistoric earthwork. Excavation has shown it to be post-Roman, and this makes the name very difficult to explain, since the

Saxons (who were settled on the Middle Thames, not very far from the eastern end of Wansdyke, before the end of the Roman period) must be assumed to have known something of the circumstances of its construction. This problem is discussed in some detail in Gelling 1961, but no solution has been found which is wholly convincing. One theory which has been advanced is that the earthwork was made by pagan West Saxons and dedicated to Woden as the protector of the builders, but it is difficult to accept that the northern frontier of the West Saxons was ever as far south as this. However that may be, Woden under his nickname *Grīm* certainly had a special association with linear earthworks which are of prehistoric origin, and to a lesser extent with hill-forts and other prehistoric monuments.

It has been established that *Grīm*, meaning 'the masked one', is a nickname for Woden, alluding to the god's habit of going about in disguise; and the numerous earthworks called Grims Ditch, Grimsdyke in many parts of the country are believed to contain this nickname, either because they were believed to be the work of the god, or as a vague expression of superstitious awe concerning their origin. The use of disguise by Woden is inferred from the many instances in which the corresponding Old Norse god Othin behaved in this way. We do not have narratives concerning the Old English gods of the sort which have survived for the Old Norse deities, and there are many dangers in transferring Old Norse information of a much later date to our own relatively brief pagan period. But a major characteristic like this one seems likely to belong to both traditions.

Not all English place-names in Grims- are of this origin. *Grímr* was a common Old Norse personal name, and in the areas of England where Danes and Norwegians settled in the ninth and tenth centuries there are such names as Grimsby, Grimesthorpe and Grimscote which contain this personal name and are of no special archaeological significance. The special problem of the name Grimston in the Danelaw is discussed in Chapter 9. Even in the Danelaw, however, a Grims- name referring to an earthwork is likely to allude to the god.

Outside the Danelaw and the areas of Norwegian settlement there are a number of names in Grims-, in addition to the Grimsditch type, which contain *Grīm* in the supernatural sense and are likely to denote archaeological remains. Grimsbury OXF may have referred to an earthwork, though no prehistoric features are now to be distinguished in this suburb of Banbury. There is a hill-fort called Grimsbury Castle in Hampstead Norris BRK, and 'Grim's hill' in the Old English bounds of Hawling GLO is a hill crowned by a fort. Other prehistoric monuments with this type of name are the neolithic flint-mines called Grimes Graves in Norfolk, and the Bronze-Age enclosure called Grimspound on Dartmoor.

The original connection between Grim and Woden must be regarded as established, but it is very doubtful whether all the names in Grims- referring to ditches and other prehistoric features were coined by pagan Anglo-Saxons having a specific deity in mind. Grimspound on Dartmoor is too far west for the name to have been coined in the pagan period. It seems probable that Grim survived the conversion to Christianity, perhaps as a pseudonym for the Devil. Association with the adjective *grim* would help such a process, and some of the Grims- names are probably the equivalent of Devil's Ditch, Devil's Highway which are applied in more recent times to earthworks and Roman roads.

Less august supernatural beings denoted by such words as *pūca* and *hob*, both meaning 'goblin', may be associated with earthworks. Hobditch Causeway, south of Birmingham, is a linear earthwork of Roman or pre- Roman date, the course of which has been traced for nearly four miles, and which has its eastern end at Harborough Banks WAR. The field-names *Pouke Ditch* and *Grymshill* occur in sixteenth-century records in the vicinity of this bank. The association of puck with pits, found in minor names and field-names, particularly in the south-west Midlands, has never been explained. It is best evidenced in Gloucestershire, where such names as Puck Pit, Puckpits, Pugpit, Puckshole occur in a surprising number of parishes. The compound with *pit* occurs also in the modern form Poppets (OXF and SSX), but it is not known what type of feature is denoted. Other terms for supernatural beings which occur in place-names are *thyrs* 'giant' (Thursden LNC, Thirlspot CMB), *dwerg* 'dwarf' (Dwarriden YOW, Dwerry- house LNC), *scucca* 'demon' (Shugborough STF, Shuckburgh WAR, Shuck- nall HRE). A reference to archaeological remains is possible in some of these names, though obviously places could be haunted without being of special interest to the modern archaeologist. References to elves are relatively frequent, and it has been suggested that some of these, and some of the 'dwarf' names, refer to there being an echo at the place. There are said to be echoes at Dwarriden ('dwarf valley') in Ecclesfield YOW and at Elvendon ('elf hill') in Goring OXF.

(d) *Roman Remains*

A distinction is made here between the words discussed in Chapter 3— *camp, port, wīc* (in *wīchām*), *ecles, funta*—which may have been used to coin place-names at a time when Roman institutions were still functioning in Britain, and some other terms—*ceaster, strǣt, flōr*—which must in many instances refer to Roman remains observed by the Anglo-Saxons long after the decay of a Roman or sub-Roman way of life.

(i) *Old English ceaster, 'walled town'*.   The recent article on the use of the term *vicus* (Johnson 1975) which has been quoted in the discussion of place-names from *wīchām* in Chapter 3, says 'It is probable that in Britain, as in Gaul, the small towns which were walled were known as "castra". . . . One might see this usage as a Roman antecedent for the name "-chester".' Mr Johnson is speaking of the fourth-century Roman usage, and this late Roman sense 'walled town' suits the literary use of Old English *ceaster*, which is a loan-word from *castra*. The Old English poetic use may be illustrated by the lines:

> Ceastra beoth feorran gesyne, orthanc enta geweorc, tha the on thysse eorthan syndon, wrætlic weallstana geweorc ('Cities are visible from afar, the cunning work of giants, the wondrous wall-stones which are on this earth').

A more prosaic use is seen in the entry in the Anglo Saxon Chronicle for 577, which reads:

> Her Cuthwine and Ceawlin fuhton with Brettas . . . and genamon threo ceastra, Gleawanceaster and Cirenceaster and Bathanceaster ('In this year Cuthwine and Ceawlin fought against the Britons . . . and captured three cities, Gloucester, Cirencester and Bath').

There is no doubt that *ceaster*, or the Anglian form *cæster*, was the normal term for the Anglo-Saxons to use when they named a walled Roman town. This is demonstrated by the names formed by the addition of this word to the Romano-British place-name. Instances of this are listed in Chapter 2, and they belong to the grander categories of Romano-British towns, most of which would be walled in the later years of the Empire.

It would be difficult, perhaps impossible, to say how consistently this meaning of *ceaster* was observed in the formation of other names besides those which incorporate the Romano-British name of the town. It is unlikely that a case could be made out for complete consistency, but some of the apparent anomalies, in which *ceaster* seems to be applied to a very modest Roman site or to one which was in no sense a town, may be due to the incompleteness of our archaeological evidence. The term may appear uncompounded, as in Caister NFK, Caistor LIN, Chester CHE, or as a first element, as in Casterton RUT, WML, Chesterton in several counties, Chesterford ESX, Chesterfield DRB, STF, and a number of other compounds. As a final element, the use is not limited to the compounds with earlier place-names; it occurs occasionally with an Old English personal name, as in Chichester SSX, Kenchester HRE, Godmanchester HNT, or with Old-English and Old-Norse words, as in Acaster YOW, Bewcastle CMB, Horncastle LIN, Silchester HMP, Woodchester GLO. There are also compounds with pre-English names not known to be the Romano-British name of the town, like Dorchester OXF and Worcester WOR, and with pre-English river-names, like Alcester WAR, Ilchester SOM. Among these examples there are a number of walled towns, like Caistor-by-Norwich, Chester, Chichester, Godmanchester and Silchester; but there are also places where no Roman site has as yet been discovered, like Casterton WML, and others where a Roman site is known but is believed to be very modest, like Chesterfield DRB. There are also some, notably Woodchester GLO, where the Roman site cannot be described as a town.

In the present state of knowledge, *ceaster* can only be recommended to the archaeologist as a general indication of Roman remains, but it should be remembered that the apparent imprecision of the Old English use of the term in place-names may be due to gaps in modern knowledge. It should also be noted that some of the Chesterton, Chesterfield type of names refer to a Roman town at a short distance; Chesterfield STF is half a mile south of Wall (*Letocetum*), and Chesterton OXF is three-quarters of a mile north-west of Alchester.

There is evidence for the occasional use of *ceaster* to denote fortifications which are not Roman. As with the occasional use of *burh*, *byrig* to denote Roman forts, this is probably best evidenced in the north of England. There are three northern names—Craster and Outchester NTB and Hincaster WML—in which *ceaster* is compounded with birds' names. Craster and Outchester are both near the Northumberland coast. Outchester ('owls' fort') lies among a number of small earthworks. Craster ('crows' fort') may be a fanciful name for the rocks on the coast, but there is a promontory fort just over a mile north, and a small round 'camp' two miles to the south, so this may, like Outchester, be a settlement surrounded by small earthworks, some of which are less apparent now than they were when the name arose. Prehistoric fortifications are more probable than Roman ones at both these places. At Hinchester WML, which means 'hens' chester', there has been no identification of any remains, Roman or prehistoric. In the west Midlands, Chesterton SHR, five miles north-east of Bridgnorth, lies by a fort called The Walls, which is assumed to be Iron Age. In the south-west, Chesterblade SOM is considered to derive the Chester- part of its name from a nearby prehistoric camp. These examples from NTB, WML, SHR and SOM may indicate that in the later stages of the Anglo-Saxon settlement the term *ceaster* lost its precise association with

Roman remains and was used of any ancient fortified site. But it should be remembered that no systematic study has yet been made of English place-names containing *ceaster*, *cæster*, and such a study might bring out a more consistent pattern than has hitherto been observed.

There is occasional confusion between *ceaster* and the much less common place-name element *ceastel* 'heap'. Both may become Castle- or Caster- in modern names. Chastleton OXF contains *ceastel*, perhaps referring to some unusual feature of the camp on Chastleton Hill. It is also the first element of Chesham BUC, but here the 'heap' is the natural ring of boulders on which the church is built. It is of rare occurrence in field-names, but a number of instances have been noted in Wiltshire, including *Stanchestle* ('stone heap') in Brokenborough. Such names may be of interest to the archaeologist if they occur in an area where natural heaps of stones or boulders are improbable.

(ii) *Old English strǣt, modern street.* The best-evidenced and most reliable guide to Roman remains is Old English *strǣt*, when it occurs in major place-names. The qualification is important; in minor names of late origin, Street is likely to have the modern dialect sense 'straggling village', and in field-names and Old English charter-boundaries the reference is often to a road of uncertain age which has some signs of a made surface. Major place-names like Street, Strete, Streatham, Streetham, Stretton, Stratton, Stratfield, Stretford, Stratford, Streetley, Streatley, however, refer to the position of the settlement on or close to one of the main roads of Roman Britain. The compound with *ford* may become Strafford or Strefford, and similar assimilations sometimes occur in other compounds. Strelley NTT ('clearing by a Roman road'), on the western outskirts of Nottingham, is an apparent exception to the general rule that major names with *strǣt* as first element are on or by the main Roman roads; but this is an area where the known road network, always widely spaced, is so sparse as to suggest that our knowledge of it is incomplete.

(iii) *Paved and tesselated floors.* There is no place-name element which has been shown to refer consistently to a particular class of Roman building, such as a villa or a bath-house. The baths at Bath SOM were called *Bæthum* 'at the baths', but elsewhere, in its rather rare occurrences in place-names, the word *bæth* does not appear to have any connection with Roman remains. The only term so far noted which may have a specific reference to a single Roman building is *fāgan flōre* '(at the) variegated floor', which is the source of Fawler OXF, and which is thought to refer to a tesselated pavement in a Roman villa. The phrase occurs again in the charter-boundaries of Water Eaton OXF, which run 'along the stream till it comes to the variegated floor' when they are tracing the boundary between Water Eaton and Marston. Until recently it was assumed that Fawler near Kingston Lisle BRK was another instance of this name, but careful study of the early spellings has made it clear that it is from *flage* 'flag-stone' and *flōre*, a compound found also in two names in Nottinghamshire, Flawford and Flawforth. Since only two instances of *fāgan flōre* and three of the compound of *flage* with *flōre* have so far been noted, it appears that both compounds refer to something noteworthy, and both could denote the floors of Roman buildings which, whether paved or tesselated, would be more elaborate than those of Anglo-Saxon buildings. The royal hall which is featured in the first half of *Beowulf* is said by the poet to have a *fagne flor*.

It has been suggested that *flōre* used by itself as a place-name may refer to a pavement in a Roman villa. This name occurs in Floore NTP, and in Flower Farm in Godstone SUR; and Eastwick HRT was *Estwyk atte Flore* in the fourteenth century. It is possible that a field-name or minor name Floor(s) is of special archaeological interest.

(e) *Anglo-Saxon Paganism*

The two aspects of English paganism which concern us in this section are burial and worship, the former being known mainly from archaeological evidence, and the latter mainly from place-names. The pagan burials are our main source of information about the English settlement, and the contribution which place-name studies can make to knowledge of the burials is slight; it may be of some interest but is unlikely to be of much archaeological importance. Regarding the sacred sites of pagan times, on the other hand, archaeology has as yet nothing to tell us, and literary references are few, so that place-names constitute the main source of information about this aspect of paganism. The chances of archaeological discovery arising from the place-name evidence are slender, but not to be dismissed entirely, and it seems worth while in this section to summarize the evidence for the location of pagan shrines.

(i) *Possible references to Anglo-Saxon pagan burials.* There is circumstantial evidence for connecting the word *hlāw, hlǣw* with Anglo-Saxon barrow burials in some of its occurrences in place-names. This is not one of the commoner types of Anglo-Saxon burial, and such instances as can be firmly connected with grave-goods date from the early seventh century, which is the end of the period during which pagan burial was practised.

At Taplow BUC a mound in the churchyard produced jewelled buckles and other grave-goods which show it to be most probably the tumulus of a prince who died in the first quarter of the seventh century. Taplow means 'Tæppa's tumulus', and it seems reasonable to assume that the place-name refers to the mound in the churchyard, and that Tæppa was the name of the man buried there. It is not likely that the settlement was founded at a later date than the burial, and if the name and the tumulus are indeed connected it seems probable that an earlier place-name (either Welsh or English) was replaced by Taplow because the tumulus was an object of great note. Challow BRK means 'Ceawa's tumulus'; and here again it seems likely that the settlement was flourishing long before a Saxon burial took place, but possible that the tumulus, and the ceremonies which accompanied the burial, left so deep a mark on local consciousness that the name of the land-unit was replaced. The tumulus is mentioned in the Old English bounds of Denchworth, the neighbouring parish, so its approximate position is known, but there is now no trace of it, and a critic may fairly point out that we do not know it to have been a Saxon barrow as opposed to a prehistoric one.

Probably the firm evidence for suggesting that a name meaning 'x's low' may sometimes refer to a late pagan Anglo-Saxon monument consists of no more than the coincidence of the mound and the name at Taplow. There are, however, a number of names, particularly in the west Midlands, in which *hlāw* is combined with an Old English personal name which is either 'archaic' or has associations with the Mercian royal family; and these may be worth noting, even if there is little chance of any dating evidence being found, or even, in most instances, of an actual tumulus being located.

The most notable instance in the west Midlands of a -low place-name which may refer to an Anglian burial is Offlow, the name of a hill two miles south-south-east of Lichfield STF. This was the meeting-place of one of the Staffordshire hundreds, and the tumulus which marked the meeting-place is drawn on the first edition one-inch map, which suggests that it was still clearly visible in 1834. Unfortunately, the hill which it crowned is a slight one, the whole area is arable land, and ploughing has reduced the tumulus to a diffuse mound spread over a wide area. There has been no excavation, and no chance finds are known. The name means 'Offa's tumulus', Assuming that Offa may be the man buried there, the name cannot of course refer to the great king of Mercia, the builder of Offa's Dyke, who flourished in the second half of the ninth century, since he was Christian and came much too late for this type of burial. But the name Offa was of special significance in the Mercian royal family. Their genealogy includes a much earlier Continental Offa, king of Angeln in Slesvig and one of the chief heroes of Germanic legend, and it has been suggested that it was partly their claim to this illustrious descent which enabled the kings of Mercia to establish their dominion over the whole of the Midlands. Some other princes of the royal house probably bore the name, as well a number of humbler men. The Mercian ruling house was pagan until the death of Penda in 654, and their kings and princes may be supposed to have had burials at least comparable to that of a king of East Anglia at Sutton Hoo. It is pushing the evidence too far to suggest that grave-goods richer than those of Sutton Hoo lie under the plough-spread which is all that remains of the tumulus called Offlow; but the name deserves consideration in the context of Mercian royal burials of the pagan period, none of which has ever been discovered.

The date of the English penetration into the western division of Mercia which comprised the kingdom of the Magonsæte in north Herefordshire and south Shropshire is not known. The first recorded king of the Magon-sæte is Merewalh, who was reputed in later traditions to have been the third son of Penda, and who flourished in the second half of the seventh century. Some of his English subjects were probably in the region before the kingdom was organized, but it is likely that there was only a short period during which English paganism was practised in Herefordshire and Shropshire—perhaps only a generation. This presumed single generation of pagan Angles in the first half of the seventh century would be likely to give their leading men the rite of barrow burial, since this appears to have been the time at which it was practised. It is noteworthy, therefore, that both counties contain place-names which mean 'x's tumulus'. The Herefordshire name of this type is Wolferlow; this means 'Wulfhere's tumulus', and the tiny settlement lies near the HRE/WOR border, six miles south-east of Tenbury. In Shropshire there are seven examples, widely distributed in the county: Beslow, Longslow, Munslow, Onslow, Peplow, Purslow and Whittingslow. Beslow, a tiny hamlet in the parish of Wroxeter, means 'Betti's tumulus'. Longslow, north-west of Market Drayton, is 'Wlanc's tumulus', *Wlanc* 'the proud one' being the sort of personal name which is sometimes described as archaic (see Chapter 5). Munslow, 'Mundel's tumulus', lies in a recess in the eastern escarpment of Wenlock Edge. Onslow, 'Andhere's tumulus', is a hamlet three and a half miles west of Shrewsbury, and this, like Longslow, contains an 'archaic' personal name. Peplow, probably 'Pyppa's tumulus', lies beside the River Tern, six miles south-west of Market Drayton. Purslow, 'Pussa's tumulus', is a hamlet in the south-west of the county, three and a half miles east of Clun. Whittingslow, 'Hwittuc's tumulus', is on a hill spur overlooking Watling

Street, three miles south-west of Church Stretton. Munslow and Purslow were hundred meeting-places.

There are other names in -low in Herefordshire and Shropshire, but attention is here confined to those which have an Old English personal name as first element, as these are perhaps more likely to be Anglo-Saxon rather than prehistoric tumuli. No archaeological remains are known from any of the sites, but it does not seem too far-fetched to suggest that in Betti, Wlanc, Mundel, Andhere, Pyppa, Pussa and Hwittuc, and perhaps the Wulfhere of Wolferlow, we may have a generation of pagan Angles of aristocratic status who were among the first English settlers in the Marches.

Some jewellery of the seventh century has come from barrows in the east Midlands, in the Peak district; the records of discovery are not very satisfactory, but it is clear that in some instances the tumuli were pre-historic structures used for secondary Anglian burials. Some of the mounds have names like Bole Low, Hurdlow, White Low, but these are only known from late records, and do not appear to include any ancient names like Taplow and Offlow, in which a tumulus is associated with an Old English personal name.

A fairly common feature of Old English estate boundaries is the phrase *hǣthenan byrgels* 'heathen burial-place'. There is no general correlation between this boundary-mark and tumuli, so it seems probable that the reference is to Anglo-Saxon pagan cemeteries the position of which was remembered in the ninth and tenth centuries, though there were no mounds to mark the graves. So far, no archaeological remains have been discovered which can be equated with one of these boundary-marks. One of the difficulties in attempting such a discovery would be that while the position of the boundary-mark is often ascertainable with sufficient precision to enable the course of the survey to be followed, it is seldom possible to narrow it down sufficiently for the archaeologist, who needs to know exactly where to dig. The heathen burial-place may be the only boundary mark to be given in a half-mile stretch of boundary. It is some-times possible to be more precise than this, however, and the archaeological phenomenon which lies behind the phrase will probably be discovered eventually.

It is rare for this phrase, or similar ones, to occur in later place-names, but a few instances have been noted. Heathens' Burial Corner in Steyning ssx has Middle English spellings like *Hetheneburiels* 1279, *Hethenberieles* 1288. There is a tradition of urns being found there, but apparently nothing is now known of them. Heath Bridge in Blackthorn oxf may be a corruption of a name spelt *Hethenebergh, Hethenebouruwe* in some thir-teenth-century perambulations of Bernwood Forest, and this may be from *hǣthenan beorgas* 'heathen barrows'.

Old English *hǣthen* means 'growing with heather' as well as 'heathen', and this is at least as likely a sense in any place-names and field-names where it occurs in other compounds than that with *byrgels*.

(ii) *Pagan religious sites.* English place-names which appear to denote sites of pagan worship have long been recognized as a category which make a vital contribution to history and which have an exceptionally vivid imaginative appeal. Three important articles, Dickins 1934, Ekwall 1935 and Stenton 1941, established a sort of canon of names considered to refer either to pagan temples or to pagan deities. It was thought that the canon would be added to as place-name research progressed, and Stenton 1941 says, 'At the present time, between fifty and sixty sites of heathen worship can be identified by means of local names. It is certain that the number will be increased by further investigation.' The thirty-five years of systematic place-name study which have elapsed since that prophecy was made, however, have not produced a single new specimen, and two conclusions may be drawn from this. First, it is unlikely that the canon laid down in 1941 contained an absolutely correct corpus of available place-names with heathen connotations, and since subsequent study has failed to add to it, it seems likely that it was in fact larger than the true corpus. Secondly, since most, perhaps all, the possible candidates were known in 1941, they must fall into categories of names which had been comprehensively studied at that date; this means that the great majority are either among the major place-names studied in Ekwall 1960, or they are to be found in the boundaries of the Anglo-Saxon charters. Stenton's hope that field-name study would produce more examples has proved unfounded, in spite of the great increase in the scale on which field-names have been collected and examined for the post-war surveys of the English Place-Name Society.

Two 'prunings' of the Dickins-Ekwall-Stenton corpus have been made (Gelling 1961, 1973b). The last was perhaps a little more drastic than it need have been, but the resulting body of material has been accepted as sounder than that proposed in 1941. It contains forty-three names, some with a query. These are shown on Fig. 11. They fall into two main categories: names containing *hearg* (e.g. Harrow, Harrowden) or *wēoh*, *wīh* (e.g. Patchway, Weedon, Weoley, Willey, Wye, Wyham, Wyville), both of which elements are considered to mean 'heathen shrine', and those containing the names of the gods *Wōden* (or *Wēden*), *Thunor* and *Tīw*.

The names shown on Fig. 11 form a distribution pattern which is capable of more than one interpretation. The rarity or absence of these names in areas subject to heavy Danish settlement has not been satisfactorily explained. The western limit of the names offers less difficulty, as it is probably due to the greater Welsh element in the population. No tradition has survived of the conversion to Christianity of the Hwicce of the Severn Valley, and this may be due to their not having required conversion, the Welsh Christian element in their composition being sufficient to cause the abandonment of paganism by the Saxon and Anglian settlers. King Merewalh of the Magonsæte was said by a post-Conquest writer to have accepted Christianity in AD 660. It is suggested above that there may only have been one generation of English paganism in his kingdom, and this might not allow for the growth of noteworthy centres of pagan worship. In the areas where these place-names do occur, their distribution is uneven, and it has been suggested (Gelling 1961, 1973b) that it can be explained to some extent as showing areas where the pagan religion lingered for some decades after the acceptance of Christianity by the ruling families of the various kingdoms. Shrines which continued in use after the acceptance of Christianity by the majority of the people might be commemorated in a place-name because they were felt to be an exceptional feature of a settlement. To illustrate this point, the sites of some early bishoprics have been marked on Fig. 11. Those of Dorchester on Thames, Winchester and Selsey have cleared spaces round them on this map. Those of London and Lichfield do not, however. The pagan site near to London is Harrow on the Hill GTL, and this may have been commemorated in an enduring place-name because of its exceptionally impressive site. As regards Lichfield, the centre of the Mercian see was placed here by St Chad, and it is possible that the close proximity of unregenerate worshippers of Woden seemed an inducement to this particular saint.

Some clusters of names occur on the borders of kingdoms—the group comprising Willey, Peper Harrow and Thursley would be on the boundary between the spheres of influence of the Kings of Kent and Wessex in the seventh century, and the group in north Essex would be on the boundary between the East Saxons and the East Angles. There may have been 'no-man's land' areas, in which missionary work was particularly difficult for bishops operating under the protection of a royal house. The west Surrey names are especially interesting in relation to the monastery of Farnham, founded *c.* 685 and endowed with a great estate here. The foundation charter mentions two more names of pagan significance, *Cusanweoh*, one of the properties given to the monastery, and *Besingahearh*, where the charter was drawn up. These names have not survived, but the places may reasonably be supposed to have lain in the Farnham area, and it may be that the monastery was founded with a view to mopping up an obstinate enclave of paganism.

Fig. 11   English place-names which probably refer to pagan religious practices

Much more could be said of the possible significance of each of the names on Fig. 11; but the articles referred to above may be consulted for greater detail, and it is only necessary here to say something of the chances of archaeological discovery at any of these places.

Only two of the sites shown on Fig. 11 are outstandingly impressive, these being Harrow MDX and Wednesbury STF. In both these instances it is likely that the pagan shrine was succeeded by a Christian church. Several excavations have recently taken place in and around churches (though not at any which have this type of name). So far no excavation has produced traces of anything other than earlier Christian churches or Roman buildings of different character, but there is always the possibility that some post-hole pattern will be recognized which seems appropriate to a non-Christian religious building. There is little doubt that many churches besides those on the hills at Harrow and Wednesbury stand on the sites of earlier pagan shrines. Of the sites with pagan names where the sanctuary does not seem likely to be under the church, the most promising is probably Weedon Bec NTP. The name means 'hill with a heathen temple', and the likeliest site is Weedon Hill, a mile south-west of the village. The summit of the hill is shown on the one-inch map as free from trees, buildings and roads, and it is perhaps just possible that a timber structure might be observed as a crop-mark from the air. Patchway SSX ('Pæccel's heathen temple') is the name not of a settlement but of a meadow included in Stanmer Park, a short distance north-east of Brighton. Several fields called Patchway are shown on the Tithe awards for Falmer and Stanway, and if the exact position of these were noted it would be possible to look for significant marks on air-photographs.

This class of place-names has been more exhaustively studied than any other, but their significance is far from exhausted. It is curious that they show a dichotomy similar to that noted in the *wīchām* names (Chapter 3) of being estate centres or being situated on an estate boundary. Patchway, Thunderfield, *Thunorslege, Thunresfeld, Thunreslea* (two examples), *Tislea, Tyesmere* all occur in charter-boundaries, and as such names are not found in later field-names scattered about in the areas of parishes, this characteristic seems significant. Three of the examples marked on Fig. 11 —*Wodneslawe* BDF, *Thunreslau* and Thurstable ESX—were the names of hundred meeting-places.

Chapter 7

Personal Names in Place-Names

Three topics require discussion under this heading: first, the nature of Old English personal names; second, the extent to which personal names enter into place-names; third, the situation which led to the coining of place-names like Brighton ssx ('Beorhthelm's estate or settlement') and Basildon esx ('Beorhtel's hill').

The introductory volume to the English Place-Name Society's publications contains an essay by Sir Frank Stenton (Stenton 1924) which has the same title as this chapter. Its orientation is different, however. Stenton was concerned mainly with the recovery of Old English personal-name material, and he saw the place-names as a quarry from which items might be extracted. Here we are concerned rather with the historical significance of place-names which incorporate personal names. Stenton's views on this last topic seem to the present writer to be mistaken; but the first half of his 1924 article, in which he studies the principles of Old English personal-name formation, is the best explanation which has been written for the non-specialist. Old English personal names are difficult to explain, as the reader will agree if he peruses the next few paragraphs, and Stenton's brilliant account is a most helpful starting point. It will be summarized here with the addition of some information from other authorities, in particular Redin 1919.

After observing that English personal names form part of the general stock of Germanic personal nomenclature, Stenton discusses the main division into two great classes, compound names composed of two elements, and simple names composed of one. Compound names form a well-defined class, which includes such items as *Ealhmund, Tīdhelm, Cynewulf, Ælfrǣd*. Simple names are not a homogeneous class, and must be divided into several distinct types. Some of them are the short forms of compound names; these include **Hycga* (found in Hitcham BUC), which is considered to be a short form of *Hygerǣd*; *Cūtha*, which alternates with *Cūthwine* in the Anglo-Saxon Chronicle and is assumed to refer to the same West Saxon prince; *Sæba*, which Bede cites as a form used by the sons of King *Sæberht* in referring to their father; *Bucge*, recorded as a familiar form of the name of an Abbess *Hēaburg* or *Ēadburg*; and *Gode*, used in a number of sources for Edward the Confessor's sister *Godgifu*.

It is difficult to say how many of the uncompounded personal names existed in their own right, and how many of them originated as short forms of longer names, but it seems likely that original uncompounded names are a large class. They can be derived from nouns, like *Beorn* 'man, warrior', *Cēol* 'ship', *Hengest* 'horse', or from adjectives, like *Beald* 'bold', *Frōd* 'wise, old', *Snell* 'smart, strong, bold', *Swēt* 'sweet'. Feminine uncompounded names include *Bēage* 'ring', *Hild* 'battle', *Hwīte* 'white'.

Another class of uncompounded personal names consists of one of the recognized name-forming elements with the addition of a suffix, such as *-il*, *-el*, *-ul*, *-ol*, *-(i)la*, *-ele*, *-uc*, *-oc*, *-(i)ca*. These suffixes are used to form hypocoristic names—the equivalent of modern Tom, Dick and Harry. Old English names in this class include *Berhtel*, *Esla*, *Hemele*, *Hwituc*, *Hereca*. Sir Frank Stenton devoted several pages of his discussion to this type, and it is clear that he realized, even before the county place-name surveys began to appear, that an understanding of these hypocoristic formations would prove to be of crucial importance for the interpretation of many place-names.

Another category consists of names in *-ing*, some of which may originally have been patronymics (see Chapter 5), but most of which became independent names. These include *Brūning*, *Dēoring*, *Lēofing*. There is a small group of uncompounded names which refer to racial origin, including *Dene* and *Scot*, and probably *Franca* and *Seaxa*. Other racial names, such as *-gēat* and *Peoht-*, occur in compound personal names. On the problem of *Wealh* and *Welisc*, see Chapter 4.

It is assumed that all the elements used in the formation of personal names were at one time meaningful, although a fairly high proportion of those recorded, especially of the uncompounded names, are unintelligible to us, and a number seem ambiguous. How far the meaning influenced their use it is impossible to say. Many of the short names, like *Crispa* 'curly', *Hwīta* 'white', *Swift* 'swift', could be nicknames which had replaced a man's original name. The choice of elements from which a compound name was made was certainly influenced by other considerations than that of sense. Stenton 1924 (pp. 168–9) gives examples of compound names formed to indicate family connections. Alliteration (the use of names beginning with the same consonant, or all beginning with a vowel) was sometimes practised in aristocratic families. The influence of alliteration on a sequence of family names is seen, e.g. in the genealogy of the kings of Northumbria—'Ælle wæs Yffing, Yffe Uxfreaing, Uxfrea Wilgilsing, Wilgils Westerfalcing, Westerfalca Sæfugling, Sæfugel Sæbalding, Sæbald Sigegeating, Sigegeat Swebdæging, Swebdæg Sigegaring, Sigegar Wægdæging, Wægdæg Wodening'. Alliteration is the commonest indication of family connections, but Stenton quotes instances of the combining of one element from the father's and one from the mother's name to give such a compound as *Hereswīth*, the name of the daughter of *Hererīc* and *Breguswīth*. Similarly St Wulfstan, the eleventh-century homilist, was the son of a man named *Æthelstān* and a woman named *Wulfgifu*. The elements used in male and female names overlap, but there are some, e.g. *-gifu, -swīth, -flǣd, -hild, -burh*, which are only used as final elements in women's names.

Something needs to be said of the grammar of personal names, as this affects the form of the place-names in which they occur. The different ways of forming the genitive, which are the main concern of the place-name student, are determined both by the gender of the name and by its grammatical classification. Feminine names do not have *-s* in the genitive, and in addition to this it is important to note that not all masculine names have genitives in *-s*. The major divisions into which Old English nouns and personal names fall are those of 'strong' and 'weak', and it is only strong masculine names which have *-s* in the genitive. Many weak masculine names end in *-a* (e.g. *Æsca, Beorna, Dudda, Cēna, Goda, Hwīta*), and such names take *-n* in the genitive. Strong names like *Beorn* take *-s*. Thus Barnsley YOW is 'Beorn's wood or clearing', Barnwell CAM and Barnwood GLO may be 'Beorna's spring and wood'. Final *-a* in a personal name is most likely to be a characteristic of a weak masculine name; this can be confusing for the uninitiated modern reader, who may be surprised to find a king named *Anna* put forward as one of the candidates for the Sutton Hoo burial. Feminine names take *-e* in the genitive if they are strong, and *-n* if they are weak. The *-n* genitive, which is appropriate to the weak masculine and feminine names, is sometimes confused with *-ing-*. It is possible for place-names to be formed by adding such elements as *tūn, hām, worth* to an uninflected personal name. This has happened, e.g. in Alfreton DRB ('Ælfhere's estate or settlement'), and it is much more common in the northern half of England than in the south.

It is often difficult to say whether the first element of a compound place-name is a personal name or a significant word. It is not always possible to say whether the first element is in the genitive, since some genitive endings leave no conclusive trace in Middle English spellings; and even if the first element is definitely genitive this does not tell conclusively in favour of derivation from a personal name, as other types of element, such as a significant word or another place-name, may be used in this way. A very important Swedish book, Tengstrand 1940, is a comprehensive study of genitival composition in place-names recorded in Old English sources. Tengstrand sets out material proving that the type of formation is well-evidenced in compounds which do not contain personal names. He observes (p. lxii) that *Fiscesburna*, 'stream of the fish', occurs too many times to be plausibly explained as containing the personal name *Fisc*.

It will be seen from the few examples quoted above of recorded Old English personal names that the stock of elements used included words for wild creatures and for domestic animals. Because of this, there is no way of knowing whether such a compound as Ravensdale DRB means 'valley of the raven' or 'valley of a man named Raven'. Toponymists usually give one etymology or the other according to the nature of the second element. Thus, Ravenscroft CHE is rendered 'Hræfn's enclosure', Ravenstone BUC and LEI 'Hræfn's settlement'; but Ramsbury (see Chapter 6) is translated 'fort of the raven'. It seems satisfactory to interpret Barsham NFK and SFK as 'village of a man named Boar', but to give 'hill of the boar' for Boars Hill BRK; but these are inferences based on the sense of the compound, rather than scientific deductions from philological evidence. If the early spellings show the first element to be in the genitive plural, the reference can safely be taken as being to a bird or animal; thus Hunton HMP, which is recorded *c*. 909 in the form *Hundatun*, is 'settlement where hounds are kept', and Oxford, Old English *Oxenaforda*, is 'ford of oxen'. But a first element of this kind which is in the genitive singular is always ambiguous, and if there are only Middle English spellings it may be impossible to decide whether a first element is the genitive singular of a weak personal name, such as *Hunda* or *Wulfa*, or the genitive plural of a strong noun, such as *hund* or *wulf*, as the inflections appropriate to both will usually have been reduced to -*e*-.

The stock of words used in Old English personal names includes adjectives, like *hēah* 'high' and *hwīt* 'white'; and this also makes for ambiguity in place-names, as many of these adjectives could be applied to topographical features, and some, like *hwīt*, to buildings. Adjectives had strong and weak declensions in Old English, and it is the weak form which is usual in place-name compounds. The inflections of the weak declension of adjectives correspond closely to those of the weak nouns, which means that they have -*an* in the genitive and dative singular. In consequence it is often impossible to say whether a place-name contains an adjective in the dative singular, or a weak personal name in the genitive. Here again, it is usual to give the etymology which seems best suited to the sense of the compound. Whitchurch Canonicorum DOR is *æt Hwitancyrican c*. 880, and this, like the less well-recorded instances of the same name, is rendered 'white church', though '*Hwīta's church*' would be philologically acceptable. The same ambiguity characterizes many names in Whit-. Reading BRK is always rendered 'the people of Rēad(a)', on the assumption that *rēad* 'red' is used here as the basis of a personal name or nickname; but little or no allowance is made for the possible occurrence of such a personal name in other place-names in Rad- or Red-. Radford is usually translated 'red ford', and this is perfectly acceptable, especially in instances where the local soil is the right colour, but *ford* is often combined with personal names, and 'Rēada's ford' is equally possible on philological grounds. Obviously this problem arises in respect of a great many place-names. The constant citing of alternatives (e.g. 'old cottage' or 'Ealda's cottage', 'high hill' or 'Hēaha's hill') would be tedious and is not usually practised, so it is important to note that many etymologies given in the reference books represent a choice between such alternatives, and that there can seldom be a conclusive philological reason for the decision.

The problems outlined so far have been relatively simple. We know that animal and bird names are used as personal names, so we often have to decide between a reference to ravens and to a man named Raven, remembering that the use of the genitive singular is appropriate to both, and that either can be used without any inflection at all. We know that adjectives in place-names may be personal names or may be descriptive of the place. These factors produce nothing worse than ambiguity. Much more serious complications arise in respect of place-name elements which are not easily explicable from our knowledge of the language. Our knowledge of Old English vocabulary and of Old English personal names is incomplete, and with regard to obscure place-name elements there is wide scope for speculation about unrecorded topographical terms and about unrecorded personal names. Excessive recourse to etymologies involving unrecorded personal names is the reproach most easily levelled at English toponymists, while some Swedish scholars have laid themselves open to the criticism of excessive ingenuity in reconstructing hypothetical topographical terms. Ekwall, the greatest of the Swedish scholars who have devoted their time to English place-name studies, sided with the English school in this perennial controversy.

The system adopted by the editors of the English Place-Name Society's county volumes for distinguishing between personal names which are on independent record and those which are not was to attach asterisks to the latter. In the pre-war volumes, names whose existence 'can be inferred from evidence other than that of the particular place-name in question' were given one asterisk. 'Those for which no such evidence can be found

are marked with a double star.' These quotations are from the introductory remarks to the list of 'Personal Names compounded in Buckinghamshire Place-Names' which occupies pp. 252–6 of the first county
survey, that of Buckinghamshire, published in 1925. Without virtually
revising *The Place-Names of Buckinghamshire* it would be difficult to say
how many place-names there considered to contain personal names would
be differently interpreted by a modern author; but it will be instructive to
look briefly at some of the personal names which have single and double
stars in the Buckinghamshire list.

Single-starred names include:

Biccel, in Bigstrup Farm in Haddenham parish (*Bikelestorp* 1179). This
would be a hypocoristic form of the recorded *Bicca*. The second element is
throp 'hamlet', which is certainly compounded with personal names in a
number of other instances, and there is no reason to question this etymology.

Bledda, in Bledlow. This would be a short form of a compound name in
Blǣd-, which is evidenced as a personal-name element. For the compound
with *hlāw*, see Chapter 6.

Briddel, in Burston in Aston Abbots parish (*Bridelestorn* 1227). *Bridd*
'bird' is recorded as a personal name, and *Briddel* would be a hypocoristic
form. The suffix -*el* could, however, be used to make diminutive nouns as
well as hypocoristic personal names. The second element of Burston is
thorn 'thorn-bush', and the first could be a noun *briddel 'little bird'. The
image of a thorn-bush full of birds is convincing, and Tengstrand has
shown that comparable genitival compounds occur.

Byrna, in Burnham. This name is more likely to contain *burna* 'stream'.
The contours suggest that a stream may once have flowed past Burnham
Abbey to the Thames.

Byttel, in Biddlesden. This would be related to the recorded *Byttic*.
Biddlesden and several other place-names have more recently been derived
from a noun meaning 'building' (Ekwall 1960, Smith 1956), but the
suggested personal name is possible.

Cærda, in Charndon and in Chartridge in Chesham parish. Other
suggestions have been made for these names. Ekwall 1960 suggests Welsh
carn 'rock' for Charndon, and *ceart* 'rough ground' seems possible for
Chartridge, though this is rejected by Smith 1956 (Part 1, p. 91).

Ceacca, in Chackmore in Radclive parish. Subsequent authorities have suggested an Old English noun *ceacce* 'lump', applied to a hill, as first element of some place-names in Check-, Chack-. Tengstrand 1940 (p. 217) suggests a bird-name of onomatopoeic origin for some of them. This last is convincing, but if there were such a bird-name it could, of course, be used as a personal name or nickname.

Col, in Coleshill. This is discussed below.

Cott, in Cottesloe in Wing parish. This would be the strong form of the recorded personal name *Cotta*. Cottesloe was a hundred meeting-place of the type discussed in Chapters 6 and 8, and there is no reason to question this etymology.

Cub(b)el, in Cublington. It is argued that this is one of a group of hypo-thetical personal names—*Cybba*, *Cybbel*, *Cubba*, *Cubbel*—contained in various place-names, including Cubley DRB, Cubbington WAR, Kipling Cotes YOE. No evidence is brought forward to support the personal name except its occurrence in place-names.

Cwēn in Quainton. Ekwall 1960 gives *cwēne-tūn*, 'queen's manor', as the source of this name.

   Double-starred names include:

**Balla* in Balney in Hanslope parish. Some names in Bal(l)- are now derived from an adjective *balg* 'rounded, smooth', which is possible here. Such an adjective could, of course, be the base for a personal name.

**Doder* in Doddershall in Quainton parish. The second element is *hyll* 'hill'. Ekwall 1960 accepts the probability of a personal name for Dodder-shall, but says 'no such name is known elsewhere'. For Dodderhill WOR the same authority suggests an Old English form of the plant-name *dodder*. The greater and lesser dodder are parasitic climbing weeds, and it would be interesting to have a naturalist's opinion as to whether either plant was likely at Dodderhill or Doddershall. The Old English use of a plant-name does not have to correspond exactly to the modern use. Dodder is recorded as a modern dialect term for corn spurrey and black bindweed, both edible plants.

**Sandhere* in Saunderton. The objection to *Sandhere* is that there is no evidence for the use of *Sand-* in Old English personal names. The Berkshire charter boundary-mark *sandan dene* quoted in *The Place-Names of Buckinghamshire* as evidence of a short name **Sanda* is not relevant. Another manuscript containing these bounds has *santan dene*, probably from *sandihtan denu* 'sandy valley' (Gelling 1976b, p. 656). Probably Saunderton is 'sandy hill' from Old English *sanden* and *dūn*. Mr J. F. Head informs me that there is a spread of sand on Lodge Hill. The early spellings for Saunderton are similar to those for Sanderstead SUR, except that for Sanderstead we have pre-Conquest references *sonden stede*, *sondenstyde*, which show that *-r-* is a later corruption of *-n-*.

**Smēawine in *Smewnes*, a lost place in Great Brickhill. This personal name only needed one star, or possibly could have appeared without any. There were men called *Smewin* in England from Edward the Confessor's reign onwards, and several appear in Domesday Book. On the other hand, it should not, on the evidence of the place-name *Smewnes*, have appeared in a list of *Personal Names compounded in Buckinghamshire Place-Names*. *Smewin* became a surname (Smewing is the modern form), and *Smewnes* is a manorial name of Middle English origin, of the type in which the owner's family name is used in the genitive as a place-name.

It would be possible to argue one's way in this fashion through the lists of personal names in all the county surveys, and the exercise would be instructive, but is clearly appropriate to another book than this one. The above examples from the first county survey may serve as illustrating the approach to this vexed question adopted by Sir Allen Mawer and Sir Frank Stenton at the beginning of their great enterprise, when there was very little comparative material on which they could draw.

The Place-Names of Buckinghamshire was in many respects a pioneer work, and the editors cannot be accused of unreasonable dependence on unrecorded personal names. Some of the names which they suggested (e.g. **Cott*) have been well evidenced in place-names investigated subsequently, others (e.g. **Sandhere*) have not; but the great majority of the hypothetical personal names which they brought forward were a reasonable starting point for future discussion. The division into the two categories of single-starred and double-starred names, reasonable in theory, seems difficult to carry out satisfactorily. This distinction was abandoned in *The Place-Names of Cumberland*, the first survey to be published after the war, and since then only one of the seven surveys to be issued has observed it. The abandonment of the classification, and the recognition only of 'recorded' and 'unrecorded' categories, is in theory accompanied by a more critical consideration of the evidence for all hypothetical personal names. The most recent surveys, of Cheshire and Berkshire, were scrutinized in manuscript by Dr Olof von Feilitzen, who was the leading authority on Old English personal names, and it is unlikely that many specimens have slipped through for which there is no basis whatsoever. It must be admitted, however, that some hypothetical personal names which were adduced rather casually in pre-war county surveys have continued to be cited because they offer an easy solution, and because their appearance in print gives them a spurious authority. (It is a major difficulty of place-name study that the early county surveys, whose main purpose was to provide material on which sound etymologies could be based in the light of comparative evidence, are cited by everyone as authoritative sources for etymologies only intended as tentative.) We have not yet attained a sufficiently rigorous attitude to the unrecorded personal name, and it is time to look at the criticisms brought by some Swedish scholars against English toponymists in this matter, and to consider some notable instances in which a hypothetical personal name has been revealed as a significant term. The last point may be considered first.

As more material became available for the study of place-names it became apparent that some compounds which had been explained as containing unrecorded personal names recurred rather frequently. Windsor and Ludgershall are the standard examples of this. Windsor BRK, Old English *Windlesoran*, was at one time considered by the editors of the English Place-Name Survey to mean 'river-bank belonging to a man named **Windel*', and to be connected with Windlesham SUR, seven miles away, which was rendered '**Windel*'s village'. The personal name was explained as a diminutive of another hypothetical personal name **Wind(a)*, which was inferred from Wyndham SSX; and the possible existence of Old-German personal names *Windo*, *Windulo* was adduced in support. There are, however, six certain and two possible examples of the name Windsor, and only two names—Windlesham SUR and *wyndelescumb* in Topsham DEV—in which this hypothetical personal name is compounded with other elements than *ōra* 'river-bank'. The six certain examples are Windsor BRK, PEM, WAR, Winsor DEV, HMP, Broadwindsor and Little Windsor DOR; the two possibles are Windsor in Nether Wasdale CMB and a lost *Windesore Mill* in Breadsall DRB. A Swedish scholar, A. Fägersten, pointed out in 1933 that the supposed name **Windel* was compounded surprisingly often with *ōra*, and this objection was noted in the discussion of Windlesham in *The Place-Names of Surrey*, but discounted on the grounds that if **windel* were a meaningful term it would be unlikely to appear always in the genitive. The problem was solved brilliantly by Professor Ekwall with the suggestion of a noun **windels*, possibly the Old English form of Modern English *windlass*. The compound **windels-ōra* 'river-bank with a winch for pulling up boats' has been generally accepted as the most satisfactory origin for all the instances of the place-name Windsor. As the proposed noun has the ending *-els*, there is no need to assume a genitival compound. It is still possible to prefer a personal name **Windel* for Windlesham SUR.

If a personal name, recorded or unrecorded, is found in regular combination with a particular topographical term, there are obvious grounds for suspecting that the first element is not a personal name but a word, and that the recurring compound is an appellative, not an *ad hoc* description of a single place. The five place-names which derive from Old English *lutegareshealh* furnish another good example of this phenomenon. The names are Ludgershall BUC and WLT, Luggershall GLO Lurgashall SSX and a lost *Lotegareshale* in Arkesden ESX. The editors of the place-name surveys clung rather desperately to the belief that the first element was a personal name **Lutegār*, though they admitted when discussing Ludgershall WLT that it was surprising that this personal name should be compounded five times with *h(e)alh* 'corner of land, sheltered place', and only evidenced in one other compound, *Lutgaresberi*, which was the old name for Montacute SOM. A much more satisfactory solution was proposed in Tengstrand 1940. Tengstrand suggested an Old English compound noun **lūtegār*, meaning 'trapping spear', *gār* being the ordinary word for a spear and **lūt(e)* an unrecorded term related to the verb *lūtian* 'to lie hid, lurk'. The image he suggests is that of a hollow, perhaps in a hill-side, where a trap was set which shot itself off when an animal disturbed it. This explanation is accepted in Smith 1956. As Tengstrand observes, the use of the genitive of **lūtegār* in all instances might be taken as indicating that the whole compound, meaning 'hollow of the trapping spear', had become a common noun.

Windsor and Ludgershall are names which occur so many times that the possibility of the first element being an unrecorded personal name strains credulity beyond reasonable bounds. There are a number of other instances in which compounds with the same first element, apparently in the genitive, have been noted three or four times; and here it is more difficult to decide whether the coincidence of an unrecorded personal name being associated several times with a particular topographical feature is or is not beyond the bounds of probability.

The name Coleshill occurs in BRK, WAR, BUC and FLI, and there has been much discussion about its etymology. The first element has been variously considered to be a river-name, a personal name and an unrecorded word **coll* 'hill'. The most recent discussion (Gelling 1974c, pp. 356–7) takes the view that the names are not identical. Coleshill WAR is 'hill by the R. Cole (Old English *Coll*). Coleshill FLI has only Middle English spellings in *Coles-*, with no sign of *-ll-*, and for this the best etymology is probably a personal name **Col*, the strong form of the recorded *Cola*. Only four early spellings have been assembled for Coleshill BUC, and these are not sufficient evidence on which to assess a difficult name. For the BRK Coleshill, which is *æt Colleshylle c.* 950, there is little ground for preferring any one of the three suggested sources, personal name (which would be the recorded *Coll* in this instance), river-name, or hill-name.

There are three place-names—Chadlanger in Warminster WLT, Chaddlehanger in Lamerton DEV and Channy Grove in Hurley BRK—which can be explained as deriving from a personal name **Ceadela* and the word *hangra* 'wood on a slope'. This unrecorded personal name is well evidenced in other compounds, including Chadlington OXF, Chillington DEV, Chadenwick WLT and Chaddleworth BRK. The latest discussion (Gelling 1973a, p. 62) takes the view that for three men called **Ceadela* to be associated with woods on hill-sides is not too much of a coincidence to be believed. If any more instances of 'Ceadela's wood on a slope' are found, it will be necessary to think again.

It is unnecessary to adduce further instances of these groups of place-names. The Windsor, Ludgershall, Coleshill and Chaddlehanger groups are sufficient to give an idea of the problems involved. Interested readers could pick out from the county surveys groups which have not yet attracted critical discussion. There is, for instance, a tendency for a man named **Amma* to have an association with brooks, rivers, and springs. The English Place-Name Society has been shown to be mistaken in specific instances, such as Windsor and Ludgershall, and it is now time to inquire whether the admitted preference for personal names which led to a defence of the indefensible in these two instances, is a serious weakness in the Society's general approach.

The pragmatic answer is that the alternative approach, that of always preferring a topographical term, has led to worse results. The great exponent of this alternative approach was a Swedish scholar, Professor R. E. Zachrisson, who published a number of articles between 1932 and 1934 attacking the prevailing method of interpreting English place-names. In an article published in 1934 he summed up the results of his investigations under six headings, of which point four is the most relevant to the present discussion. This is: 'That the vast majority of Old English place-names contain in their first elements descriptive words which are often found with a meaning identical with or akin to the topographical one in English dialects or in other Teutonic languages. Not seldom these significative words have the same etymological origin as well-recorded short-names [i.e. personal names].' The above quotation is taken from Tengstrand 1940 (p. xlvii), and Tengstrand's comment on it is 'Zachrisson's views can only be correct on the assumption that the gen. sg. of descriptive words played an enormous part in Old English place-name formation'. If Zachrisson's claims had been less extreme his theories would probably have been taken more seriously by the editors of the English Place-Name Society's volumes, and this would have been to the benefit of the study. Some Scandinavian scholars are at present endeavouring to redress the balance by finding more topographical terms and fewer personal names in English place-names, and this revival of the alternative approach will be considered after some comments have been offered on the most whole-hearted of several attempts which have been made to carry out county place-name surveys in the light of Zachrisson's teaching.

Two works by Dr J. K. Wallenberg (Wallenberg 1931 and 1934) have become, rather unfairly, a quarry for anyone wishing to ridicule Professor Zachrisson's approach to the interpretation of English place-names. Wallenberg's area of study was Kent: his 1931 work discussed all the Kentish names recorded in Old English sources, and the 1934 book deals with the mass of names for which recorded evidence starts in 1086 or later. He worked under Zachrisson's guidance, and stated his initial position in the Introduction to the 1931 book:

> In my opinion a considerable part of these names have without quite convincing reasons been explained from a personal name basis. I have made it my task to examine, taking due account of the topography of the relevant places, whether there are not sometimes other possibilities of interpreting obscure place-names than the one that implies the existence of sometimes very dubious personal names. . . . As regards the general trend of this work revealed in the reaction against the exaggerations of the prevailing tendency of interpreting place-names from personal name bases, my indebtedness to Prof. Zachrisson is here duly acknowledged. For possible exaggerations in the opposite direction . . . I bear of course the sole responsibility.

The introduction to the 1934 work shows a retreat from this position of accepting Zachrisson's conclusions and being prepared to go even further in the same direction. In 1934 Wallenberg said:

> It may, however, be questioned whether Zachrisson has not been too radical in his underrating and even negation of the possibility that in Old English there may have existed, by the side of the actually recorded mono-thematic names [i.e. personal names], a considerable and even larger number of unrecorded names of the same type, names that also may form part of place-names. . . . The investigation of the names one by one seems

to me to indicate that an interpretation on these lines gives, as a rule, more plausible solutions for the difficult names than an explanation that tries to account for the names as toponymics. In my attempts at an interpretation of the Kentish place-names I have tried both ways to unveil the origin of the names, but I do not hesitate to pronounce in most cases in favour of the former alternative.

This 1934 statement is the voice of experience; and long experience of working on place-names often leads the specialist to a belief in certain principles, while the investigator who has not served such an apprenticeship may not feel convinced that one approach is more valid than another. Having ascertained Wallenberg's position in 1931 and 1934 it is appropriate to quote some of his place-name etymologies from both works.

The bounds of the Bromley charter of AD 862, which mention the *weard setle* discussed in Chapter 6, refer to the contiguous estates in such phrases as *modinga hema mearce* ('boundary of the dwellers in Mottingham'), *cystaninga mearc* ('boundary of the people of Keston'), *bromleaginga mearc and liofshema* ('boundary of the people of Bromley and of the dwellers in Lewisham'). Some of these phrases use the term *-hǣme*, 'dwellers', which is added to the first part of a place-name, and this means that the bounds do not give us the full forms of the names Mottingham and Lewisham, but there are other Old English references which give these as *Modingaham* and *Lievesham*. For these names all authorities are now content with the etymologies 'village of Mōda's people' and Lēofsa's village'. *Mōda* is not on independent record, but compound names in *Mōd-* are evidenced, and *Mōda* is an obvious short form of those. *Lēofsa*, also unrecorded, would be a short form of *Lēofsige*.

Wallenberg's discussion of Mottingham in 1931 is a classic of its kind. He withdrew it in 1934, so it may seem unfair to quote it, but there is no better way in which his own sad experience of trying to find toponymic terms wherever possible can be turned to general advantage. It runs:

Ekwall . . . and Karlström . . . suggest derivation from a pet form of Old English personal names in *Mōd-*, *-mōd*. This stem is not well evidenced in Old English as a first element of personal names. Mottingham is on a protuberance of the ground and there are streams in the neighbourhood. It is perhaps not impossible also to derive the name from a nature-name formed from the same stem as Old English *mōd* 'courage, pride, power'; Old English *mōdig* 'bold, impetuous, proud'. It is generally assumed that the original meaning of the Indo-Germanic root *$*mō$* was 'to strive, make an effort'. . . . Perhaps the original meaning of the stem *mōd-* may equally well have been 'to swell'. . . . May perhaps some root connection exist between Old English *mōd(ig)* and *mōdor* 'mother'? . . . The stem may have been applied to things of a swollen, roundish appearance, possibly also to a roundish protuberance of the ground. All this is of course very uncertain but the possibility of forming toponymics from the base suggested should not be dismissed off-hand.

For Lewisham Wallenberg suggested a river-name *Lēwse*, from the same stem as Old English *lēf* 'feeble', perhaps connected with Modern English *left*, meaning 'wry, crooked'. This etymology also was withdrawn in 1934, in favour of a personal name *Lēofsa* or a personal name or nickname *Lēfsa* from the same stem as *lēf* 'feeble'. Keston is easily explained as 'Cyssi's stone', the form from the 862 charter showing contraction of *Cysses stan* to *Cystan-*. *Cyssi* is not recorded, but would be a regular derivative of the recorded *Cussa*, and *stān* is compounded with a personal name in a number of other place-names, including Boston LIN. Wallenberg, however, gave the following discussion in 1931, and did not withdraw it in 1934:

> The most remarkable feature of the topography of Keston is the hill situated to the south-east of the village of Keston which reaches a height of over 600 feet. Perhaps this hill was called *Cȳs* or *Cyss*. Perhaps this place-name contains the hill-name element from the basis of *kūs-* assumed for *cusincg dene*. . . .

Discussing *cusincg dene* he says:

> Cf. Middle Low German, Low German *kûse* 'club', Middle Dutch *cûse*, Modern Dutch *kuis* 'lump, stock', Norwegian *kūs* 'hump, hunch', Swedish *kūse* 'loaf, bun'. . . . The primary sense seems to be 'something thick, swollen'. . . .

No systematic analysis has been made of the types of toponym proposed by Wallenberg and other Swedish scholars using the same approach. I have a general impression that hill-names from roots meaning 'to swell' and river-names from roots meaning 'to wind' are the most numerous categories. The dangers of the approach are obvious, and it must be stressed again that Wallenberg perceived very quickly that many of his suggestions in the 1931 book were too nebulous to be useful. This type of etymologizing must have been known in the eighteenth century, as it is satirized by Swift in *A Voyage to Laputa*:

> The word, which I interpret the *Flying* or *Floating Island*, is in the original *Laputa*, whereof I could never learn the true etymology. *Lap* in the old obsolete language signifieth *high*, and *untuh*, a governor, from which they say by corruption was derived *Laputa*, from *Lapuntuh*. But I do not approve

of this derivation, which seems to be a little strained. I ventured to offer to the learned among them a conjecture of my own, that *Laputa* was *quasi lap outed*; *lap* signifying properly the dancing of the sunbeams in the sea, and *outed* a wing, which however I shall not obtrude, but submit to the judicious reader.

Wallenberg's experience has shown that it is not profitable to try to identify the first element of every compound place-name as a toponym. The English Place-Name Society's approach of postulating personal names when no obvious toponym is on record has proved a better starting point for future discussion. It keeps the argument brief, whereas the Zachrisson-Wallenberg approach results in many pages of what can only be described as waffle. Many of the English Place-Name Society's etymologies were only intended as suggestions, the main purpose of the county volumes being to make collections of early spellings available. The etymologies can be challenged, and the hypothetical personal names can be discarded if better suggestions are made by later commentators. The reasons for replacing an etymology involving a personal name with one involving a toponym should be either that the supposed personal name occurs too often with the same topographical word, or that a toponym which suits a place-name is discovered in a hitherto unnoted document. Examples of the first phenomenon have been given above. The second—the finding of a toponym in a hitherto unexamined source—is rarer, but can still occur. Childrey BRK, for instance, Old English *cille rithe, cilla rithe, cillan rithe*, was derived in Gelling 1973a (following earlier authorities) from *rīth* 'stream' and a personal name, either feminine *Cille* (on record as a short form of *Cēolswīth*) or masculine **Cilla*. This was quickly challenged by Gillis Kristensson, one of the Swedish scholars who are now trying to redress the balance between personal names and toponyms. Dr Kristensson has assembled evidence for a Middle English word *chille* meaning 'spring', one of his instances being from a document of 1306 which mentions 'quendam fontem qui vocatur Chill'. He considers that this Middle English term derives from an unrecorded Old English **cille*, which was earlier postulated by Zachrisson as a variant of Old English *ceole* 'throat, gorge'. Childrey Brook, an affluent of the River Ock whose upper course is interrupted by the line of the Berkshire-Wiltshire Canal, appears to have risen near Childrey village, and the suggestion that the spring from which it rose was called **Cille* is convincing, though there is probably not enough surviving evidence to reveal whether the spring had special characteristics which could account for the use of this rare term for it. Dr Kristensson thinks that **cille* 'spring' is also likely to be the first element of Chilham KNT and Chillington STF, and this is possible, though the etymology is not as compelling in relation to those two names as it is for Childrey.

The points to be noted are that there is some evidence for an Old English toponym **cille* 'spring', and that the village of Childrey lies at the source of the brook called *cillan rith*. In view of these two facts, the etymology 'stream of the spring named *Cille*' is better than 'stream on the estate of a woman named *Cille*'. This type of reasoning is different from that displayed in the discussion of Mottingham in Wallenberg 1931. Evidence of this kind will probably continue to be brought forward, and to lead to revision of some etymologies given in Ekwall 1960 and in the volumes of the English Place-Name Society. It is doubtful, however, whether convincing evidence will be brought forward for wholesale revision of the kind proposed by Zachrisson.

Something must be said of the category of place-names in which (according to the English Place-Name Society) a personal name is linked to a habitative word, usually *tūn*, by the syllable *-ing-*, which, in this type of formation, is considered to be a connective particle. The main body of these formations constitute the category of *-ingtūn* names, which are shown on most of the English Place-Name Society's distribution maps by a symbol distinct from that used for other names in *-tūn*.

Readers of this book will already be aware that the syllable *ing* had a number of functions in Old English (see Chapter 5); its use as a connective particle is yet another. Much has been written on this, and opinions up to 1956 are summarized in Smith 1956 (Part I, pp. 291–8). Smith's conclusion is that:

> The editors of the English place-name survey have always accepted and still adopt views . . . that in most instances *-ing-* denotes the association of a place with a particular individual and in the broadest sense has something of a genitival function without necessarily implying possession; *Teottingtūn* is by this to be interpreted as 'farmstead associated with *Teotta*', *Ælfrēding-tūn* 'farmstead associated with *Ælfrēd*', rather than 'farmstead belonging to *Teotta* or *Ælfrēd*' which would be *Teottantūn* and *Ælfredestūn*.

Professor Whitelock has pointed out (Whitelock 1955, p. 487 n.7) that there is evidence in a charter dated AD 857 for the use of *-ing-* with merely genitival force. This charter disposes of an estate in London called *Ceolmundinghaga* (*haga* 'enclosure' is regularly used of town properties), which was purchased for one pound from Ceolmund the prefect, and this certainly implies that 'Ceolmund's enclosure' is the correct translation of the place-name. In addition to this example, Smith (pp. 293–4) gives several others of names in *-ing-* which 'incorporate the names of identified persons'. One of these, *Badenothing land*, occurs as a contemporary endorsement to a Kentish charter, dated 845, by which King Æthelwulf grants land near Canterbury to a man named Badanoth. The charter mentions a purchase price, and gives Badanoth the right to bequeath the estate freely; so here, as in *Ceolmundinghaga*, the *-ing-* particle seems to denote straightforward possession. There is no reason to suppose, however, that either of these phrases became enduring place-names, as neither has been found in later sources. Other *-ing-* formations occur in the boundaries of *Badanothing land* (*deoringlond, alingmed*), and all these may reflect a short-lived use of the particle in the south-east in the mid ninth century, which need not be seen as proof that the purely genitival sense was universal, and likely to be found in all the *-ingtūn* formations which survived as settlement-names. In Smith's other instances of *-ing-* names connected with known persons, the identity of the person in the place-name with the person in the record is less certain. For Kemberton GLO (Old English *Cyneburgingctun*) Smith later withdrew the suggestion of a connection with an Abbess of Gloucester. Wolverley WOR (Old English *Wulfferdinleh*) is not certain to be named from the *Wulferd* who was concerned with it in a charter of 866, and Simeon of Durham's suggestion that Rennington NTB was named from a certain *Reingualdus* is not necessarily based on evidence. It is probably sound to connect Tredington WOR with the thegn called *Tyrdda* said in a charter of 757 to be a previous holder of the estate. If this last example be accepted, it could be held to accord with a use of *-ing-* in cases of temporary overlordship. The evidence for the precise meaning of *-ing-* furnished by these names is too slight to build on, but there is little room for doubt that *-ing-* denotes an association of a place with a particular individual.

One of the less acceptable doctrines adhered to in Ekwall 1960 is the belief that *-ingtūn* in place-names was a reduction of original *-ingatūn*, showing the use of *-inga-* discussed in Chapter 5. In accordance with this belief Ekwall regularly translates such names as Harlington GTL and Bebington CHE as 'the *tūn* of Hygerēd's people' or 'the *tūn* of Bebbe's people', where other commentators would say 'farm or estate associated with Hygerēd or Bebbe'. The English Place-Name Society's editors only recognize *-ingatūn* in names which have Old English spellings showing that exact form, or a reasonable proportion of Middle English spellings in *-ingetone*. Such names are rare. One example is Essington STF, which is *Essingetun* 996, *Eseningetone* 1086; here there is no reason to question Ekwall's rendering 'the *tūn* of Esne's people'. But most *-ington* names do not have such spellings, and are better interpreted as 'estate connected with x'.

A recent contribution to the personal name versus topographical term controversy is concerned with the category of *-ingtūn* names. This is

Fellows Jensen 1974, an article by an English scholar working in Denmark, which argues that many place-names considered in the English Place-Name Society's volumes to consist of a personal name and -*ingtūn* can be better explained in other ways. In many of the names considered, ambiguity arises from the use for personal-name formation of nouns and adjectives which are appropriate also in place-names. The particle -*ing*, which is a place-name forming suffix, could be added to topographical nouns, as in Cowling YOW from *coll* 'hill', or to adjectives, as in Deeping LIN from *dēop* 'deep', to give meanings like 'place by the hill' or 'marshy place'. It is possible to postulate such formations as the first elements of -ington names like Blatchington SSX and Whittington DRB, GLO, LNC, LEI, NTB, WAR, WOR; these could be '*tūn* at *Blæcing (the dark place)' and '*tūn* at *Hwīting (the white place)' rather than 'estate associated with a man named *Blæc* or *Hwīt*'. A lot of -ington names are ambiguous in this way, if one is prepared to postulate a great many -*ing* place-names which have only been preserved as the first part of names in -*tūn*.

Dr Fellows Jensen's arguments would, if accepted, imply that the singular place-name ending -*ing* was used much more frequently in English place-name formation than has hitherto been supposed, and that many of these names had been deemed to require the addition of *tūn* before their first appearance in records. She stresses the frequent recurrence of some -ington names, such as Donnington or Dunnington of which twenty-one instances have been noted, and considers that these are much more likely to be formed by the addition of *tūn* to a place-name *Dūning meaning 'place by the hill', than to arise from the association of a number of estates with men named *Dun(n)*. A possible objection to this argument is that if a place-name *Dūning 'place by the hill' were sufficiently common to father twenty-one place-names in -*tūn*, one might have expected it to be on record once or twice without the addition of *tūn*. There does not appear to be an instance. Possibly the best approach to the questions raised by Dr Fellows Jensen would be a fresh study of the singular place-names in -*ing*. This should try to differentiate them from the plural names in -*ingas*, and endeavour to obtain a reliable estimate of their frequency and distribution in England, and to estimate the proportion in which they were formed from toponyms, plant and animal names, adjectives or personal names. Such a study might provide a sounder basis than we have at present for deciding whether a substantial number of -*ing* formations are likely to be the basis of -ington names.

There is not space here to do justice to Dr Fellows Jensen's arguments, but it may be noted that there is a considerable range of probability in her suggested revised etymologies. The suggestions for -*ing* formations from a dithematic base are less convincing on the whole than those for which a monothematic base is postulated. For instance, she suggests that Brightwalton BRK (Old English *Beorhtwaldingtune*) may be '*tūn* by *Beorhtwalding', this last being an *-ing* formation from a wood-name *Beorhtwald 'bright wood'. This would be an unusual place-name. The adjective *beorht* is hardly evidenced in place-names except with *wella* 'spring', and *wald* never occurs as a final element in Berkshire. The personal name *Beorhtwald*, on the other hand, occupies three columns of Searle's *Onomasticon Anglo-Saxonicum*, so 'estate associated with Beorhtwald' seems much more likely for Brightwalton. It is sometimes useful to consider together a single category of names assembled from all areas; but something is lost as compared with the process of taking names in their geographical setting. In the latter method, seen in the county surveys, the whole nature of the nomenclature of the district is taken into account in assessing the likelihood of an etymology, and the anomalous nature of a hypothetical wood-name *Beorhtwald in Berkshire is immediately apparent.

The reader will have observed that the problem of the extent to which personal names enter into English place-names is possibly the most vexed question in the whole field of the study. It is perhaps because so much energy has been expended on the problem of whether first elements are personal names or not that there has been no adequate consideration of the historical significance of the personal names which undoubtedly do occur. Most reference books either state or imply that the usual relationship between a man whose name occurs in a place-name and the settlement to which the name belongs is that of the founding father, or at least of an early settler who was the dominating force in the farming life of the community. This belief was expressed in Stenton's earliest work on place-names, Stenton 1911, and a passage from that deserves quotation. This runs:

> *The seignorial implication.*—For this is what is really implied by the personal element in local nomenclature. We may dispute at length about the exact position in which Wulfric stood with regard to the land of Wulfric's *tūn*, the origin of Woolstone; but no probable explanation of the appearance of his name compounded in that of the village can refuse him rights of some kind over the village land and over the men who tilled it, and the simplest theory about the eponymous lord is precisely that which would give him the most extensive rights—rights of ownership rather than of superiority. We may see in the original Uffington the house and farm steading of Uffa, standing with the cottages of his labourers in the middle of his fields and pasture land; or, if we so prefer, we may imagine a group of ceorls, personally free, but economically dependent, rendering dues or services to Uffa, the great

man and leading settler of the township; in either case, the lord is there, and with him the starting-point for the future manorial organization. It may never be possible for us finally to decide, in any given case, between these alternatives; our external evidence is too scanty, and too poor in quality. The essential fact is that in regard to numberless English villages we have to reckon with a lord of some kind as an integral and original force in the development of the agrarian community. When at last English place-names as a whole have undergone detailed investigation, the most notable result of the work will be the recognition of the seignorial idea as a primitive force in the organization of rural society.

It was unfortunate that Stenton chose Uffington and Woolstone in Berkshire as the concrete illustrations of the relationship he believed to have existed between eponymous lords and the settlements named from them. Subsequent research, of which a full account is given in Gelling 1976b, has made it clear that these two adjacent parishes were known until *c.* 955 as *Æscesbyrig* from the hill-fort (now Uffington Castle) on their common boundary, and that the Wulfric from whom Woolstone is named was a thegn who, in 960, owned eight villages in Berkshire, five in Sussex and two in Hampshire. Wulfric may be acquitted of any personal involvement in the management of the fields and pastures of the village named after him, and he and Uffa came too late to have anything to do with the history of settlement. The ironical chance of Stenton's picking on this example does not, however, invalidate his general argument. He knew, of course, that some 'x's *tūn*' names arose in this way, and he goes on from the passage quoted above to discuss other examples in which *tūns* are named from eleventh-century overlords who were in the same category as we now know the Wulfric of Woolstone to have been. His argument is that the later type of manorial overlordship, represented by the relationship of King Edward the Confessor's staller, Esgar, to his manor of East Garston BRK (earlier *Esgareston*), could have evolved from an earlier, more organic, relationship between villages and overlords who were resident leaders of the community, not outsiders given the estate by the king; and that these early overlords will only be known to us from place-names.

I believe this to be a very unlikely interpretation of the place-name evidence, but it cannot be proved wrong. It is possible to point to a growing and quite impressive number of instances in which an 'x's *tūn*' place-name is firmly connected with a man or woman mentioned in a charter of tenth- or eleventh-century date, or with an overlord who appears in the Domesday Survey. To these may be added the probable naming of Tredington WOR from the thegn Tyrdda, who held the estate before 757, and—the most impressive piece of evidence bearing on this matter—the history of the name Bibury GLO. This last is important because it takes the process of the naming of villages from overlords who were not leading peasants back as far as could be hoped for, given the starting date of written grants and leases to laymen, and because it shows that the incorporation of feminine names in place-names need not have the significance which Stenton tried to place upon it (Stenton 1943b).

Bibury GLO, which probably contains *byrig* in the sense 'manor house', is named from Beage, the daughter of Leppa, to whom the estate is leased in a document dating from 718–45, for their two lives. The estate is not named in the lease, but is identified as 'by the river called Coln'. This may indicate that the river-name was at one time used for several settlements. The parishes east and west of Bibury are Coln St Aldwyn and Coln St Denis. The name Bibury, first recorded in a charter of 899, may have come into use *c.* 750, when Beage, having inherited the lease, may have built a new manor house, referred to by the local people as *Bēagan byrig*.

Stenton 1943b lists eleven place-names in which *burh, byrig* is combined with the genitive of a feminine personal name. There is some evidence that *burh* included among its various meanings that of 'monastery', and Stenton is inclined to think that names of the Bibury type refer to early monasteries founded by pious ladies. The evidence for Bibury, however, accords well with a sense 'manor house'. Fladbury WOR, 'Flǣde's *byrig*', is the earliest of these names to be recorded. A large estate here was granted in the late seventh century by the King of Mercia to the Bishop of Worcester in order that monastic life might be re-established there as when the land was first granted. The estate had presumably been in lay hands for a time, and the likeliest explanation of the name Fladbury seems to me to be, not that it was the name of the decayed monastery, but that it referred to a manor house built by the widow or daughter of a thegn. Since we have documentary evidence for the coining of Bibury in the mid eighth century, it is perfectly reasonable to postulate the same process involving a feminine personal name in the mid seventh century.

The question is, are we justified in inferring from the known origin of Bibury in *c.* 750, the probable origin of Tredington at the same date, and the more substantial number of names which can be shown to have arisen in the period between *c.* 950 and *c.* 1100 that all the place-names which have meanings like 'x's *tūn*', 'x's *byrig*', 'x's *worth*', 'x's *cot*' arose from the granting by a king, nobleman or bishop of a viable estate to a man or woman who was not a peasant farmer? I think we are, though obviously there can be no question of proof. The number of surviving pre-Conquest documents in which evidence for name-formation might be incorporated is less than 2000 (see Sawyer 1968, which catalogues 1875 items). These are very unevenly distributed over the country, and large areas of England have no pre-Conquest documentation at all. Feilitzen 1937 (pp. 32–3) lists over thirty instances of place-names in which the first element is the name of the last pre-Conquest holder of the estate, as recorded in Domesday Book, but the chances of information surviving which throws light on the formation of place-names from the names of earlier manorial owners are slight, and two early instances together with a respectable number of tenth-century ones seem to me to be acceptable statistically, and not too few to be used as evidence for the probable origin of the whole category of place-names. It is important to note that our documentation suggests that Bibury replaced Coln as the name of the estate, and that from the tenth-eleventh centuries we have evidence proving such replacements as that of Collingbourne by Aughton, Lambourn by East Garston, *Æscesbyrig* by Uffington and Woolstone (see Chapter 5).

It seems reasonable to associate names which mean 'x's *cot*', 'x's *wīc*' and 'x's *worth*' with the 'x's *tūn*' names, though there is no direct evidence bearing on these earlier than Domesday Book. More problematical are names like Amersham BUC, in which the genitive of a personal name (in this case *Ealhmund*) is combined with the word *hām* 'village, estate', which is probably, in some areas, the earliest English habitative term (see Chapter 5). Because of the earlier origin of most names in -*hām* it may be felt that the suggestion made here about the 'manorial' nature of the 'x's *tūn*' names is not appropriate to the 'x's *hām*' category. I would consider these names also as probably arising from the gift of estates to king's thegns, but this can never be more than speculation, and it is perfectly reasonable to prefer the older image of Ealhmund as the founder of Amersham, or as the Saxon leader who took it from the British.

Whether or not it is the whole explanation of our 'x's *tūn*', 'x's *byrig*' place-names, the gift of land to a king's thegn, or to a woman of the same class, certainly gave rise to some of them. The system whereby land was provided for the support of the king's companions and their families is described in Stenton 1943 (pp. 298 ff.). Stenton says:

> At the middle of the seventh century Benedict Biscop, as a young companion of King Oswiu, was offered an estate appropriate to his rank by his lord. There can be no doubt that similar grants had been made by the sixth-century kings under whom the English peoples had been established in Britain. . . . It was in the lands which kings had given to their companions that the changes began which created the manorial economy of the middle ages.

On pp. 302–3 Stenton discusses the type of land-grant, necessarily later than those of the sixth and seventh centuries, of which we have records in our surviving Anglo-Saxon charters. Of these he says:

> They were not in the strictest sense grants of lands. Each of these gifts
> empowered the man who had received it to exact within a definite area the
> dues and services which the local peasantry had formerly rendered to the
> king himself. A king's companion thus rewarded received the food-rent
> which the land of his endowment had previously yielded to the king. . . .

Whatever the exact terms of such land-grants (and this is a matter on
which historians are not in total agreement) the broad nature of the relationship between a thegn and his estate is clear enough, and it is quite
different from the relationship which Stenton felt in 1911 to be recorded in
the 'x's *tūn*' place-names. The suggestion that in most such place-names
the relationship of the eponymous lord is the 'manorial' one will, if
accepted, compel revision of some doctrines which were followed in the
Introductions to the earlier volumes of the English Place-Name Survey. It
will mean that such place-names are not likely to be the primary English
names of the settlements concerned, and that the personal names should
not be used as evidence for the date of the first English settlement or the
racial affinities of the settlers. It also means that the personal name may be
that of a woman without this implying that women played a leading part in
settlement or assarting. One of the reasons why thegns needed estates was
that their wives and families had to reside somewhere while they themselves attended the king. The estate might seem to the people of the
countryside to be more closely associated with the thegn's womenfolk than
with the man himself.

There is another class of habitative place-names which arises from
manorial ownership of the kind here postulated for the 'x's *tūn*' type. This
is the class in which a habitative term is compounded with a word like
cyning 'king', *biscop* 'bishop', *ealdorman* 'chief officer of a shire' in the
genitive singular, or with the genitive plural of such words as *cild* 'young
nobleman', *cniht* 'retainer'. Probably the most common of these names is
Kingston, which may fairly be translated 'royal manor'. 'Bishop' occurs in
Bishopstone, Bishton and Bushton, also with other habitative terms, for
instance Bishopsworth SOM, and sometimes with topographical terms, as in
Bishopton WAR (*Biscopesdun* 1016, 'bishop's down'). Bispham LNC is
from a recorded appellative *bisceophām* 'episcopal estate'. 'Alderman'
occurs in Aldermaston BRK and Alderminster WOR (earlier *Aldermanneston*).
Chilton and Knighton ('estate of the young noblemen/retainers') are both
common names, and *cild* and *cniht* occur also with *cot* and *wīc*. In these
names, as in some instances of the common Preston 'estate of the priests',
the reference is likely to have been to the use of the profits of the estate for

the upkeep of a group of people who were not themselves farmers. It is not likely that all these places were founded or managed by a commune of men of the class indicated. The origin suggested above for the 'x's *tūn*' names would place them in the same broad category as Knighton, Chilton, Kingston, which must also have displaced earlier names for the estates they designate. Charlton, Carlton or Chorlton, 'estate or farm of the free peasants' is slightly different, as the peasants in question probably did live and farm at the places named from them. This place-name is discussed in Finberg 1964b, and his conclusion (pp. 157–8) deserves quotation:

> We must think of places like Axminster, Wantage and Mansfield as being not only the administrative centres of districts covering a hundred hides or more, but also as the headquarters of agrarian units which may comprise any number of appendant villages and hamlets. But very early in the history of these great estates a process of erosion sets in. Provision has to be made for the king's younger sons; great noblemen demand favours; old companions in arms expect their reward; and there are churches to be endowed. Piece by piece the royal domain is granted away. Whether or not this process impoverishes the Crown, it greatly enriches local nomenclature. Many of the component villages, hitherto undifferentiated by name, or differentiated only by reference to their geographical features, now have the names of their new owners permanently attached to them. The *tun* granted to Sibba becomes known as Sibton; Tyrdda's becomes Tredington and so on. Presently all but one of the settlements on the original estate have acquired distinctive names of one kind or another. The one exception is the subordinate *tun* which the king has not granted out, but keeps in hand because without the food-rents and the agricultural services rendered by its husbandmen the economy of the central manor would break down. If the central estate has its home-farm, this will quite possibly be worked by slaves, but we may be sure that at busy seasons of the year the peasants of the subordinate village will be called in to lend a hand. This village, geographically distinct from the king's *tun*, and tenurially distinct from the alienated *tuns* which now pay dues to other lords, becomes known as Charlton because it is where the king's own husbandmen live, tilling the soil partly on their own account, but partly also, and perhaps chiefly, for the king.

This picture, like much of Finberg's historical writing, is perhaps more precise than the available evidence will vouch for, but its general outline is convincing, and the implied suggestion that the Kingston, Brighton, Preston, Charlton types of place-name belong together, and should all be seen in the context of manorialization rather than of settlement, has much to recommend it.

There remains the problem of the place-names in which a personal name is compounded with a topographical term. To take two Berkshire examples, are the *Cēol* of Cholsey and the *Frithela* of Frilford to be regarded as temporary manorial overlords, like the owners of the *tūns* discussed above, or are they more likely to have been the leading settlers at the time of the first coming of the English? It is doubtful whether there is any method of investigation which would enable an objective answer to be given to this question. Each investigator will probably incline to one answer rather than the other for subjective reasons, based ultimately on his own instinctive approach to this period of history. There are several instances of a possible connection between people mentioned in charters and settlement-names of this type, but no early ones which are entirely convincing. Feilitzen's list of place-names which probably incorporates the name of the last pre-Conquest holder of the estate (see above) includes two English topographical names (Wadshelf DRB and Brinsley NTT), and two with Old Norse *holmr*. These, with *Biscopesdun* (see above) and the compounds of *ceorla* with topographical terms (as in Chorley) might be seen as some justification for associating this class of names with the 'x's *tūn*' type. It would be interesting to have statistics for the types of second element used in these compounds, but such an investigation would be hampered by the problems discussed in the first half of this chapter. It is likely that most reference books overestimate the number of topographical settlement-names in which the first element is a personal name rather than a significant word. It is certain that *ford* is often compounded with a personal name, and a recent study of names containing *lēah* which are recorded in Old English sources (Johansson 1975) shows that personal names are very frequent with that element. Other topographical terms with which this type of compound is well evidenced are *ēg* 'dry ground in a marsh, island', *feld* 'open land', and *dūn* 'hill'. It is possible that such compounds arose through the granting of estates to thegns at an early date, when *tūn* had not yet attained its overwhelming popularity as a final element, or that a close investigation would show many of them to be concentrated in areas where *tūn* is scarce. There is little objective evidence for regarding these names as manorial in origin, however, and no reason why the people commemorated in some of them should not be early settlers.

Specially difficult problems arise with regard to place-names in which the personal name could be that of a saint. Boston LIN ('Bōtwulf's stone'), Guthlaxton LEI ('Gūthlāc's stone'), and Oswestry SHR ('Oswald's tree') have been considered to refer to Saints Botulf, Guthlac and Oswald. These names are discussed in Gelling 1970, and it is suggested there that since there are other place-names in which personal names are associated with stones (e.g. Allerston YON, Axton KNT, Aylstone HRE, Brixton SUR, Cuddlestone STF, Keston KNT, Keystone HRE, Tilston CHE) and trees (e.g. Brain-tree ESX, Austrey and Coventry WAR, Elstree HRT) it is probably unsound to accept a dramatic derivation of those in which the personal name happens to have historical associations. Church dedications, like that of Oswestry to St Oswald, are very likely to arise from a place-name which did not originally refer to the saint. An instance of this can be found in Warburton CHE. 'Wærburg's farm or estate', where the religious house established in the twelfth century was dedicated to St Werburgh, doubtless because the place-name suggested it. The suggestion that a similar process may have happened at a somewhat earlier date at Oswestry is a shocking heresy to the people of that town, and they will doubtless continue to believe that Oswestry is the place where St Oswald, the Christian King of Northumbria, was killed by Penda, the heathen King of Mercia, in AD 641. Old English *trēow* 'tree' could mean 'wooden cross', and the Welsh name for Oswestry, *Croesoswald*, which is recorded in 1254, shows that the tradition was accepted by Welsh-speaking people in the area. The dedication of the church at Atcham SHR to St Eata may have been suggested by the place-name, which means 'the village of Eata's people'.

Saints and other historical personalities are probably not involved in the formation of such names as Boston and Oswestry. Even if the traditional explanation is retained for some of them, the whole class of names presents difficult problems which cannot be solved in this way. It is difficult to understand the choice of trees and stones as the defining characteristic of a settlement. Some topographical features, such as a *ford*, which is of importance to the surrounding countryside, a *dūn*, *lēah* or *feld*, which covers a wide area, or an *ēg*, which might determine the site of a village in wet ground, may be mentioned in a place-name in association with an owner's name because this was felt to be a compound not entirely different from the 'x's *tūn*' type. But the association of a person with a tree or stone or other small item in the landscape, and the use of the resulting compound to name a settlement, is more difficult to understand.

A clue may lie in the occurrence of such phrases as *burgilde treowe* and *cenelmes stan* in the charter-boundaries which are discussed in Chapter 8. Stenton 1943 tried to use charter-boundary names in which feminine personal names are combined with such elements as *dīc*, *trēow*, *stān* as evidence that 'the part which women had taken in the occupation of new lands for settlement had been by no means inconsiderable', but the use of personal names in boundary marks will not bear that interpretation. It must be considered together with the use of terms like *ealdormannes-*, *biscopes-*, *cinges-*. In the bounds of part of Kingston Lisle BRK the names *cincges scypene* and *cinges thornas* occur, and since there is not likely to have been royal participation in the erection of cow-sheds or the planting of thorns the only sensible translation is 'cow-shed and thorn-bushes on the boundary of the king's estate'. A similar phrase such as *burgilde treowe* will mean 'tree on the boundary of the estate belonging to the lady called *Burghild*'. This sense can be proved to be the correct one in one of the boundary marks, *Leppan crundlas*, of the estate at Bibury granted to Leppa (see above), and it is the obvious one in the numerous occurrences of such phrases as *ælfheages gemære*, *ælflæde gemære*, which means 'boundary of the estate belonging to Ælfhēah/Ælflǣd'.

Some of the place-names of the Coventry-Elstree type may refer to settlements which have grown up on boundaries, and their names may originally have referred to boundary marks of the type well evidenced in the charter surveys. It is possible that some such settlements grew up at meeting-places. The two elements on which this discussion is centred, *trēow* and *stān*, are both well represented in hundred-names, and as meeting-places were often deliberately sited on boundaries, the names may have referred both to boundary marks and to meeting-places. Brixton SUR, which means 'Brihtsige's stone', is the name of a hundred as well as of a settlement. Two Herefordshire hundred meeting-places named from trees have become hamlets; these are Bromsash ('Brēme's ash-tree'), a hamlet at a cross-roads on the boundary of Upton, Weston and Linton parishes, three miles east of Ross, and Webtree ('Webba's tree'), a hamlet at the junction of Clehonger, Haywood and Allensmore parishes, three miles south-west of Hereford. A detailed study of all settlement-names in *trēow* and *stān* would be required in order to ascertain whether a significant proportion of the places referred to were likely to fit into this rather special category of secondary settlements on boundaries, perhaps at ancient meeting-places.

Finally, something must be said of the attitude of the Venerable Bede and of the compilers of the Anglo-Saxon Chronicle to the question of whether first elements which are in the genitive are more likely to be personal names than anything else. Bede makes this assumption fairly frequently, but he shows clear awareness of other possibilities. He translates Selsey into Latin as *Insula uituli marini* 'island of the seal'. This name probably has the collective use of the genitive singular seen in Tengstrand's example, *Fiscesburna* (see above). The editors of *The Place-Names of Sussex*, writing in 1929, were influenced both by unwillingness to disagree with Bede and reluctance to admit this use of the genitive, and they commented, 'The island probably gained its name from the stranding of a seal there on some memorable occasion, rather than by their common presence there'. It is not very likely that a seal would be stranded, or that such an event would be memorable. The genitive is probably collective here, though the resemblance of a piece of land to the shape of a seal might be a possible alternative.

For *Streanæshealh*, assumed to be the Old English name of Whitby YON, Bede gives the Latin translation *Sinus Fari*, which means 'bay of the lighthouse'. This offers formidable difficulties, not yet resolved. The same place-name occurs in Strensall, also in YON, and in a charter boundary mark in WOR, *Streoneshalch*, near Bengeworth. There is also a boundary mark *on streon halh, be streonen halæ* in a survey of Wick Episcopi near Worcester. There is no question of lighthouses in these names, and the *halh* must be an inland hollow. In *The Place-Names of The North Riding of Yorkshire* (1928), A. H. Smith suggested that the first element was Old English *strēon*, one of the meanings of which is 'strain, descent', used as a personal name, and that Bede's *fari* was a mistake for *farae*, genitive of Medieval Latin *fara* 'strain, descent'. It is, however, unlikely that four men called *Strēon(a)* would be associated with hollows or valleys. This is a group of names comparable to the Windsor-Ludgershall groups discussed above. The evidence does not suggest that Bede thought *Streoneshalh* contained a personal name.

For some other names where the first element is in the genitive singular, Bede probably does postulate a personal name. In this category are *Uilfaresdun* 'id est Mons Uilfari', and *Cnobheresburg* 'id est Vrbs Cnob-heri'. *Wilfær* and *Cnofhere* appear in Searle's *Onomasticon* on the strength of these two renderings, as do some other names from Bede's translations of place-names. *Denisesburn* is rendered 'Riuus Denisi', which possibly means that Bede thought it was named after a man whose name would be *Denisus* in Latin. Rendlesham SFK is translated 'mansio Rendili', and *Rendel* has been regarded as an 'archaic' personal name formed with *-el* from *rand* 'shield-border'. A diminutive noun meaning 'little shore' would suit the place, however. Bede's 'Degsastan, id est Degsa lapis' is rendered by modern translators 'Stone of Degsa', but Bede may have meant 'stone (or rock) called *Degsa*'.

Instances in which Bede makes it quite clear that he thinks the first element is a personal name include Rochester, which he says was named 'after one of their former chiefs whose name was Hrof' (see Chapter 2). He derives Bamburgh (Old English *Bebbanburh*) from Queen Bebbe, and he says that *Tunnacæstir* was named from an Abbot called Tunna. A tanta-lizing statement occurs when he is discussing the deacon James; he says 'there is a village near Catterick in which he often used to dwell, which is still called by his name', but the place has not been identified and we have no way of knowing exactly what the place-name was.

Bede's use of personal names to explain Old English place-names is a good deal more cautious than that of the compilers of the early annals of the Anglo-Saxon Chronicle. The confusion of personal names and place-names in these annals presents particularly difficult problems. Something has been said in Chapter 3 about the improbable chieftain Port from whom Portsmouth is said to be named. Other more or less improbable characters include Natanleod, Wihtgar and Wipped. Much could be said both for and against the claims to independent historical existence of these and other early Saxon and Jutish leaders mentioned in the Chronicle. Whatever decision is reached about each of the individual names, it will remain doubtful whether the early annals constitute sound evidence for the use of personal names in place-names at the date of the Anglo-Saxon settlement.

Chapter 8

Boundaries and Meeting Places

The ecclesiastical parishes of the English countryside correspond in many cases to land-units of the Anglo-Saxon period. This has been demonstrated beyond any possibility of doubt by the study of the boundary surveys incorporated in Anglo-Saxon charters. A series of articles by G. B. Grundy, published in the 1920s and 1930s, made this relationship between the charter estates and the modern parishes clear, and a considerable body of work on the charter boundaries which has been published since 1940 has confirmed the general picture.

Work on charter boundaries is not exclusively the preserve of the toponymist, but place-name identifications and interpretations are a crucial factor in the study, and the subject is worthy of a section in this book on that account. It is relevant also because the study of land-units has an important bearing on the topic discussed in Chapters 2 and 3, the problem of the degree of continuity which can be traced from the period before the coming of the English.

Some examples are given here of Old English boundary surveys, attached to Latin charters, which have a close correspondence with modern parish boundaries. These are chosen from a large number of possible examples. Not all charter surveys have been identified on the ground, and by no means all of those which can be located fit modern land-units as neatly as the four quoted here. Nevertheless, these four are by no means atypical, and it follows from evidence of this kind that many of the administrative areas of modern times have had the same boundaries since the ninth and tenth centuries AD. If these units have kept their identity for a thousand years, surviving the major upheavals of the industrial and agricultural revolutions in the eighteenth century, it is reasonable to suppose that they were already of some antiquity when their boundaries were written down for incorporation in Anglo-Saxon land grants.

Some historians and historical geographers feel that continuity from prehistoric and Romano-British times may be manifested more clearly in

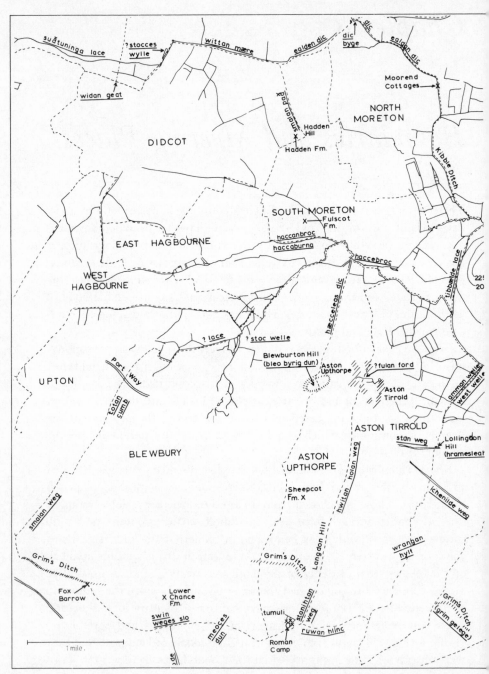

Fig. 12   The Old English bounds of Blewbury BRK

the administrative geography of the countryside than in the history of the villages. Settlements may move about within the areas of their land-units, while the boundaries remain constant. Each land-unit is part of an interlocking pattern which could hardly be changed by a piecemeal process; and even if a village disappears (as some did in the late Middle Ages) the parish named from it does not necessarily vanish from the map. A glance at Sheet 132 of the one-inch map shows Warwickshire instances such as Chapel Ascote (GR 415565) and the adjoining Hodnell, where there is in the first instance nothing, in the second instance only a Manor Farm, to account for the dotted outline of the parish boundary which surrounds each name. The parish outlines which belong to a lost village may have been preserved by the irregular, interlocking outlines of the adjoining parishes. Those surrounding an existing village owe their continuity to the fact that in the days of subsistence farming they enclosed an area of land which had been proved by long experience to be capable of yielding the necessities of life for a farming community. The varied and irregular shapes of the parishes are explicable mainly in terms of the need for each community to have its share of certain types of land.

The boundaries written down for incorporation in the Latin charters of the Anglo-Saxon period are those of estates, that is viable agricultural concerns over which a religious house or a lay nobleman was given certain rights. The problem of whether a manorial owner is an original feature in such a concern—a founding father of the village and responsible for the initial agreement about the estate boundaries—or whether these irregularly shaped land-unit patterns are the creation of peasant farmers, and are only subjected to manorial overlords at a later stage, is touched upon in Chapter 7. Many historians speak in terms which suggest an organized sharing-out of newly acquired kingdoms among the followers of the first English warlords, with many estate boundaries being laid down at that time. Recent work on parish and township boundaries has suggested, however, that many of these units have been preserved from the Roman period or earlier.

An original and stimulating paper by D. J. Bonney (Bonney 1972) has demonstrated that in Wiltshire there are pre-Roman linear earthworks, particularly Grim's Dyke on the Grovely Ridge west of Wilton, which are likely to have served as estate boundaries since they were built, in or before the Iron Age, whereas post-Roman earthworks, in particular the eastern part of Wansdyke, cut across parishes in a way which suggests that the parish units are earlier than the earthwork. Roman roads can be shown to be used as parish boundaries in areas of Wiltshire where there is little or no sign of pre-Roman habitation, and where the Roman road was probably

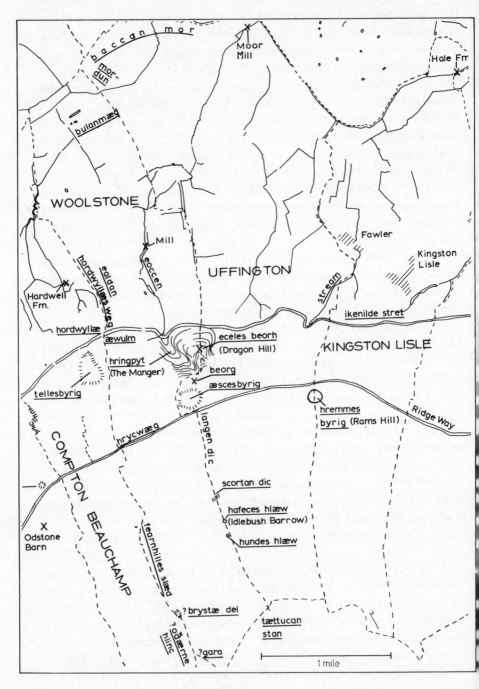

Fig. 13   The Old English bounds of Uffington BRK

the first feature in the development of the landscape; but they are consistently ignored in areas where habitation can be shown to go back before Roman times. This study takes the subject a good deal further than Mr Bonney's earlier paper (Bonney 1966), which had established the probability that many parish boundaries were fixed before the end of the pagan Anglo-Saxon period, because of the high proportion of pagan burials which lay on or near them. Bonney 1976 further suggests that many of the component units of large parishes, the townships, had boundaries of comparable antiquity.

It would be excellent to have studies of this kind for other parts of the country, and this is another exercise which can be recommended to local historians. The persistent ignoring of Offa's Dyke by the boundaries of the west Midland parishes which it crosses was taken by Sir Cyril Fox to show that the parishes were much later than the Dyke, but it seems more likely that the units were ancient when the Dyke was made, and that their survival in spite of it is a phenomenon comparable to that observed by Bonney in relation to Wansdyke. If the land-units were laid out after the earthwork was made, even at a date when it was without political significance, the convenience of having it as a boundary rather than as an obstacle would surely have caused more parishes to lie wholly on one or the other side. The modern spectacle of cows standing on bridges over our new motorways, watching the traffic as they pause in their journey from one part of a farm to another, is a reminder of the manner in which great linear features driven through an ancient farming landscape will bisect ancient land-units but will not cause their outlines to be re-drawn.

In Berkshire, where a brief study of the type pioneered by Mr Bonney has recently been attempted (Gelling 1976b, pp. 807–10), the limited use which is made of the known Roman roads by the boundaries of modern parishes and pre-Conquest estates seems to be a significant historical feature. The only part of Berkshire in which the land-units are laid out with some regard to a Roman road is on the heathlands traversed by the Devil's Highway east of the Roman town of Silchester. The parishes of Stratfield, Swallowfield, Sandhurst and Winkfield make use of the road, and this is one of several reasons for believing that a belt of land south of Reading was newly broken in for agriculture during the Anglo-Saxon period (see Chapter 5). West of Silchester, on the other hand, the use of the Roman road for boundaries ceases almost entirely; on the long stretch between the east boundary of Aldermaston and the west boundary of Lambourn there is no coincidence which is more than a mere touch, and this is true also of the Roman road which branches off between Welford and Kintbury.

Other approaches to this question of persistence of land-units from pre-historic times, particularly that advocated by Professor Glanville Jones, may be discussed after some Anglo-Saxon charter boundaries have been presented. Four sets have been chosen, relating to Blewbury, Uffington and Shellingford in Berkshire, and to Witney in Oxfordshire. They are given in translation here, with the modern forms of those place-names which have survived, and Modern English renderings of those which have not. Figs 12–15 should make it possible to follow the course taken by the surveys.

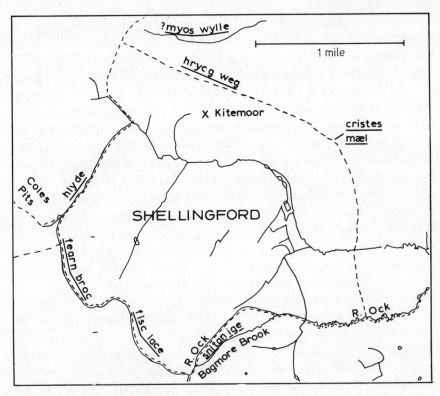

Fig. 14   The Old English bounds of Shellingford BRK

The Blewbury survey, one of the most detailed of its kind, is attached to a Latin charter dated AD 944, by which King Edmund grants an estate of a hundred hides to Bishop Ælfric of Ramsbury. The number of hides an estate was considered to contain is a matter of great interest. The hide, which originated as the amount of land considered adequate for the support of a single household, had become a formal unit of assessment by the tenth century, and by the time of the Domesday Survey the hidage given foi each estate is a note of its liability to taxation. In spite of many

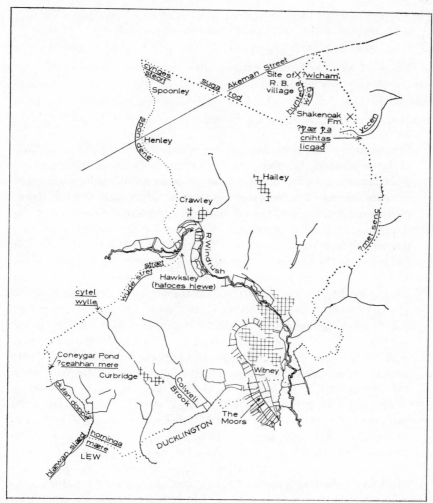

Fig. 15   The Old English bounds of Witney OXF (from Gelling 1967, by permission of the Society for Medieval Archaeology). Approx. 1 inch to 1 mile

anomalous hidage assessments, there is often a fairly clear relationship between hidage and area, and between hidage and the relative importance of the estate. An assessment of a hundred hides, in addition to indicating that the Blewbury estate of this charter was a large and important one, probably indicates that the area was an early administrative unit. It is almost certainly the Blewbury Hundred which survived till the twelfth century, and was then dismembered because a new hundred was created from the scattered estates of Reading Abbey. The administrative units called hundreds are discussed further in the second half of this chapter.

The survey describes the five modern parishes of Blewbury, Aston Tirrold, Aston Upthorpe, North and South Moreton. This unit did not continue much longer as a single estate. Aston Upthorpe is the subject of a grant of AD 964, so it was a separate estate by then, and there were a number of manors in the area of the four parishes at the time of the Domesday Survey. In 944, however, the four parishes constituted an estate of a hundred hides with the following boundaries:

> First to the east side of the estate at Amwell, then south straight to the ditch of the water-slade, then along the ditch to the south end to the true estate boundary, then up to the great tumulus beneath wild-garlic wood, then from the tumulus up along stone way to the tall crucifix at hawk thorn, then from hawk thorn to the tall thorn tree at Icknield Way, then to the third thorn tree at bog-myrtle hanger, from the thorn to the fourth thorn tree which stands on the front part of crooked hill, then forward to the fifth thorn tree, to the olive tree, then west along the little way up to the thorn tree, up to hill of trouble, then west to the rough lynchet, along the rough lynchet to the heathen burial-places at the old ditch, then along to the plantation, then from the plantation straight on to the broad barrow east of the stump of fugitives, then to fugitives' stump, then from fugitives' stump to Mēoc's down, to the burial, from the burial to the water-channel at swine path's slough at the junction of ways, then up to the landslip to Fox Barrow, from the barrow west along the bank of the ribbon to the Ridge Way, along the way to the red stone, from the stone north along the narrow way to Tadcombe at the barrow, then north straight along the narrow way to the main road, then to the end of the lynchet, then forward north along the way to Ordstān's ditch, then along the ditch, from the ditch to the north of the ploughed land, then by the ploughed land to the stream which leads to tree-stump stream; then from tree-stump stream north along the brook to the ditch which the king's son marked out, then along the ditch to the sheep-wash on Hakka's Brook, then along Hakka's Brook to Hudd's island, then forward north along the brook to the west of Hudd's island, then up along the headlands to the end of the little ditch, and then north along the head-lands to the tall crucifix at Hadden, then north along the narrow path to the ditch hurdles to the studfold, then east along the old ditch to Athelstān's plantation to the bend of the ditch, then south-east along the ditch by Brightwell boundary, then south-east over the marsh to Mæring's thorn tree, from Mæring's thorn tree to plough-gate, from plough-gate by the edge of the hill to the red-leafed maple tree, from the maple tree to the stream, then straight to West Well which by another name is called Amwell.

As can be seen from Fig. 12, this survey starts at the north-east corner of the estate, which is not one of the commonest starting-places. The Berkshire surveys show a marked preference for a corner as starting-point, but the south-east and south-west corners are more common than the northern ones. The Blewbury bounds resemble the vast majority in Berkshire and elsewhere, however, in running clockwise. Among seventy-four Berkshire charter surveys only one runs anti-clockwise, and while the anti-clockwise circuit may be slightly better represented in other regions, it is certainly a rarity, and should only be assumed if there is strong evidence to support it. Not many of the boundary-marks in the Blewbury survey have become surviving place-names, but those which have done so are fairly evenly distributed round the circuit, so that there is no doubt of the general line followed, and other boundary-marks can be identified with reasonable certainty from the topography.

The starting-point, Amwell, is one of a network of small streams draining a marshy area. The name survived into the present century (and may still be known) as that of a spring in Cholsey parish which must have been the source of the watercourse named in the Old English bounds. The Icknield Way is the next precisely identified point, then Fox Barrow, a tumulus marked on the one-inch map a good deal further round the circuit. Several intermediate points have been marked on Fig. 12 on the basis of the topography. The term *drægeles bæc*, here translated 'bank of the ribbon', which follows Fox Barrow, refers to Grim's Ditch, an unusual linear earthwork on the Berkshire Downs, which differs from other prehistoric ditches by its modest scale and its indirect course. The next point, the Ridge Way, is not now on the boundary of Blewbury, so there is an apparent discrepancy of about a fifth of a mile between the Old English survey and the modern boundary; but the Ridge Way may have been a much wider track, or collection of tracks, than it is today. Tadcombe, on the west boundary of Blewbury parish, is the next name to have survived, at least until the 1920s, when G. B. Grundy noted it. After Tadcombe, the survey mentions a *herepæth*, literally 'army path', which may fairly be translated 'main road', and is clearly the road to Wantage known as the Port Way which crosses the Blewbury boundary here. Hakka's Brook is marked on some O.S. maps; other Old English boundary surveys call it *hacceburnan* as well as *haccebroce*, and it is the stream from which the villages of East and West Hagbourne are named. The name Hadden (Old English *hǣth-dūn* 'heath-hill') has survived as that of a modern farm, so there is no doubt that the survey is going round South Moreton parish; and a subsequent reference to Brightwell boundary makes it clear that North Moreton is included also.

Since the Blewbury charter of AD 944 enables us to reconstruct the exact area of a great estate which was also a hundred, and which contains six or more ancient centres of habitation, it provides a good text for speculation about a 'hierarchy' of place-name types. Something has been said of this in Chapter 5. The whole unit was known by the name Blewbury, which means 'variegated fort', and which was the Old English name of the hill-fort on Blewburton Hill, believed to have been so called from the creamy-white chalk soil, which would give a variegated appearance when the hill was under cultivation. As can be seen from Fig. 12, the hill-fort is fairly central to the whole unit. The village of Blewbury, still the largest settlement in the five modern parishes, lies a mile to the west of the fort. Aston Upthorpe and Aston Tirrold, though they have given name to separate modern parishes, are two halves of the same village, and this village lies immediately east of the hill-fort and one and a half miles east of Blewbury village. Aston means 'east farm'. North Moreton and South Moreton, on the other hand, are distinct villages, lying a mile apart, as well as being distinct parishes. Moreton means 'marsh farm', and the meadow provided by the wet ground at this northern end of the estate must have been an important factor in the estate economy. Moreton is probably not just a topographical statement about the setting of the *tūn*, but also a reference to the part it played in the organization of the whole unit. This is an area of nucleated settlement, so there are not many farms or hamlets within the five parishes. No farm in Blewbury parish, in North Moreton, or in either of the Astons has a name which is recorded before the sixteenth century. South Moreton however, contains Fulscot Farm, which is a settlement of some antiquity, being recorded in the Domesday Survey as a small estate with a population of nine families and with the valuable asset of thirty acres of meadow. This is a property by no means to be despised, but the use of *cot* in the name, which means 'Fugol's cottages', probably indicates that it was always regarded as of subsidiary status to the Astons and Moretons. As mentioned above, the name *hǣth-dūn* in the boundaries has survived as that of Hadden Farm. This lies just outside the boundary of South Moreton, in Didcot parish. It is not recorded in the Domesday Survey, and is almost certainly a settlement resulting from relatively late agricultural encroachment on heath land used as rough pasture in the pre-Conquest period.

It is from the boundary survey attached to a charter of AD 964, which grants Aston Upthorpe as a separate estate, that we know that *blēo byrig*, the Old English form of Blewbury, was the name of the fort on Blewburton Hill. This is by no means the only instance of a feature which was once central to an estate being left on a boundary by the splitting of the great estate into smaller units. The same thing happened to Uffington Castle, the hill-fort which lies above the Berkshire White Horse, and the next set of bounds to be studied is one of several documents from which we can recover the identity of an estate which took its name from this hill-fort.

The Anglo-Saxon charters relating to Berkshire include three grants of land at a place called *Æscesbyrig*, and it is clear from the boundary surveys attached to these and other grants in the vicinity that *Æscesbyrig* was the Old English name of Uffington Castle, which besides being used specifically of the hill-fort was used of the estates on either side of it until these became known by the new names of Uffington and Woolstone in the second half of the tenth century. The new tenth-century names refer to manorial overlords, one of whom, the *Wulfrīc* of Woolstone, is a king's thegn mentioned in a number of sources (see Chapter 7). Some confusion has arisen among modern commentators on these charters because *Æscesbyrig* was taken to be the Berkshire parish of Ashbury, a few miles west of Woolstone. Ashbury, however, is from Old English **Æscbyrig*, 'fort where ash trees grow', while *Æscesbyrig* is probably 'fort belonging to a man named *Æsc*'. It is instructive to note that while these two names seem confusingly alike to the modern eye, the distinction was probably perfectly clear to the finer linguistic perceptions of our forefathers. One of the estates called *Æscesbyrig* was granted in AD 953 with the following bounds, which fit the modern parish of Uffington:

> First in at the south gate and out at the north gate, to Dudda's tumulus, and then to ?church tumulus, and then to ring pit, and then to the headlands, and then to the chalk pits, and thence to the broad pool, and thence along the ditch to clean meadow, and then to the broad way, round marsh hill, to *thyreses* stream, and thence to the north part of bog pool, and then along the marsh by the north stone, and then crosswise over the marsh to Bula's ditch, and so along the ditch to Æthelfrith's boundary, to the end of Bula's ditch, to the thorn stump, and then to *Teale* brook, and thence to the holy place, and so up along the brook to the west part of Æthelfrith's boundary, and so along the boundary to Rams Hill to the north gate and out at the south gate, to Hod's tumulus, and then to stone tumulus, and then to the red hollow, and then to the dark hollow, and so by the slope, and then to Dunfrith's headland, to Tættuca's stone, and then to hound's tumulus, and then to hawk's tumulus, and then to the short ditch, and then to the long ditch, to Æsc's camp again to the south gate.

The surveys we have for the *Æscesbyrig* estates may describe portions of a large composite estate comparable to the Blewbury one just discussed. If so, the splitting-up process was earlier here, the earliest surviving *Æscesbyrig* charter being one which grants the western half of the modern parish of Woolstone in AD 856. The combined area of Woolstone and Uffington parishes is similar in its north/south dimension to that of the great Blewbury estate, but it is much smaller from east to west, and it is possible that more of the long, narrow parishes which lie athwart the escarpment of the Downs in north-west Berkshire were part of the original *Æscesbyrig* estate. This is speculation, however, as we have no evidence for an estate large enough to be a hundred which had Uffington Castle as its centre. If such a unit did exist, it would have been similar in several ways to the Blewbury estate. The largest village in the area is Uffington, and this was certainly called *Æscesbyrig* in 953. The estate also resembles the Blewbury one in having a large area of marshy land at its northern end, but there is no settlement corresponding to Moreton, perhaps because Uffington itself occupies slightly raised ground in this area of *mōr*. The Uffington estate was assessed at thirty-three hides.

Special interest attaches to this survey, and to others which adjoin it, because of the evidence they supply for the Old English names given to the striking archaeological and topographical features of the White Horse area. There is no reference to the White Horse itself, but the artificially flattened hillock now called Dragon Hill was named *eceles beorh*, which may contain *ecles* 'Celtic Christian church', discussed in Chapter 4. The dramatic natural hollow now called The Manger was known as *hringpyt*. The hill-fort to the east of Uffington Castle was called *hremnesbyrig* 'raven's fort', and the first part of the Old English name survives in the modern Rams Hill. This name is discussed in Chapter 6. Two surviving prehistoric tumuli south of Uffington Castle are called *hundes hlǣw* and *hafoces hlǣw*, 'hound's tumulus' and 'hawk's tumulus'. The significance of this is obscure, but the names may be jocular, hound and hawk being thought of as things which went together. It is clear from the survey that other tumuli and earthworks have disappeared since the tenth century. The limitations of these surveys as precise guides to ancient monuments are illustrated by the use of *langen dic* 'long ditch' for what is probably a geological feature— a low cliff running alongside the parish boundary for about 700 yards south of Uffington Castle. The 'gates' referred to at Uffington Castle and at Rams Hill are probably gaps made in the ramparts in Saxon times, not the original entrances. The boundary between Uffington and Woolstone, which now makes a detour round the camp, went through it until 1777, when the camp became part of Uffington under an Enclosure Act.

The charter of AD 969 by which King Edgar granted to one of his thegns thirty hides at Witney in Oxfordshire has a boundary survey which contains several points of exceptional interest. The area described is that of the four modern parishes of Witney, Curbridge, Crawley and Hailey, an area which is perhaps a little less than half that of the Blewbury grant, but it is still a large estate with several ancient centres of habitation. The survey runs:

First from hawk's tumulus to Windrush, to the willow row, to nut slope, from the slope to Henley, then to Langley way, along the way, then to Spoonley, then to wood-chipping way, along the way until it reaches the north part of king's tail of land, thence to marsh clearing, along the clearing to huntsmen's way, along the way till it reaches *wīchām*, thence always by the edge to *ofling* acre, thence to old way, along the way to *cycgan* stone, from the stone to the green way, along the way, then to open land by the *Yccen*, from open land by the *Yccen* to the hedge-row, along hedge-row to *met sinc*, along *met sinc* to the upper part of Ecgheard's hill, along the edge to Windrush, along Windrush to the east side of foul island, thence following the boundary to Tīdrǣd's ford, thence to Occa's slippery place, thence to the southern part of Witta's marsh, thence to Colwell Brook, from the brook to the old ditch, from the ditch to bird valley, from the valley to the stone bridge, along the brook to the old way, from the way to the boundary of the Hornings, thence to the southern part of the slope with weirs, thence along the valley to Tyca's pit, along the brook to the junction, from the junction to jackdaw's pond, thence to small earthwork, from the earthwork to the headlands, from the headlands to kettle spring, from the spring to the paved road, along the paved road to hawk's tumulus, from the tumulus again to nut slope where it started.

This set of boundaries and another of AD 1044 which describes the same estate have been studied with special care because the circuit includes at its north-east corner an area of particular archaeological interest. Excavations in 1967–70 in the vicinity of Shakenoak Farm produced Roman and Anglo-Saxon material in a relationship the nature of which is still being debated. The bounds were examined carefully for possible traces of Romano-British linguistic survival, and it was suggested (Gelling 1972) that the name *wīchām* and the use of *yccen* for a small tributary of the Evenlode were specially significant. The association of *wīchām* with Romano-British settlements of the sort believed from surface finds to have existed a mile north of Shakenoak Farm is discussed in detail in Chapter 3. The term *yccen* in *yccenes feld* is probably a pre-English river-name other instances of which have become Itchen in Hampshire and Warwickshire. This is an area where only a few major rivers have kept their pre-English names, and the survival into the Old English period of the pre-English name for a small brook suggests an unusual amount of contact between English-speaking settlers and their British predecessors in the immediate vicinity of Shakenoak. The name *yccenes feld* survived into modern times in the form Edging Field, which is given in an Enclosure Award for ground along this stream. The later version of these bounds, in a charter of AD 1044, mentions a place in *yccenes feld* 'where the young men (or servants) lie' (*thær tha cnihtas licgath*), and this seems likely to refer to some remarkable burials found in the Shakenoak excavations. Another name in this north-east corner of the circuit which is of special interest is 'huntsmen's way', referring to the road from Delly End to Wilcote. There was in Elizabethan times a traditional Whit Hunt, centred on Burford but involving Witney, Hailey and Crawley, and the late Mrs Wickham Steed informed me that this 'huntsmen's way' was the starting point. If the tradition continued from 969 till *c*. 1600, it is reasonable to suppose that it extended at least as far back into the period before 969.

The rest of the circuit contains several points of interest. The starting point is another 'hawk's tumulus' (Old English *hafoces hlewe*), the same name as that given to Idlebush Barrow in the bounds of Uffington. In this instance the name survived as Hawksley in the Curbridge Tithe Award, and there is a record of some digging in a long burial-mound here in 1857. A number of the names in this set of bounds appear in later records, including the 'nut slope', Old English *hnut clyf*, which is *Notley* in a survey of 1552, the 'high clearing' (Old English *hean leage*) which is Henley in an Enclosure Award, and the 'wood-chipping clearing' (Old English *spon leage*) which is Spoonley in the same source. The 'king's tail' (Old English *cynges steorte*) is called *Sharpesterte* in a survey of part of Wychwood Forest in 1300. The use of *horninga mære* 'Hornings' boundary' for the Lew/Curbridge boundary is interesting. The Hornings were the people who lived in the angle of the old county of Berkshire which lies west of Oxford, a district called 'the horn' because it is enclosed by the great loop of the Thames between Cumnor and Abingdon. This area formed the Hundred of Hormer, named from its meeting place which was a marshy pool called **Horningamere* 'pool of the Hornings'. The Abbot of Abingdon was temporarily the owner of Curbridge, which he exchanged in AD 956 for Kennington in Hormer Hundred. Probably he moved some tenants from Hormer Hundred to Curbridge, causing part of the Curbridge/Lew boundary to be called *horninga mære*. This is a useful warning against the too confident acceptance of sporadic *-inga-* place-names (discussed in Chapter 5) as indications of the exact location of Old English tribal units which had *-ingas* names.

Another noteworthy point about the western side of the circuit is that while no reference is made to the major Roman road, Akeman Street, a road leading to the tumulus at Hawksley is called *stret* (here translated 'paved road'). It is necessary to remember that while *strǣt* in settlement-names (like Streatham, Stretton, Stratford) seems always to be a major Roman road, the word is used in the charter boundaries of roads of much more lowly status, probably not always of Roman origin.

The area of the Witney estate includes marshy land by the Windrush and wooded land on the edge of Wychwood Forest to the north. Witney ('Witta's island') shows the characteristic use of *ieg* for a raised site in marshy land, and these bounds reveal that the surrounding marsh was called *Wittan mor*, presumably from the same landowner. Ancient settlements are more numerous in the southern part of the estate. Witney parish contains Cogges ('hills') which was a separate estate in the Domesday Survey, and Curbridge ('Creoda's bridge') contains Burwell and Caswell ('manor spring' and 'cress spring'), which are evidenced in 1226 and 1166 respectively. The two northern villages of Crawley and Hailey, 'crow wood or clearing' and 'hay clearing', are first recorded in 1214 and 1241, and they may have been new settlements of the Anglo-Saxon period. The frequent occurrence of *lēah* (for which see Chapter 5) in names in the northern part of this area is partly responsible for the development of *hafoces hlewe* and *hnut clyf* to Hawksley and *Notley*. Place-names often influence each other in this manner.

It is not apparent from the records what the North Berkshire estates did for woodland. It is clear from the Blewbury and Uffington surveys quoted here that they had very little wood within their boundaries, though both were well provided with meadowland which would produce the vital hay crops. Wood and meadow were both important—the latter essential—to subsistence farming, and a number of Anglo-Saxon land grants give the boundaries not only of the main estate but also of areas of wood and meadow situated at some distance. The later Witney survey, not quoted here, mentions 'the mead which belongs to Shilton'. Shilton lies six miles west of Witney, in dry limestone country, and this outlying meadow near Witney remained a detached portion of Shilton long enough to be marked as such on the first six-inch map. Many instances could be cited of the persistence of such pre-Conquest arrangements into the present century, when they appear as detached portions of parishes. Again, it is legitimate to suggest that arrangements which are known to have lasted for a thousand years were already of very great antiquity when they were first recorded.

Probably the main focus of settlement in this part of Oxfordshire in early Anglo-Saxon times was by the Windrush, and Crawley and Hailey represent later agricultural encroachment into forest, but it is important to note that this Witney estate includes a corner of an area of dense Romano-British settlement. The Shakenoak Roman villa is on the edge of a famous group of villas which includes those at North Leigh and Ditchley. The forest used and cleared by the Anglo-Saxons may have been to some extent a re-growth since the Romano-British period. Reasons are given in Chapter 3 for thinking that the Romano-British settlement referred to as *wīchām* in the Witney bounds may have been the centre of a land-unit before it was left stranded on a boundary.

There is abundant evidence from Anglo-Saxon charters that large estates which comprised settlements subsidiary to the main village were subject to a process whereby some subsidiary settlements became the centres of independent estates, and then evolved into modern parishes, so that there may be four or more modern parishes within the area of a single pre-Conquest estate. This breaking up of large units may have been at an advanced stage by the date of our earliest records in Oxfordshire and Berkshire. Much work has been done, especially by Professor Glanville Jones and Professor G. W. S. Barrow, on the identification of large multiple estates in the north of England, and both authorities believe that such units were formed long before the coming of the English, and that some of them preserved their identity from Roman to medieval times. These studies of great estates in the north postulate much bigger units than the Berkshire and Oxfordshire ones outlined here. Jones 1971 may be consulted for a study of such an estate at Kirkby Overblow YOW. Here Professor Jones postulates a 'relatively small multiple estate' which was 'a subdivision of the larger multiple estate of Knaresborough'. He believes that such great estates are the origin of the shires of Northumbria (like Norhamshire and Islandshire NTB, Aucklandshire DRH), and that they are represented by the multiple estates of medieval Wales to which the term *maenor* was applied. A convenient summary of these views is provided in Jones 1976. The first chapter of Barrow 1973 pursues this theme, and postulates royal lordships 'based upon a unit known variously as lathe, soke, shire or *manerium cum appendiciis*' which can be traced in the whole country from Kent to Northumbria. Historians have not yet endeavoured to apply these theories in much detail to southern English counties, though Jones 1976 cites Malling SSX as a possible example. These remarks are inserted here in order to indicate that the study of Anglo-Saxon charter boundaries, which are concentrated in the southern counties, may have an extra dimension of providing evidence for pre-English territorial units. The presence of a hill-fort as the central point in the Blewbury and *Æscesbyrig* estates could be seen as specially significant in this connection.

Attention has been focused so far in this discussion on sets of charter boundaries which circumscribe the area of several modern parishes, or which, like the Uffington survey, can be shown from the Old English name to describe part of a larger unit. It is appropriate to cite one more set of bounds as an example of the numerous surviving Old English surveys which describe a single modern parish where there is only one settlement. The bounds of Shellingford BRK, although not firmly connected with a

Latin charter and so of uncertain date, afford a good example of such a survey. These run:

> First to the Ock at the boundary of the people of Stanford, so out up-stream to snipe's island, to the northern side of the island, and so to the middle of Bagmore, so along the marsh to fish stream, into the indentation of the burrow, and then along fern brook till it comes up to the red ditch, so along the ditch to the Lyde, along the Lyde to broad marsh, from broad marsh to priest meadow, up to marsh spring, from marsh spring to the ridge way, along the ridge way to the crucifix, then south till it comes again to the Ock where it began.

The survey of this small parish starts in the south-east, Stanford being the adjacent parish to the east. The Ock divides into branches, leaving the ground called *snitan ige* ('snipe's island') between two arms of the river. The southern arm is still called Bagmore Brook, preserving the name ('Bacca's marsh') of an extensive tract of *mōr* mentioned also in the bounds of a Woolstone charter. Lyde, Old English *hlȳde* 'the loud one', was the name of the stream which flows through Lyde Copse on the west boundary of Shellingford. The term 'ridge way' is here used of the road from Faringdon to Wantage which forms the north boundary of the parish. The crucifix (*cristes mæl*) probably stood at the point where the boundary leaves this road. It is not certain what *crypeles heale*, here translated 'indentation of the burrow', refers to, but one use of *healh* in place-names is for a projecting corner of a parish, and this may be the curve in the boundary where the adjacent parish, Fernham, intrudes into Shellingford on the south-west side.

Shellingford was assessed at twelve hides in the pre-Conquest period. If its size is compared with that of Uffington, it appears that Shellingford was rather more lightly assessed in relation to its area. These hidages do, however, generally give a reliable rough guide, at any rate in the south of England, as to whether an estate was large or small. Shellingford is one of a number of parishes of roughly similar size and shape situated between the long, narrow parishes, like Uffington and Woolstone, which lie athwart the northern escarpment of the Berkshire Downs, and the River Thames. There is good reason to believe that some of these relatively small parishes were originally parts of larger units. Great Faringdon and Shrivenham in this area can be shown to have been the centres of large, composite estates, that at Shrivenham including the neighbouring parishes of Bourton, Longcot and Fernham, and that at Great Faringdon extending into Wiltshire and into Oxfordshire, where one of its members is still called Little Faringdon (Gelling 1976b, p. 831). But the process of splitting into small, independent units is well advanced by the time of the earliest records, and it would be unwise to try to fit all the jig-saw pieces, like Shellingford, into a hypothetical earlier pattern of larger units.

The study of Old English charter boundaries is linked with place-name study on the one hand and with that of administrative geography on the other. This is a book about the historical bearing of place-names, so it is not the place for a long digression on the reasons for the varied shapes and sizes of our parishes. Fig. 16, which shows the area in which lie three of the four sets of boundaries discussed here, will, however, make it clear at a glance that the pattern made by the parish boundaries is a most remarkable feature of the English countryside, and the four charter surveys quoted above may serve to establish the antiquity of some aspects of this strange pattern.

Old English surveys do not survive for all parts of the country. The distribution of estates for which Old English charters, with or without boundaries, have survived is very uneven, with heavy concentrations in Kent, Hampshire, Wiltshire, Berkshire, Gloucestershire and Worcestershire, and very little in the east and north. There is a handlist (Sawyer 1968) to the charters, and regional studies of some of them are to be found in a series of handbooks published by Leicester University Press (Finberg 1953, 1961, 1964a, Hart 1957, 1966, 1975). The numerous studies of G. B. Grundy are listed in Sawyer 1968. Local historians wishing to make a fresh study of a set of boundaries need the actual text of the survey. Sawyer 1968 lists the printed editions of each item catalogued, which will enable people with access to good library facilities to obtain them. For really detailed work, as opposed to a general appreciation, it is not advisable to accept G. B. Grundy's translations as definitive. The translation of these texts is fairly difficult, and specialized advice is worth having if possible. All the existing Berkshire boundaries are edited with maps in Gelling 1976.

The study of parish and township boundaries is a rewarding one whether or not there is an Old English survey. It is always advisable to check for nineteenth-century and modern adjustments, but where these have not operated it is safe to assume that many parish and township boundaries are of great antiquity, probably, in many cases, dating from before the coming of the English. There are many boundary surveys of later date than those attached to Anglo-Saxon charters, and some of these reproduce the style of the Old English surveys quite closely. For instance, a perambulation of Selattyn parish, made in 1752, and written on the first page of Selattyn parish register for 1783–1812 (*Shropshire Parish Registers*, St Asaph Diocese, Vol. I, pp. 378ff.) includes the following directions:

> So by a stone in a cart track to some old holly and hawthorn stumps . . .
> from thence up a purl of water westward running down a dingle formerly

called Nant Kelyn Duon, up the said dingle and with the remains of an old ditch which leads up to the Race Course upon Kern y Bwch crossing the said course in the place called the Slough to a mear stone below. . . . Cross the enclosure in a line to a forked tree . . . from the forked tree straight down Cae Freeze to a stile, leaving about two strikes sowing in the Parish of Whittington . . . with a purl of water to Maes tan y Wern with the north hedge to a crab Tree . . . from the crab Tree turn to the right to the point of the Hedge . . . by an old well to the place where formerly stood the Llwyn house through the old house place to the Gate going into the road leading from Chirk Castle to Oswestry where we began with the boundaries.

It is not only the boundaries which have remained unchanged in many cases for at least a thousand years. The names given to features recognized as boundary-marks also have a surprisingly high survival rate. It is commonplace for a name used in a charter survey of the Old English period to reappear in a Tithe Award of the mid nineteenth century, having apparently been preserved by oral tradition over the intervening centuries. Sometimes a name in a charter boundary is found to be still in use locally, though there is no written evidence for it. Many discoveries of this kind are doubtless still to be made by local investigators, but for this type of investigation it is essential to study the Old English text of the bounds (since names survive in a form derived from the Old English one, not in a modern translation), and it is important to be sure that the resemblance of names is more than a coincidence. Specialist advice is worth having about whether a modern field-name is likely to preserve an Old English boundary-mark.

The pre-Conquest estates, which are the subject of the charters, were grouped for administrative purposes in larger units. In much of England these were known from the tenth century onwards as hundreds. In some counties in the Danelaw the unit corresponding to the hundred was called the wapentake. The origins of these administrative divisions constitute a complicated historical problem, which cannot be discussed here. A convenient summary as regards the hundred can be found in Whitelock 1955 (p. 393). What does deserve brief discussion here is the contribution made by place-name studies to our knowledge of the functioning of hundreds and wapentakes. These divisions had names, and in many instances the name is that of the place where the meetings of the men of the hundred or wapentake were held. Many hundreds were re-named from an important manor in their area, so that the name of the ancient meeting-place may be lost; but other hundred-names preserve rich evidence for the siting of the outdoor assemblies which met to settle matters of local administration and justice.

The typical hundred meeting-place, as revealed by the names of the hundreds, was in a sort of 'no-man's-land', as far away as possible from the settlements of the community it served and on the boundary between two or more estates, but often near a main road or a river-crossing. A tumulus (see Chapter 6), a stone, or a tree were the sort of objects likely to be chosen as markers for the spot. Despite the primitive nature of the meeting-places, which are naturally suspected of having served older units than the hundreds, the administrative units themselves continued to function throughout the Middle Ages and, for some limited purposes, into the modern period. Because of their continuing administrative importance the units were liable to much adaptation and re-arrangement. This took the two main forms of rationalization, such as that which created hundreds of regular size and taxation-assessment (that is, containing estates whose assessments totalled a hundred hides) in Worcestershire in the second half of the tenth century, and special concessions to privileged landowners, such as that which created the Hundred of Reading in Berkshire in the thirteenth century from a number of scattered estates belonging to Reading Abbey (see Fig. 16). Even in counties much affected by such alterations, the names of some hundreds may still reveal the nature of the ancient meeting-place, as in the Worcestershire Doddingtree ('Dudda's tree'), but the ancient names are best studied in counties like Staffordshire, Hereford-shire and Shropshire, where the early units have been subject to less drastic interference.

Pre-Conquest estates in Staffordshire have much lower hidage assess-ments than estates of similar area in the southern counties, and the hundreds of Staffordshire are much larger than those of the surrounding counties, and have been much more stable. All the five hundreds into which the county was divided at the time of the Domesday Survey have kept their outline, practically unchanged, down to modern times. The names of the five hundreds are Seisdon, Cuttlestone, Offlow, Pirehill and Totmonslow. Seisdon may mean 'Saxon hill', with reference not to the presence of English among Welsh (as in Pensax, see Chapter 4), but to the presence of some Saxons in a predominantly Anglian community. The village of Seisdon, which lies six miles south-west of Wolverhampton, is overlooked by a small hill, which was presumably the meeting-place. There is a junction of several parishes on the other side of the hill from the village. Cuttlestone means 'Cuthwulf's stone', and the name survives in Cuttlestone Bridge, one mile south-west of Penkridge. This is not on a parish boundary, though it may be at a junction of township boundaries; it is typical in other ways, as there is no settlement there and it lies at a junction of roads and waterways. Offlow ('Offa's tumulus') has been discussed in Chapter 6. The hill lies on the north boundary of Shenstone, with Watling Street a short distance to the south. Pirehill (possibly 'look-out hill') is a small hill two miles south-south-west of Stone, of similar size to the hill at Seisdon, but a fairly commanding eminence in thinly settled, marshy land. A parish boundary touches the west side of the hill, but the site looks atypical as regards access, as there are only minor roads and lanes in this patch of moorland south of the River Trent. Totmonslow ('Tātmonn's tumulus') is a hamlet in Draycott in the Moors, two miles south-west of Cheadle. This is another high spot in thinly settled moorland.

The Shropshire and Herefordshire hundreds are smaller than the Staffordshire ones, so too numerous to list here, but some examples may be cited from each county. One of the Herefordshire units has the unusual name of Wolphy, earlier *Wulfheie*, 'enclosure in which wolves are caught'. The name is lost, but there is a hamlet called The Hundred at the junction of the parishes of Eye, Middleton on the Hill and Kimbolton, north-east of Leominster, which is probably the meeting-place. Grimsworth Hundred, which lay between the rivers Lugg and Wye north-west of Hereford, is believed to preserve an old name of Credenhill hill-fort. The name (earlier *Grimeswrosen*) means 'the knot of Grim', and is one of the names discussed in Chapter 6 in which the god Woden is associated with ancient earthworks. Broxash Hundred is in the north-east of Herefordshire, east of the Lugg, and the name ('Brocc's ash tree') survives in Broxash Wood on the boundary of Little Cowarne and Ullingswick parishes. There was another ash-tree marking the meeting-place of the Domesday Book Hundred of *Bremesesce* ('Brēme's ash tree'), and this name survives in Bromsash, a hamlet at a cross-roads on the boundary of Upton, Weston and Linton parishes, three miles east of Ross, though the hundred was later merged in the Hundred of Greytree ('grey tree' or 'Grǣga's tree'). Webtree Hundred ('Webba's tree') met where the hamlet of Webtree now stands, at the junction of Clehonger, Haywood and Allensmore parishes, three miles south-west of Hereford. Trees are particularly common in the Herefordshire hundred-names, but a tumulus was used for the marker of Wormelow Hundred, which met at Wormelow Tump, six miles south-south-west of Hereford. This lies at a junction of three parishes and a convergence of six roads, and is a good example of the type of site favoured. Although it is first mentioned in Domesday Book it is difficult to imagine a Norman administration choosing such a place, so it is probably much more ancient. Wormelow is not one of the 'dragon' names discussed in Chapter 6; Worm is here the ancient Welsh name of the stream, Worm Brook, which rises a short distance to the north of the hamlet.

Of the names of the fourteen modern hundreds of Shropshire, four may

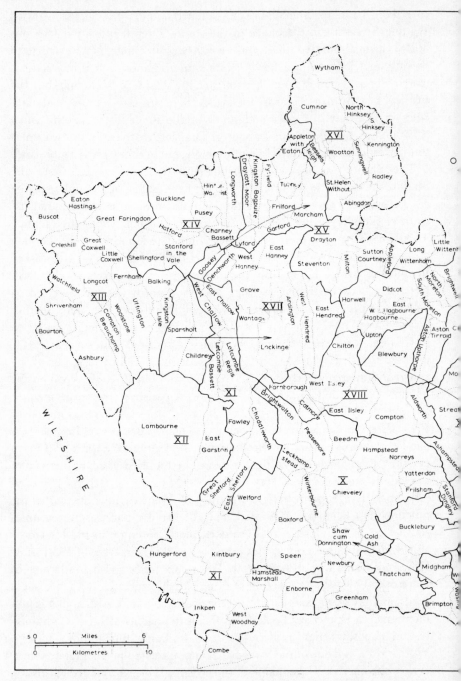

Fig. 16 Index-map to the parishes and hundreds of Berkshire (from Gelling 1974c, by permission of the English Place-Name Society)

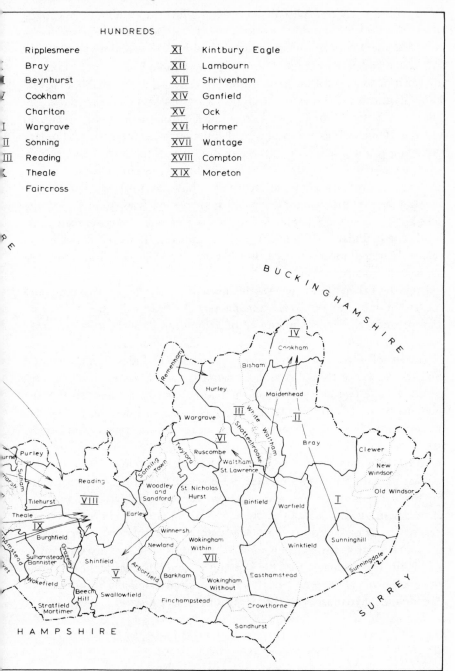

HUNDREDS

Ripplesmere		XI	Kintbury Eagle
Bray		XII	Lambourn
Beynhurst		XIII	Shrivenham
Cookham		XIV	Ganfield
Charlton		XV	Ock
Wargrave	I	XVI	Hormer
Sonning	II	XVII	Wantage
Reading	III	XVIII	Compton
Theale		XIX	Moreton
Faircross			

be instanced as giving especially interesting information about the meeting-places. Pimhill Hundred lies north of the River Severn. The name is not recorded in Domesday, where a unit roughly corresponding to the later Pimhill is called Baschurch Hundred; but although the name does not appear in records until the early thirteenth century, it is probable that Pim Hill ('Pymma's hill') was the meeting-place from a much earlier date. The hill is in Preston Gubbals parish, five miles south-south-west of Wem, an isolated eminence just south of a road-junction, with the parish boundary diverging to include it. Brimstree Hundred lies in the east of the county, and the name ('Bryni's tree') survives in Brimstree Hill, a mile south of Shifnal. The site is a low eminence in what was probably heath-land. Purslow and Munslow Hundreds are both named from tumuli, and the sites are discussed in Chapter 6. Purslow is a hamlet at a cross-roads, just inside the boundary of Clunbury parish. Munslow, however, is not now a typical Hundred meeting-place, as it has developed into a village and given name to a modern parish.

Even in urban areas, where the ancient landscape is obscured and modern administrative arrangements may be drastically different from ancient ones, the approximate site of a hundred or wapentake meeting-place can sometimes be identified by place-name evidence. The Middlesex Hundred of Ossulstone, for instance, which includes Willesden and Fulham in its western part and Westminster and Stepney in its eastern, seems to have met at a spot about half way down Park Lane, on the east side just beyond South Street. A map of 1614 marks a field-name *Osolston* at that point. The name, 'Ōswulf's stone', is of the same type as Cuttlestone STF.

Since meeting-places are often on boundaries, the evidence which enables us to locate a hundred meeting-place and to provide an etymology for the name is sometimes gleaned from charter boundaries of the type discussed in the first half of this chapter. Brixton Hundred in Surrey is one instance. The name means 'Brihtsige's stone', and there is a reference to the actual stone as the starting-point of an Old English boundary survey of Lambeth. It is probable that the 'Ōswulf's stone' of Ossulstone Hundred and the 'Brihtsige's stone' of Brixton Hundred originally stood in 'no-man's-land', like most of the other meeting-places discussed above.

Chapter 9

Scandinavian and French Place-Names

A great many place-names in the north and east of England are in the language spoken by the Vikings, whose raids and invasions disrupted English history in the ninth–eleventh centuries. This language is known to modern scholars as Old Norse. The Vikings who came to Britain were from two Scandinavian countries, Denmark and Norway, where different dialects of the Old Norse tongue were spoken. This means that there are some differences between the place-name-forming vocabulary of the Norwegian settlers in the Orkneys, Man, the Scottish Isles and north-west England, and that used by the Danes in the part of England which became known as the Danelaw (see Fig. 17). One important difference is that the word *thorp* is not used in Norwegian names.

The vocabulary of Old Norse is in many respects similar to that of Old English, and because of this it is not always possible to say with certainty whether a name is Norse, or is an older English name which has been slightly altered by Scandinavian pronunciation. A few examples will illustrate this. Nunburnholme YOE was earlier *Brunum* or *Brunnum* (*Nun-* is a late addition, referring to the Benedictine Nunnery there). This is generally explained as Old Scandinavian (*i*) *brunnum* 'at the streams', from the dative plural of *brunnr*, the Norse word which corresponds to Old English *burna*, modern *burn*. The etymology is probably sound, but a devil's advocate could make out a case for the name being a much older one, derived from an Old English dative plural, *burnum*, from *burna*, and later adjusted by Scandinavian speech. Lythe YON could be from Old Norse *líth* 'slope' or from Old English *hlith*, with the same meaning. Sneith YOW is, as it stands, from Old Norse *sneith* 'slice' (thought to refer in this instance to land cut off by the River Aire), but it could be a Scandinavian adaptation of a name from Old English *snǣd*, a related word used in a similar manner in English place-names. Many more examples of this

kind could be cited. Sometimes the early spellings make it probable that
the name was Old English, although the modern form is Scandinavianized.
A number of names beginning with Sk-, like Skeckling YOE, Skelbrooke,
Skellow, Skibeden, Skirlaugh YOW, have early spellings in *Sch-*, which
suggests that they are English names in which the initial sound would have
developed to *Sh-* if it had not been affected by Scandinavian speech, and
some names in Stain- (e.g. Stainburn, Stainforth YOW) have Domesday
Book spellings in *Stan-*, which suggest that the first element is Old
English *stān* 'stone', replaced by the cognate Scandinavian *steinn*.

Although there are some names of apparently Scandinavian form which
could be Old English in origin, there are many others which must be Old
Norse because they contain words which have no English cognate. These
include names like Wasdale WML and Watendlath CMB, containing *vatn*
'lake', Forcett and Fossdale YON containing *fors* 'waterfall', and many
names containing *lundr* 'grove', and *thveit* 'clearing, meadow'. Others,
such as Howsham YOE (earlier *Husum*) 'at the houses', can safely be considered Scandinavian because, although there is a corresponding Old
English word, it is hardly ever used in place-names outside the areas of
Scandinavian settlement. Many Old Norse personal names used in place-
names cannot be adaptations of Old English personal names. The standard
Scandinavian word for a settlement, *bý*, which becomes -by in place-
names, has no English equivalent, and offers little difficulty as regards
identification, though there are a few instances, mostly on the fringes of the
Danelaw, in which a name in -by can be shown to be an adaptation of an
earlier English name in -bury. Rugby WAR is *Rocheberie* in Domesday
Book, and Badby NTP is *Baddan byrig* in an Anglo-Saxon charter. No one
has suggested that this origin is plausible for a significant number of names
in -*by* inside the areas of Danish and Norwegian settlement, but the status
of the numerous names in -thorp(e) in the Danelaw has been questioned
recently (Lund 1975, 1976), on the grounds that many of them could be
adaptations of names containing the Old English equivalent, *throp*. This
suggestion, which is considered more fully below, is unsound, but the
ambiguous linguistic origin of many names in the north and east of
England does need to be borne in mind when the historical significance of
Scandinavian place-names in England is under consideration. It is possible
that the number of certain Scandinavian names has been somewhat over-
estimated, but, when all possible adjustments have been made, the body of
Scandinavian material will remain considerable, and the historical bearing
of this material is a question of great importance for the history of a large
part of England. The modification of earlier English names by Scandinavian speech implies Scandinavian presence in the neighbourhood, so that

Legend:

o   Burhs of the Burghal Hidage
□   Burhs of Edward & Aethelflæd
▲   Danish boroughs
▦   Areas of strong Danish settlement
▨   "   "   "   Norwegian settlement
–·–·–   Alfred/Guthrum boundary

fig. 17   The Scandinavian settlement (from H. R. Loyn, *Anglo-Saxon England and the Norman Conquest,* by permission of Longman)

even if some names hitherto accounted new formations of the Viking
period are re-classified as Scandinavianized English ones, they still have
to be taken into account in any attempt to calculate the density of Viking
settlement. Modification of English names by Scandinavian pronunciation
implies a Scandinavian local presence. The effects of Norman French
pronunciation (see Chapter 1), on the other hand, are to be interpreted

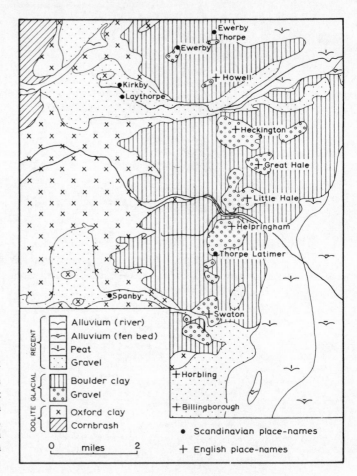

Fig. 18 Geology
and settlements
in south-east
Kesteven (from
Cameron 1965,
by permission
of Nottingham
University)

partly in terms of a bureaucratic administration, and do not imply the
presence of French-speaking people in the countryside to anything like the
same extent. It is noteworthy, also, that French influence on field-names is
very slight, while Scandinavian influence on field-names is extensive in
some areas.

There is a large measure of disagreement among scholars concerning the
density of the Viking settlement. This is a question which generates a

certain amount of acrimony, and in this it is somewhat akin to the question discussed in Chapter 4, that of the density of the Anglo-Saxon settlement. Discussion about Viking settlers has centred more on the late ninth-century events in the Danelaw than on the Norwegian colonies in the north-west. A great deal of ink has been expended on the question of how many Danes settled in the Danelaw, and the arguments deployed by the protagonists are complicated; but the approximate state of the parties can be explained quite briefly. A more detailed account of the dispute, and a full bibliography, can be found in Fellows Jensen 1975.

The historical events which led to the settlements began with an invasion of England in AD 865 by a Danish army which was more coherent than the bands of Viking raiders which had plagued the British Isles and western Europe for many years. This army remained in the country,

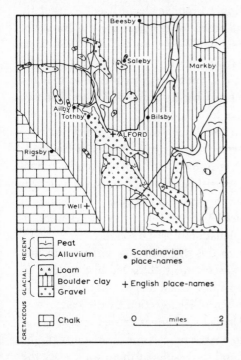

Fig. 19 Geology and settlements around Alford LIN (from Cameron 1965, by permission of Nottingham University)

camping in winter and raiding in summer. There were subsequent invasions in 878 and 892. The invasion of 865 led to a period of political confusion, culminating in the elimination or partition of all the English kingdoms except Wessex, of which King Alfred became ruler in AD 871. King Alfred kept Wessex intact, but his peace with the Danish King Guthrum in 886 was based on a partition of Midland England which had as its boundary the line of the River Thames, then that of the River Lea, then a line from the source of the Lea to Bedford, then the River Ouse, then Watling Street (see Fig. 17). After much fighting in the first half of the tenth century King Alfred's successors won the political control of the areas ceded to King Guthrum, but a large part of eastern England continued to be known as the Danelaw into the post-Conquest period, because the customary law observed in the shire courts of this region had acquired a strong individuality from the Danish influences which had once prevailed there. The English re-conquest of the Danelaw was not accompanied by any expulsion of Danish settlers. The Danelaw comprised four main regions: Northumbria; the shires dependent on the Five Boroughs of Lincoln, Nottingham, Derby, Leicester and Stamford; East Anglia; and the south-eastern Midlands.

The historical sources from which our knowledge of these events is derived, particularly the Anglo-Saxon Chronicle, have been accused by Professor Peter Sawyer (Sawyer 1958, 1962) of exaggerating the gravity of the Viking invasion, and giving unreal figures for the size of Viking fleets and armies. Sir Frank Stenton (1943, p. 241n. 1) stated firmly that the armies should be reckoned in thousands, but Sawyer's conclusion that the largest Danish armies in the ninth century hardly numbered more than two or three hundred men appears to have found general acceptance. The men of the army of 865 are known from the Anglo-Saxon Chronicle to have settled, when they grew weary of army life, in three regions of England: in Yorkshire in 876, in eastern Mercia in 877, and in East Anglia in 879. When historians believed that there were thousands of men in each army it did not appear entirely unreasonable to ascribe the Norse place-names of eastern England mainly to these retired Vikings, but if the armies were, in fact, much smaller, then another explanation must be sought.

Professor Sawyer's initial answer to this dilemma was virtually to discount the place-names as evidence of settlement. This led him to take up a position which was not tenable, and from which he has since retreated to some extent. The need to reply to his initial rejection of the connection between Danish place-names and Danish settlement caused specialists in Scandinavian place-name studies to make intensive examinations of the Norse place-names of the Danelaw, and the results of these studies are the main concern of the present chapter.

It seems likely that there will always be historians who do not believe that the appearance of a large number of place-names in a new language is evidence of a large-scale settlement by the speakers of the new language. Scholars whose main field of study is place-names find this intellectual position impossible to understand, but it is not a subject on which argument brings the disputants closer together. It continues to be argued in some quarters that both the English and the later Danish place-names of England could be due to the power and prestige of a small aristocracy, who were not much engaged in farming. I believe this to be impossible, but readers must decide for themselves whether they regard it as credible. Whatever stance is taken about the general principle, it is clearly desirable that the nature and probable number of the Norse place-names, and their

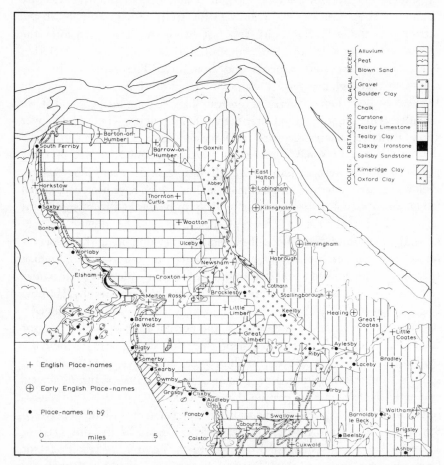

Fig. 20   Geology and settlements in north-east Lindsey (from Cameron 1965, by permission of Nottingham University)

relationship to the English ones in the same areas, should be studied with great care, and much progress has been made with this task in the last ten years.

The numerous wholly or partly Scandinavian settlement-names of eastern England can be divided into three main categories: names in -by,

names in -thorp, and those in which English *tūn* is combined with a Norse
personal name. In addition to these three main categories, each of which
has been the subject of a special study by Professor Kenneth Cameron,
account must be taken of the (relatively few) village-names from Scandinavian topographical terms, and of those names which, although
certainly or probably English in origin, have been drastically altered by
Scandinavian pronunciation. Professor Cameron's Inaugural Lecture
(Cameron 1965) was devoted mainly to the study of names in -by in the
territory of the Five Boroughs, this last being the term used after the
Danish settlements for the areas administered from the towns of Derby,
Nottingham, Leicester, Lincoln and Stamford. The statistics for -by
names in this region given by Cameron (p. 7) are impressive: 'Here, in
Domesday Book alone, there are no less than 303 names . . . and if we
included others first recorded later than 1086, the figure would rise to over
360'. Of the 303 names recorded in Domesday Book, Cameron considered
that 207 had a personal name as first element, and that 192 of these
personal names were Scandinavian. (It has recently been suggested in
Fellows Jensen 1976 that some of the -by names which have been considered
to contain personal names are equally likely to be derived from significant
terms.) Many of the names show typical Scandinavian grammatical inflections, the most impressive piece of evidence of this kind being the preservation of the voiceless *s* of some genitive singular inflections, where English
speech would have had a voiced *z* sound. It is remarkable that some names
retain this Scandinavian characteristic today: examples are Braceby, Haceby,
Laceby, Rauceby, Ulceby and Winceby, which would all have developed a
-*z*- sound if they had been treated in the normal English way. Professor
Cameron accepts Sawyer's statement that the Viking army should be
reckoned in hundreds and not in thousands, and agrees that the retired
soldiers cannot have founded or re-named all these villages, but he rejects
emphatically Sawyer's suggestion that the great majority of Scandinavian
settlement-names represent expansion and extension of settlement between
877 and *c.* 1050 by the Norse-speaking descendants of the tiny class of
retired Vikings who established themselves in the area in 877. Professor
Cameron says (pp. 10–11): 'Such a hypothesis must be wrong, for
it involves the assumption of a rate of growth of settlement sites, which
is surely impossible, in such a period as this, from an economic point of
view alone.'

It should be noted that the belief in a great expansion in the number of
settlements after 877 is no longer part of Professor Sawyer's approach to
this period. He has in recent years shown a disposition towards the belief
discussed in Chapter 8 that most features of the English countryside,

including settlements, show continuity from pre-English times. His recent statement (Sawyer 1974, p. 108) that 'the rural resources of England were almost as fully exploited in the seventh and eighth centuries as they were in the eleventh' is presumably to be taken as cancelling his earlier statement (Sawyer 1962, p. 155) that in the period between the taking of English land by the Danish army and the compilation of Domesday Book, i.e. between 876 and 1086, 'many new settlements were formed and some of these were given Scandinavian names'. It is only fair to add that my own views on this matter of how many villages and hamlets represent new foundations of the middle and late Anglo-Saxon period, and how many have a continuous history going back to Roman or pre-Roman times, have, like Professor Sawyer's, changed drastically since *c.* 1960. Belief in continuity has become much more prevalent, and has affected most historical thinking. Probably few of us would wish to be held to an opinion on this matter expressed earlier than 1965, but Sawyer's statement in 1962, and Professor Cameron's rejection of it in 1965, serve to bring out the question which is crucial to the study of Scandinavian settlement-names in England: how many of them refer to new settlements, and how many to ancient villages re-named by Norse speakers?

At the date of Professor Cameron's lecture in 1965 it had for some time been recognized that some areas of eastern England where Norse settlement-names occurred in dense clusters were not the areas where the best farming land was to be found. Professor Sawyer used this fact, very reasonably, in support of his claim that the Norse place-names did not denote the settlements of the members of a victorious Viking army (Sawyer 1962, pp. 164–5). Professor Cameron's lecture developed this theme of the inferior nature of the land in areas where Norse names are densest, and placed the whole study on a much sounder and more precise footing with a far-reaching and detailed comparison of the soils which underly Danish- and English-named villages. Professor Cameron's findings are here very briefly summarized, and illustrated by three of his maps (Figs. 18–20).

The method perfected by Professor Cameron is that of relating the place-names to the drift geology of a region. It is argued that in most regions there will be areas which are, for geological reasons, particularly desirable as the sites of villages, other areas which are acceptable but less inviting, and areas which are definitely not attractive for this purpose. Villages occupying the most desirable sites are probably the oldest in the region, and those on the less attractive ground are probably later establishments. If it can be shown that some types of place-name consistently refer to villages with better sites, and other types to villages on less good sites, this will provide a reasonable basis for estimating the relative chronology of the place-names.

The simplest situation is that of the region in which there is a great deal of clay, with patches of sand and gravel dotted about in it, and belts of alluvium along the streams. The alluvium is seldom encroached upon (except by villages at river-crossings), and in such a region the preferred sites for villages will be on the islands of sand and gravel rather than on the clay. These islands are slightly raised above the surrounding clay, and they offer a warmer, drier foundation for a village, which serves as a comfortable base for the cultivation of the heavy clay soil. Very large areas of sand and gravel are not favoured, as the soil tends to be thin and poor, and the best situation is the central one on a medium-sized gravel island. This geological situation can be seen in Figs. 18 and 19, Professor Cameron's maps of Geology and Settlements in south-east Kesteven and around Alford LIN. A more complex situation is illustrated by Fig. 20, Professor Cameron's map of Geology and Settlements in north-east Lindsey. Here the most desirable land for settlement is the relatively narrow band of clay which lies at the foot of the eastern escarpment of the Lincolnshire Wolds. This is different from the clay of the regions shown in Figs. 18 and 19, because it is made lighter by chalk washed down from the Wolds; and the soil is more fertile than that of the other main belt of settlements, the thin strip of gravel on the western side of the Wolds.

The English and Danish place-names in these three regions bear a remarkably consistent relationship to the drift geology. There is no doubt that English-named villages have the most desirable sites, the Danish-named villages being (as in Fig. 18) dotted about among them on smaller gravel islands, at the edge of the larger islands, or out on the clay, or (as in Fig. 20) situated on a belt of less desirable land.

In Fig. 18 the reluctance to use clay or alluvium for village-sites is very clearly illustrated. The glacial gravel seems to be the most favoured soil. The medium sized islands of this are occupied by Heckington, Great and Little Hale, Helpringham and Swaton, all English names. The gravel which borders the alluvium in the south of the map has Horbling and Billingborough, both English names of early type, situated upon it. Helpringham, an *-ingahām* name (see Chapter 5) appears to have the best site of all, with the Scandinavian Thorpe Latimer lying on the very edge of its island. The Scandinavian names Ewerby and Ewerby Thorpe are related to tiny patches of gravel in the boulder clay. The patches of gravel which occur in the Oxford clay are not much settled, but the three Scandinavian-named villages of Spanby, Kirkby and Laythorpe lie on these. Kirkby requires special consideration (see below). The only English-named village on this map which is not comfortably on gravel is Howell, and here the name, which has as second element *welle* 'spring', suggests that the site had a special attraction in the form of water-supply.

Fig. 19 shows a region in which one of the two English-named villages, Alford, occupies the best site, at the centre of a gravel island. The other English-named settlement, Well, is (like Howell on Fig. 18) obviously sited to take advantage of a spring. Of the more numerous Danish-named villages, Ailby and Tothby are on the northern tip of the gravel island to which Alford is central, Saleby is related to a very small island, and Beesby, Bilsby and Markby are out on the boulder clay. Rigsby, at the junction of chalk and boulder clay, is similarly situated to Well, but lacks the benefit of a spring.

When such regions as these are studied on the Ordnance Survey maps or on the ground, it is noticeable that the English-named villages, which have on the whole the best sites, are often larger than the Danish-named villages. Alford (O.S. one-inch 105, G.R. 455760) is much larger than the surrounding places with names in -by and -thorpe; and there are regions of the east Midlands where the English-named villages, on their larger patches of sand and gravel, look plump and prosperous compared with the Danish-named villages and hamlets, which have on the whole remained small unless some special factor of modern history has operated in their favour. This can be observed in the country east of Leicester.

Fig. 20 shows the northern end of the Lincolnshire Wolds, and the belts of settlements on either side of the high ground. Down the western escarpment (which, as explained above, is the less attractive side) runs a remarkable series of names in -by; thirteen are shown on this map, and the series continues for a few miles to the south. This tendency for names in -by to occur in lines or clusters is noteworthy; cf. Cameron 1965 (p. 12): 'There are few really isolated names in *-bȳ*'. This phenomenon suggests that there was a colony of Danish-speaking people occupying neighbouring villages, and the Danish place-names would arise in the speech of this community. The -by names on the western escarpment of the Lincolnshire Wolds are interspersed with a few English names—Horkstow, Elsham, Melton and Caistor being the ones shown on Fig. 20. Horkstow is the site of a Roman villa, and the land here may have remained in cultivation and so become an English farm. Elsham (a name in *-hām*, see Chapter 5) has a better position than most along the escarpment, being in a sheltered coomb at a point where the slope is much gentler than elsewhere and the stretch of cultivable land broader. Professor Cameron did not comment on Melton, but it can be seen from his map that Melton and the English-named villages Croxton and Kirmington to the north-east occupy valleys in the Wolds (Kirmington, south-east of Croxton, is accorded a symbol but not named on the map). Caistor is the site of a Roman town. It seems fair to assume that apart from the sites of Horkstow, Elsham, Melton and Caistor, the western escarpment was settled by Danes, using Danish place-names. Many of the -by villages in this series have remained small, especially the ones south of Elsham. On the east side of the Wolds the English-named villages predominate heavily, and may be seen from the map to have apparently had the first choice of site.

His brilliant study of names in *bý* in the territory of the Five Boroughs led Professor Cameron to the conclusion that while these place-names were not the settlements of the men of the victorious Danish army which took political control of the region in 877, they were due to an immigration of Danish-speaking people which took place as a result of the Danish conquest. There are too many Danish settlement-names to be either the result of settlement by the retired Viking soldiers, or the result of expansion from a few settlements made by such men. The founders of these villages came as colonists, developing virgin land and founding new settlements, mostly on sites which would not have been their first choice if the choice had been entirely open. Most of this colonizing immigration may be assumed to have taken place during the space of two generations in which Watling Street was the boundary between Danish and English England.

The only point in this analysis which seems to me to need slight qualification is the use of the term 'virgin' for the land settled by the Danes. It is possible that 'disused' would be better. As mentioned in Chapter 8 there are a number of regions where intense Roman occupation was succeeded by forest; and some of the 'second-best' land where the Danish-named villages lie may have been under cultivation in a number of earlier periods. Professor Cameron's thesis is not damaged by the fact that Roman and even very early Anglo-Saxon remains sometimes occur in the same area as Danish place-names.

The second of Professor Cameron's studies (Cameron 1970) was an examination of place-names in *thorp* in the territory of the Five Boroughs. He concluded that as a group the names in *thorp* denote settlements of lesser importance than those whose names are derived from *bý*, and that as a whole they seem to belong to a later stratum of name-giving than the *býs*, pointing to a time when greater integration had taken place between Dane and English. The evidence of first elements, including personal names, in compound names in *thorp* points to this last conclusion. Not all names in *thorp* are compounds, as the term (unlike *bý*) could be used alone as a place-name, but where there is a first element it is quite frequently an English, not a Danish, word or personal name, though there are, of course, a good number of full Danish compounds. It seems clear that *thorp* was used in the territory of the Five Boroughs, as it was in Denmark, in the sense 'a secondary settlement, an outlying farmstead or a small hamlet dependent on a larger place'.

The treatment of *thorp* as a specifically Danish place-name element has recently been criticized on the grounds that in many instances *thorp* may be a modification of the corresponding Old English word *throp*. This criticism cannot be evaluated until we have a detailed study of the English place-name element. The best study available in print is that in Smith 1956 (Part II, pp. 214–16). This discussion was supplemented by one of the distribution maps supplied with Smith 1956, which purports to show all English place-names derived from *throp* known in 1956. Neither the map nor the discussion should be treated as definitive statements; both were compiled in some haste as part of a much bigger undertaking, and the information is now, of course, twenty years out of date. Professor Smith's map and his discussion of the distribution of English names in *throp* requires some revision. His statement, for instance, that the element is concentrated in Wiltshire, Gloucestershire, Buckinghamshire, Berkshire and Oxfordshire, and is found occasionally also in the adjacent counties of Essex, Bedfordshire, Warwickshire, Staffordshire, Worcestershire, Somerset, Dorset, Hampshire and Surrey, only partly accords with the information now available. Berkshire has four surviving names in *throp* and two lost ones, so it is not clear why it should be included, along with Gloucestershire, which has twenty-five examples, in the group of counties where the element is concentrated; nor why Surrey and Hampshire should both be listed as counties where *throp* occurs occasionally, when Surrey has only two instances (one lost), and Hampshire has eight.

These sample statistics will serve to give an impression of the sort of frequency with which *throp* occurs in districts outside the Danelaw. In the territory of the Five Boroughs, which comprises the counties of Derbyshire, Nottinghamshire, Leicestershire and Lincolnshire, Professor Cameron found that 109 *thorps* were recorded in the Domesday Survey or earlier. By the same criterion of inclusion in Domesday Book the numbers of English names in *throp* available for comparison would be very small; for example, only three of the twenty-five Gloucestershire examples are recorded by 1086. The element is used in parts of the Danelaw with a frequency of an entirely different order from that of the English names in *throp* in wholly English counties.

The suggestion that many *thorp* names in the Danelaw are really earlier English names in *throp* arises partly from a feature of the distribution pattern of *throp* as shown on Professor Smith's map. This shows a concentration of *throp* names in north Oxfordshire, north Buckinghamshire, east Warwickshire and south-west Northamptonshire. The density of the group is exaggerated by the small scale of the map, and a large-scale distribution map, with all the specimens checked before inclusion, is needed before this phenomenon can be properly studied. There certainly is a concentration of English names in *throp* in the adjoining parts of these four counties, but the numbers involved are not great: ten names in south-west Northamptonshire, six in north Oxfordshire, three in east Warwickshire and five in north Buckinghamshire. The argument in favour of many *thorp* names in the Danelaw being Scandinavianized English *throps* is partly based on a claim that this cluster of *throp* names near the English/Danish border can be seen as evidence that the frequency of the English word becomes greater at about the boundary. This means that although we cannot now separate the English and Danish elements in the Danelaw, there may have been many more English names in *throp* east of Watling Street in the tenth century than there were elsewhere in England (Lund 1975). Place-name specialists do not find this convincing. They are prepared to concede that more allowance should have been made for some of the Danelaw names being really earlier English ones, but even if (on the analogy of the numbers in such counties as Oxfordshire and Warwickshire) a maximum of ten names were allowed to fall into this category in each Danelaw county, the residue of the material which is almost certainly Scandinavian would still be impressive.

Another point which would require consideration in any serious study of this problem is the likely date of the English names in *throp*. Professor Smith's discussion in 1956 (p. 216) implied that, at any rate in West Saxon territory, it was an ancient term, which had fallen into disuse before the progress of the settlement westward into Devon and Cornwall. This is only a passing suggestion, based on one aspect of the very patchy distribution of the element, and a more thorough study might lead to a different conclusion. The use of *throp* in Berkshire, where none of the six names is recorded by 1086, could be held to be consistent with its being used in late place-names rather than early ones. The argument is a sterile one as long as it is based on information taken from Smith 1956. If a serious case is to be made out for the widespread use of English *throp* in place-names in eastern England before the date of the Danish settlements, this needs as a basis a fresh study of the use of the element outside the Danelaw.

Professor Cameron's third study of Scandinavian names in the territory of the Five Boroughs (Cameron 1971) was concerned with the large class of names known as Grimston-hybrids. This term is applied to those place-names in which the first element is a Scandinavian personal name and the second element is Old English *tūn* 'farmstead, village'. It is unfortunate, for reasons discussed below, that Grimston should have been chosen as the type-name for this class, but there is little hope of establishing another term for them now. If an attempt were to be made, Barkston- or Foston- or Flixton-hybrids would be possible alternatives, since these names occur several times; though neither these nor any other comparable compound approaches Grimston in frequency. Probably the class must continue to be called Grimston-hybrids, though this now needs to be prefaced by 'so-called', which gives any reference to them an awkward, pedantic, air.

Old English and Old Norse personal names do not overlap a great deal, so there is not much difficulty in classifying the personal names considered to occur in these hybrids as belonging to one or the other language; such names as *Tófi* (in Towton YOW), *Flík* or *Flikkr* (in several Flixtons), *Gamall* (in two Gamstons NTT) are certainly Norse. There is, however, a possibility of misunderstanding concerning late Old English or post-Conquest place-names which have as first element a Continental personal name of ultimate Scandinavian origin, and this has given rise to the erroneous inclusion of some bogus Grimston-hybrids lying well outside the areas of Scandinavian settlement on the Ordnance Survey Map, *Britain before the Norman Conquest*, issued in 1973. This map marks all Grimston-hybrids with a small red dot, and it is surprising to see a small number of these dots straggling across western England, as far as Devon and Herefordshire. One of the stragglers turns out, on investigation, to be the Berkshire name East Garston (earlier *Esgareston*), discussed in Chapter 7. It is quite true that Esgar, who was a court official of Edward the Confessor, bore a name of ultimate Scandinavian origin, as did many Continental people at this date; but he was neither a Viking nor a settler, and his presence in England in the mid eleventh century had nothing to do with the Scandinavian invasions and settlements of the ninth and tenth centuries. The other 'Grimston-hybrids' shown on the map which are well outside the areas of Scandinavian settlement are Arkston HRE, Grimstone DOR, Spaxton SOM, Swainston IOW, Thorverton DEV, Thruxton HMP and HRE, and Thurloxton SOM. Thorverton DEV is a doubtful starter; the English Place-Name Society's volume gave a personal name *Thurferth* as first element, but Ekwall 1935 gives the rather more satisfactory etymology 'thorn-ford *tūn*'. Of the other names, the only one to be recorded in Domesday Book is Spaxton SOM, which means 'Spak's estate'. None of the others is recorded before the late twelfth century. With the exception of Thorverton, which is not certain to contain a personal name, and possibly Spaxton, these names should be placed in the same category as East Garston; that of late manorial names in *tūn*, formed at a time when the stock of personal names in use among the upper classes was the mixture, found in Domesday Book, of Old English, Scandinavian and Old German items, with a very small number of Celtic, Latin and Scriptural ones (Feilitzen 1937, pp. 13–31). They have no relevance to the study of Viking settlement in Britain. It is well known that in the west and south-west of England the formation of *-tūn* names with the Christian name or surname of an estate-owner went on well into the post-Conquest period. Forston in Charminster DOR, for instance, earlier *Forsardeston*, is from the family-name of William *Forsard*, who was the owner in 1285. Egliston DOR means 'Eggelin's estate', and Eggelin's widow was in possession in 1202. Walter-stone HRE is named from Walter de Lacy, who held the manor soon after the Norman Conquest. The occasional *tūn* name in southern and western England which has a Norse personal name as first element is likely to belong to this sort of context. Spaxton SOM, which is a Domesday estate, may, however, be earlier than the others. The personal name is not a common one in eleventh century England, as are *Swein* in Swainston, *Thorkell* in Thruxton, *Grímr* in Grimstone, and *Arnkell* in Arkston. A stray Viking from south Wales might conceivably have established himself at Spaxton.

In addition to these erroneous symbols for Grimston-hybrids, *Britain before the Norman Conquest* marks a few bogus names in *bý* outside the regions of Scandinavian settlement. The most shocking is Fairby, in the middle of Devon. This is a straightforward mistake, not a misunderstanding such as the one discussed in the last paragraph. There are six place-names in Devon—Brambleby, Fairby, Grammerby, Huccaby, Treby and Veraby—which have as final element Old English *byge* 'bend'. Mercifully only one of them has been accorded a large red dot on the map. Another mistake is the large red dot south-west of Coventry WAR. This represents Kirby Corner, a group of houses lining a road-junction; the name does not refer to an ancient settlement, and it has no known history beyond its appearance on the first edition one-inch map. Evidence for Viking activity is shown in red on *Britain before the Norman Conquest*, which causes it to stand out with particular clarity. It is a great pity that the red symbols which are outside the area where they might be expected were not care-fully checked before the map was published.

The digression about the bogus Grimston-hybrids on *Britain before the Norman Conquest* leads into one of the points which needs discussion in a consideration of the genuine names of this type. Historians seeking to discount the evidence for Scandinavian settlement in the Danelaw have pointed to the late manorial type of *tūn* name, which occurs sporadically in all regions, and have suggested that this may be the explanation of the

Grimston-hybrids. By this interpretation, the Flík of Flixton would be a king's thegn, of comparable standing to the Wulfríc of Woolstone BRK (see Chapter 7), in no sense a settler, and only incidentally a farmer. It is argued that the large number of Norse personal names in compounds with *tūn* inside the Danelaw only shows that the upper classes in the Danelaw favoured Norse personal names, not that there was a mass of farming settlers.

It is true that after the Danish Conquests some Englishmen bore Scandinavian personal names. But here, as in the argument about names in *thorp*, the answer to the proposal outlined in the last paragraph lies in the numbers of the relevant place-names. There are too many Grimston-hybrids in the Danelaw for them all to have a similar origin to Woolstone BRK and Aughton WLT. Counting only names recorded in Domesday Book, Professor Cameron (1971, p. 149) finds at least fifty-seven Grimston-hybrids in the counties of Derbyshire, Nottinghamshire, Leicestershire and Lincolnshire which make up the region of his study. Dr Gillian Fellows Jensen (1972, pp. 122–30), also using only names recorded in Domesday, counts thirty-seven Grimston-hybrids in Yorkshire, excluding six examples of Grimston itself (see below). Since these place-names contain Scandinavian personal names which were not current in England before the Danish wars, and since they are all recorded in 1086, the period in which they could have been coined is from *c.* 880 to *c.* 1080. If a significant proportion of them are to be considered comparable with the Woolstone type, which is known to be of mid-tenth-century date, then they should occur in numbers comparable to those in which the Woolstone type occurs in counties outside the Danelaw.

The English county which has been surveyed most recently is Berkshire, and the numbers of possible late manorial names in *tūn* in that county may be compared with the figures in the last paragraph. There are about twelve Berkshire names which consist of a personal name and *-ingtūn* (for this type of formation see Chapter 7), but these are not relevant to the present discussion, as the *-ingtūn* formula is not likely to have been used in names formed in the tenth century. Berkshire names in which *tūn* is compounded with a personal name number only eight, of which five appear in Domesday Book. Of these five, Woolstone and Uffington are certainly of mid tenth-century date, and a similar context, after AD 900, seems reasonable for the formation of the others, two of which contain feminine names. It can therefore be stated that this type of name-formation was happening in Berkshire between 900 and 1080, but it was only producing a handful of place-names. In Nottinghamshire, one of the Danelaw counties studied by Professor Cameron, there are nineteen Grimston-hybrids in Domesday

Book, and to give a fair comparison with Berkshire this must be added to the number of Nottinghamshire names which consist of *tūn* with an English personal name, which would nearly double the Nottinghamshire total. The suggestion that many of the Grimston-hybrids can be explained as 'ordinary' manorial names comparable to such names as Woolstone BRK fails to convince because of the much greater numbers in which they occur. It seems necessary to accept that many of them arise from a particular historical situation which did not occur outside the Danelaw.

As with the names in *bý* and *thorp*, the clue to the historical significance of the Grimston-hybrids is to be found in the siting of the settlements concerned. Professor Cameron's study demonstrates that these hybrid names occur intermingled with English-named settlements, and are not well represented in the areas where there are clusters of names in *bý*. His other main conclusion is that the Grimston-hybrids usually share the topographical characteristics of the English-named settlements among which they occur. These observations led him to suggest in 1971 that the Grimston-hybrid names belonged to ancient English settlements taken over and partially re-named by Danes. More recently (Cameron 1976) he has made the specific suggestion that the Danes who took over these English villages may have been the retired Vikings of the army of 865. The villages may have belonged to them in the late manorial manner which is evidenced for villages named from English thegns. This makes excellent sense as regards the general distribution pattern and the individual siting of most of these villages with hybrid names. The greater number of such late manorial names in the Danelaw than in the English counties is explicable as due to the sudden arrival of several hundred new 'manorial' overlords when sections of the army were disbanded. Some of these new Danish overlords were possibly more closely related to the farming life of the communities from which they derived their income than were the king's thegns from whom some ancient settlements were renamed in the English shires. Some men of the Viking armies possibly came from more basic farming stock than the men who made up the court of an English king in the late ninth and early tenth centuries. But some of the Danish over-lords would have administrative duties in the years when the Danelaw was outside English government, and their position in the community may have been comparable to that of the less powerful English thegns. This is the sort of identity which may now be envisaged for such men as the Thorketill of Thurcaston and the Thormóthr of Thurmaston, two settlements which lie to the north-east and north-west of Leicester.

Occasional reference has been made in the preceding paragraphs to Dr Gillian Fellows Jensen's book *Scandinavian Settlement Names in*

Yorkshire. This important study extended to Yorkshire the methods used by Professor Cameron for studying Scandinavian names in the territory of the Five Boroughs, adding some other methods, such as the consideration of Domesday Book taxation assessments, and of later information concerning lost villages. Since 1972 Dr Fellows Jensen has (in discussion) acknowledged the possibility that a few of the 155 names in *thorp* in Yorkshire recorded by 1086 may be adaptations of earlier English names, rather than new Scandinavian coinages. She has also published a paper (Fellows Jensen 1976) in which she explores the possibility that a number of *bý* names in Yorkshire and elsewhere which have been considered to contain Scandinavian personal names are at least as likely to contain Old English or Old Norse appellatives. These subsequent thoughts do not, however, seriously affect the main conclusion she reached in 1972, which was that her work in Yorkshire confirmed the broad outlines of the picture which had emerged from Professor Cameron's studies. She agrees with Professor Cameron that the settlements with hybrid names in which Old English *tūn* is combined with an Old Norse personal name are most likely to represent the taking over of established English settlements by the victorious Danes of the great army, that the majority of names in *bý* and *thorp* represent colonization of land not in use at the time of the Scandinavian settlements, and that the names in *thorp* are as a class later than those in *bý*. Her study brings out more clearly than earlier ones the anomalous nature of the settlements called Grimston.

Most of the so-called Grimston-hybrids in Yorkshire have, like names of this type in the east Midlands, situations comparable to those of the English-named villages among which they lie. In contrast to this general situation, there are in Yorkshire eleven Grimston-hybrids whose situations are demonstrably inferior to those of neighbouring English villages, and five others whose situations have certain disadvantages as compared with those of their neighbours. Of these sixteen names, five are actually called Grimston. Four of these Grimstons are lost villages, and Dr Fellows Jensen notes that Grimston NTT and Grimston SFK are lost villages, and there is a lost *Grimyston* in the parish of Quorndon LEI. It seems unlikely that Vikings named *Grimr* regularly became overlords of less prosperous villages than their fellow Vikings, and Dr Fellows Jensen suggests that in some of these names the use of the term *Grim* is comparable to that noted in English names for prehistoric remains. It is possible that if *Grim* were still in use as a term for the Devil, an appellative **Grimestūn* could be coined for a particularly depressing settlement. As stated earlier, it is unfortunate that this name, because it is so common in eastern England, should have been used in the coining of the term Grimston-hybrid, which is now well established as the accepted term for the whole class of hybrid *tūn* names, the great majority of which have sites and histories quite different from those of the unfortunate Grimstons. *Grímr* was a common personal name, and probably occurs in Grimsby and some other Danelaw names in Grims-. It is only when there is something outstandingly poor about the situation of the place that recourse need be had to the alternative explanation.

Another common Scandinavian name which does not fit into the general pattern is Kirkby or Kirby, 'church village'. This name is often borne by villages with particularly desirable situations, and it is likely that in many instances it replaces an older English, or perhaps Celtic, name. It is possible that *kirkjubý* was an appellative, liable to be applied by Scandinavian speakers to any village with a noteworthy church, so that these names are in a different category from other names in *bý* which in most instances are newly-coined names for new settlements.

The work on Scandinavian settlement-names of Cameron and Fellows Jensen, of which a very brief summary has been given in this chapter, has yielded results which have not yet been fully assimilated by historians. There has been some immediate (and perhaps ill-considered) criticism from historians who had previously committed themselves to a belief that there was no substantial Danish peasant settlement in eastern England. More detached criticism and serious assessment of the historical significance of these findings will doubtless be made in due course. There will also be more studies of this type. The work cannot be completed swiftly, but similar studies are needed for other areas, notably East Anglia, and north-west England where the Norwegian names of slightly later date await consideration.

The particular historical challenge presented by the Scandinavian place-names in England has led to these methods being perfected, but the relevance of these studies may be much wider. It is likely that much interesting information would be brought to light if a similar approach were used to study the relative age of place-names in an area where these are almost entirely in the English language. A limited experiment on these lines has recently been published (Gelling 1974b), and the map from this is reproduced here as Fig. 21.

The area chosen for this small experimental study lies north-east of Coventry WAR, and includes part of the Danelaw, of which Watling Street formed the boundary. The map shows the area surrounding the crossing of the two Roman roads called Watling Street and the Foss Way, some ten miles north-east of Coventry. The drift geology of this area, as shown on the Ordnance Survey geological map sheet 169, somewhat resembles that of the area shown in Fig. 18, having large areas of clay with slightly raised patches of sand and gravel and belts of alluvium along the streams. It is immediately apparent that most of the villages shown on Fig. 21 are sited so as to avoid the clay. There is a similar avoidance of the larger areas of sand and gravel, probably because the soil in the central part of these is poor, but the medium sized sand and gravel patches are very heavily settled and several of the very small ones have a settlement also.

An attempt to establish some general relationship between types of settlement-name and sites of villages led to the following conclusions. First, most of the wholly or partly Scandinavian names (underlined on the map) have either 'second best' sites, like those of Wibtoft and Bittesby, both lying at the edge of the sand and gravel patch on which the English-named villages of Claybrook Magna and Parva are more securely situated, or they are out on the boulder clay like Primethorpe and Ashby. The exceptions are Kirby (Monks Kirby WAR) and Copston, which both have good situations. Kirby fits into the pattern of the other examples of this compound. Monks Kirby is the name of a large parish, and the neighbouring settlement Brockhurst ('brook hill' or 'badger hill') may preserve the earlier English name of the whole area. Copston is a Grimston-hybrid.

Among the English place-names on Fig. 21, the one which has the most demonstrable claim to be early is Higham, one of the names in *hām* discussed in Cox 1973. Otherwise, the 'good' sites are occupied in roughly equal proportions by villages with habitative names in *tūn* (Burton, Bulkington, Ryton, Shilton, Stretton) or *worth* (Frolesworth), and by villages with topographical names, such as Brockhurst, Burbage, Claybrook, Combe, Easenhall, Harborough. Both types of settlement-name are well represented among settlements which were apparently able to make an early choice of sites on sand and gravel spreads. In most instances, this choice would be made long before the coming of the Anglo-Saxons, and most of the English names for these settlements are probably replacements of earlier Celtic names. The Danish names on the map, however, apart from Kirby and Copston, seem more likely to be ninth- or tenth-century coinages for new settlements on less desirable sites, which are not so likely to have been inhabited continuously from prehistoric times.

Perhaps the most interesting point to be brought out by Fig. 21 is that there are distinct categories of English place-names which belong to settlements situated on very small patches of sand or gravel or out on the boulder clay, in situations comparable to those of the typical Danish-named villages. These include some of the 'geographically related' *tūn* names, in particular Aston, probably named from its relationship to Burbage, and Sutton, in the north-east corner of the map, which lies south of Croft. They also include the three names which have *nīwe* ('new') as first element: Newnham Paddox, Newbold and Newton, all in the south-east corner. Coton ('at the cottages') lies out on the boulder-clay in the same area. It seems possible that these settlements represent a later stage of expansion or colonization than that which produced the settlements called Claybrook Parva and Harborough Parva, though these are presumably in some sense secondary to Claybrook and Harborough Magna. If these findings were confirmed by further studies of this kind, the conclusion might be that some of our 'geographically related' names in *tūn* and some names in *nīwe* arise from a process of settlement expansion of comparable date to that of the Danish colonization of areas to the east.

If this sort of study were taken up by local historians, the results might be of great interest, especially if there were co-operation with geologists. It is doubtful whether the Ordnance Survey geological maps are sufficiently detailed to be a wholly adequate base, and the series is in any case not available for the whole country. Even better results might be obtained by correlating settlement-names with the maps published by the Soil Survey of England and Wales.

The final class of place-names which merits attention in this book is the small group which are in the language of the Norman French conquerors of 1066. The smallness of this class of names affords sound evidence for the effect on place-names of the advent of a foreign aristocracy unaccompanied by a body of peasant settlers. The influence of Norman French speech on the pronunciation and spelling of English names was widespread, and some details of this are given in Chapter 1. But the number of new settlement-names coined by French speakers is very small, and there are only a handful of instances in which an older English name is replaced by a French one.

The English Place-Name Society began to give lists of French place-names in Vol. X in its series, this being *The Place-Names of Northampton-shire* which was published in 1933. Not all the names listed are new settlement-names, but the following items have been extracted as probably falling into that category, and as being probably coined by French-speaking people, as opposed to English speakers using words like *assart*, *gullet*, *laund*, which are of French origin but became part of the English language. Taking the counties in the order in which the surveys appeared, the following lists emerge for each county studied since 1933, except Cumberland, for which no list of French names was printed:

NTP: Belsize Fm (in Castor), Delapre Abbey.
SUR: Beamonds Fm (in Chertsey), Beaulieu (in Croydon), Capel, Foyle Fm (in

Oxted), Phoenice Fm (in Walton on Thames).

ESX: Beaumont (replacing English *Fulepet*, 'foul hollow'), Caidge (in South-minster), Cangle Fm (in Halstead Rural), Curry (in Bradwell-juxta-Mare), Pleshey.

WAR: Beaudesert, Beaumont Hill (in Tanworth).

YOE: Bellasize (in Eastrington), Blanch (in Warter, replacing a Norse name *Arras*, 'shielings'), Haltemprice, Ridgmont (in Burstwick), Twyers (in Preston).

HRT: Beaumont Hall (in Redbourn), Beaumont Manor (in Cheshunt), The Prae (in St Michael's, site of the Abbey of St Mary of Pre).

WLT: Devizes.

NTT: Beauvale, Belle Eau Park (in Kirklington), Palis Hall (in Norwell).

MDX: Belsize Park, *Pontefract* or *Pountfreyt* (a lost place in Poplar).

CAM: Portsand Fm in Thorney is named from the adjacent district of Postland LIN, which is French *purceynt*, 'enclosure'. Marmont Priory is a transferred name from Marmande in France.

OXF: Bruern, Rewley Abbey (in Oxford).

DRB: Beauchief, Belper, Champion (in Windley), Malcoff (in Chapel en le Frith).

YOW: Abdy (in Brampton Bierlow), Beaumont (in Erringden), Belmont (in Knaresborough), Fountains Abbey, Margrave (in Reedness), Massey Garth (in Spofforth), Missies (in Laverton), Pontefract, Richmond (in Handsworth), Roach Grange (in Kippax), Roche Abbey, Rougemont (in Harewood), Tilts (in Thorpe in Balne). In addition to these surviving names there were places called *Belasize* and *Malasize* in Bolton by Bowland.

GLO: Miserden (replacing English *Grenehamstede*). There was also a lost *Beaurepair* in Haresfield.

WML: Beacham (in Asby), Bewley Castle (in Morland), Mountjoy (in Kendal).

BRK: Beamy's Castle (in Swallowfield), Bray. Foliejon in Winkfield was earlier *Belestre*.

In addition to occasional settlement-names, most English counties can muster a small group of French field-names, which do not appear to have referred to habitation sites. Berkshire, for instance, had *Beaurepir*, *Bewley*, *Deulacresse*, all in the parish of Clewer, and a district in Theale called Malpas, which appears on the one-inch map, though it is in no sense a settlement-name.

Apart from the very limited number of French settlement-names, the striking feature of the above list is the stereotyped nature of many of the items. Names like Bellasize or Belsize ('beautiful seat'), Beaulieu or Bewley ('beautiful place'), Beaumont ('beautiful hill'), Beaudesert ('beautiful wilderness') are akin to modern house-names; they are deliberate creations of the builders of the castle or manor house, not spontaneous descriptions of the site which arose in local speech. It is probably in deliberate contrast to the *Bel-*, *Beau-* type that a much smaller

number of places were given names in *Mal-*. Massey Garth YOW was
earlier *Malessart*, 'bad clearing', and the lost *Malasize* YOW is obviously an
ironic response to *Belasize*. Other names in *Mal-* are from compound
appellatives. Malpas, which occurs at least eight times in England and
Wales, appears to have been an appellative meaning 'bad passage' which
was borrowed by English-speaking people. It usually refers to marshy
ground. Missies YOW is from French *mes-aise*, 'ill-ease', but these uncom-
plimentary names are much less frequent than the boastful ones. Some
names of monasteries, in addition to those in *Bel-* and *Beau-*, are artificial
formations. Haltemprice YOE, the site of a priory of Augustinian canons, is
from French *haute emprise*, 'great undertaking', and Dieulacres STF means
'may God increase it'; this last name is used in Clewer BRK in 1279 for an
assart belonging to Salisbury Cathedral. Some names, like Richmond
('strong hill') may be deliberate transferences of names well known in
France rather than new coinages, and this again suggests a modern
attitude to naming, in contrast to that assumed to underly the peasant
coinages of pre-Conquest times. The only surviving French settlement-
name in GLO, Miserden, can hardly have arisen on the lips of the local
farming population. The present form is a corruption of earlier *Musardera*,
Musardere, and the name was formed by the addition of an Old French
place-name-forming suffix—*(i)ere*, *-erie*, from Latin *-aria*, to the French
family-name *Musard*. The Musard family held the estate from 1086 to the
fourteenth century. Abdy YOW is from Old French *abadie*, 'property
belonging to an abbey', and this is a term not likely to have been in use in
the speech of the countryside.

Other French names, however, particularly in the north of England, do
not give this impression of having been bestowed on the manor house,
rather as a modern house-name might be fixed to the front gate. Bruern
('heath') OXF is not like this, nor is Tilts ('lime-trees') YOW. There
probably were limited areas where enough French was spoken to give rise
to some genuine local coinages in that language. But the number of new
French settlement-names of all kinds is very small, and French field-
names are extremely rare. This last point is important, as there is a marked
contrast with the field-names of the areas where Danish and Norwegian
settlements took place. Recent studies of Scandinavian field-names in
England, particularly the admirably cautious Fellows Jensen 1974b,
emphasize that the vast number of field-names using words of Scandinavian derivation are not direct evidence for Scandinavian settlement in
the way that village-names are. The Scandinavian settlement did, however,
have a marked effect on field-names, and no comparable effect resulted
from the Norman Conquest.

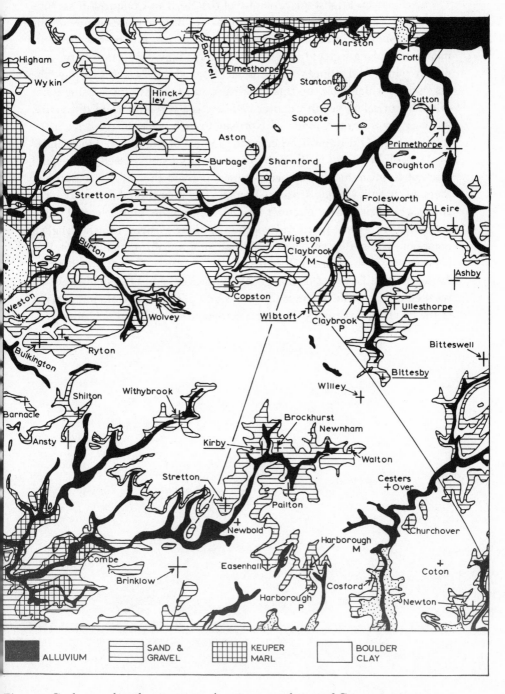

Fig. 21   Geology and settlement-names in an area north-east of Coventry WAR

The effects on English place-names of the Norman Conquest in AD 1066 may fairly be compared with the effects on British place-names of the Roman Conquest in AD 45, in that there were very few new settlement-names in the language of the conquerors, and a high proportion of the new names which did appear were of stereotyped kinds. This brings the discussions which make up this book back, in a sense, to the starting point of the historical survey in Chapter 2. There is a very important difference, however, in that the sounds of Norman French were different from the sounds of late Old English, whereas the sounds of Latin were much closer to those of British. The French conquerors did not replace the general stock of English and Norse place-names, nor did they adapt or translate them so that they made sense in French; but they brought about violent changes by their efforts to render English names pronounceable, and these, combined with the widespread addition of their surnames to the English names of manors they owned, brought about a transformation of a kind. It is important to understand that this is a different transformation from that caused by the large-scale coinage of completely new place-names which resulted in the whole of England from the English settlement, and in parts of the north and east from the Norse settlements.

Bibliography

BARROW, G. W. S.

  1973: 'Pre-feudal Scotland: shires and thanes', *The Kingdom of the Scots*. London, 7–68.

BONNEY, D. J.

  1966: 'Pagan Saxon burials and boundaries in Wiltshire', *Wiltshire Archaeological and Natural History Magazine* LXI, 25–30.

  1969: Two tenth-century Wiltshire charters concerning lands at Avon and at Collingbourne. *Wiltshire Archaeological and Natural History Magazine* LXIV, 56–64.

  1972: Early boundaries in Wessex. *Archaeology and The Landscape: Essays for L. V. Grinsell*, ed. P. J. Fowler.

  1976: Early boundaries and estates in southern England. Sawyer 1976, 72–82.

CAMERON, K.

  1959: *The Place-Names of Derbyshire*. EPNS XXVII–XXIX.

  1961: *English Place-Names*. London.

  1965: *Scandinavian Settlement in the Territory of the Five Boroughs: The Place-Name Evidence*. Inaugural lecture, University of Nottingham. Reprinted in EPNS 1975, 115–38.

  1968: Eccles in English place-names. *Christianity in Britain* 300–700, ed. M. W. Barley and R. P. C. Hanson. Leicester, 87–92. Reprinted in EPNS 1975, 1–7.

  1970: Scandinavian settlement in the territory of the five boroughs: the place-name evidence. Part II, place-names in Thorp. *Medieval Scandinavia* III, 35–49. Reprinted in EPNS 1975, 139–56.

  1971: Scandinavian settlement in the territory of the five boroughs: the place-name evidence. Part III, the Grimston hybrids. *England Before the Conquest: Studies in Primary Sources Presented to Dorothy Whitelock*, ed. P. Clemoes and Kathleen Hughes. Cambridge, 147–63. Reprinted in EPNS 1975, 157–71.

  1976: *The Significance of English Place-Names*. Sir Israel Gollancz Memorial Lecture. British Academy.

COX, B.

1973: The significance of the distribution of English place-names in *-hām* in the Midlands and East Anglia. *English Place-Name Society Journal* V, 15–73. Reprinted in EPNS 1975, 55–98.

DICKINS, B.

1934: English names and Old English heathenism. *Essays and Studies by Members of the English Association* XIX, 148–60.

DODGSON, J. M.

1966: The significance of the distribution of English place-names in *-ingas*, *-inga-* in south-east England, *Medieval Archaeology* X, 1–29. Reprinted in EPNS 1975, 27–54.

1973: Place-names from *hām*, distinguished from *hamm* names, in relation to the settlement of Kent, Surrey and Sussex. *Anglo-Saxon England* II, 1–50.

DRURY, P. J.

1975: Roman Chelmsford-*Caesaromagus. Small Towns of Roman Britain*, ed. W. Rodwell and T. Rowley. BAR 15, 159–73.

EKWALL, E.

1924: The Celtic element. *Introduction to the Survey of English place-names*. EPNS I, Part 1, 15–35.

1935: Some notes on English place-names containing names of heathen deities. *Englische Studien* LXX, 55–9.

1960: *The Concise Oxford Dictionary of English Place-Names*. (1st ed. 1936, 4th ed. 1960).

EPNS

1975: *Place-Name Evidence for The Anglo-Saxon Invasion and Scandinavian Settlements*. Eight studies collected by Kenneth Cameron, Introduction by Margaret Gelling. English Place-Name Society, Nottingham.

FÄGERSTEN, A.

1933: *The Place-Names of Dorset*. Uppsala.

FAULL, M. L.

1975: The semantic development of Old-English *wealh. Leeds Studies in English* VIII, 20–44.

VON FEILITZEN, O.

1937: *The Pre-Conquest Personal Names of Domesday Book*. Uppsala.

FELLOWS JENSEN, G.

1972: *Scandinavian Settlement-Names in Yorkshire*. Copenhagen.

1974: English place-names such as Doddington and Donnington. *Sydsvenska Ortnamnssällskapets Årsskrift*, 26–65.

1974b: English field-names and the Danish settlement. *Festskrift til Kristian Hald*. Navnestudier 13, Copenhagen, 45–55.

1975: The Vikings in England: a review. *Anglo-Saxon England* IV, 181–206.

1976: Personal name or appellative? A new look at some Danelaw place-names. *Onoma* XIX (3), 445–58.

FINBERG, H. P. R.

1953: *The Early Charters of Devon and Cornwall.* Leicester.
1961: *The Early Charters of the West Midlands.* Leicester.
1964a: *The Early Charters of Wessex.* Leicester.
1964b: *Lucerna: Studies of Some Problems in the Early History of England.* London.

FORD, W. J.

1976: Some settlement patterns in the central region of the Warwickshire Avon. Sawyer 1976, 274–94.

FRERE, S. S. and RIVET, A. L. F.

1971: Editorial. *Britannia* II, xvi–xvii.

GELLING, M.

1953–4: *The Place-Names of Oxfordshire.* EPNS XXIII, XXIV.
1960: The element *hamm* in English place-names: a topographical investigation. *Namn och Bygd* XLVIII (1–4), 140–62.
1961: Place-names and Anglo-Saxon paganism. *University of Birmingham Historical Journal* VIII (1), 7–25.
1967: English place-names derived from the compound *wīchām. Medieval Archaeology* XI, 87–104. Reprinted in EPNS 1975, 8-26.
1970: English entries in M. Gelling, W. H. F. Nicolaisen and M. Richards, *The Names of Towns and Cities in Britain.* London.
1972: The place-name evidence. *Excavations at Shakenoak Farm, near Wilcote, Oxfordshire. Part III, Site F*, ed. A. C. C. Brodribb, A. R. Hands and D. R. Walker. Oxford, 134–40.
1973a *The Place-Names of Berkshire* Part 1, EPNS XLIX.
1973b: Further thoughts on pagan place-names. *Otium et Negotium: Studies in Onomatology and Library Science Presented to Olof von Feilitzen.* Stockholm, 109–28. Reprinted in EPNS 1975, 99–114.
1974a: Recent work on English place-names. *The Local Historian* XI (1), 3–7.
1974b: Some notes on Warwickshire place-names. *Transactions of the Birmingham and Warwickshire Archaeological Society* LXXXV, 59–79.
1974c: *The Place-Names of Berkshire* Part 2, EPNS L.
1976a: The place-names of the Mucking area. *Panorama* (Journal of the Thurrock Local History Society) XIX, 7–20.
1976b: *The Place-Names of Berkshire* Part 3, EPNS LI.

GREENE, D.

1968: Some linguistic evidence relating to the British church. *Christianity in Britain 300–700*, ed. M. W. Barley and R. P. C. Hanson. Leicester, 75–86.

HART, C. R.

1957: *The Early Charters of Essex.* Leicester.
1966: *The Early Charters of Eastern England.* Leicester.
1975: *The Early Charters of Northern England and the North Midlands.* Leicester.

HOGG, A. H. A.

1964: The survival of Romano-British place-names in southern Britain. *Antiquity* XXXVIII (152), 296–9.

JACKSON, K.

1953: Language and History in Early Britain. Edinburgh.

1970: See Rivet and Jackson.

JOHANSSON, C.

1975: *Old English Place-Names and Field-Names containing lēah.* Stockholm.

JOHNSON, S.

1975: Vici in lowland Britain. *Small Towns of Roman Britain*, ed. W. Rodwell and T. Rowley. BAR 15, 75–83.

JONES, G. R. J.

1971: The multiple estate as a model framework for tracing early stages in the evolution of rural settlement. *L'Habitat et les paysages ruraux d'Europe*, ed. F. Dussart. Liège, 251–67.

1976: Multiple estates and early settlement. Sawyer 1976, 15–40.

KRISTENSSON, G.

1973: Two Berkshire river-names. *Namn och Bygd* LXI (1–4), 49–54.

KUURMAN, J.

1974: An examination of the -ingas, -inga- place-names in the East Midlands. *English Place-Name Society Journal* VII, 11–44.

LUND, N.

1975: Paper read to the Annual Conference of the Council for Name Studies in Great Britain and Ireland, London, April 1975, and to the Annual Conference for 1976 in Edinburgh.

1976: *Thorp-* Names. Sawyer 1976, 223–5.

MARGARY, I. D.

1955–7: *Roman Roads in Britain.* Vol. I, *South of the Foss Way—Bristol Channel.* Vol. II, *North of the Foss Way—Bristol Channel.* London.

MAWER, A. and STENTON, F. M. S.

1925: *The Place-Names of Buckinghamshire.* EPNS II.

MAYNARD, H.

1974: The use of the place-name elements *mōr* and *mersc* in the Avon valley. *Transactions of the Birmingham and Warwickshire Archaeological Society* LXXXVI, 80–4.

MYRES, J. N. L.

1969: *Anglo-Saxon Pottery and the Settlement of England.* Oxford.

MYRES, J. N. L. and GREEN, B.

1973: *The Anglo-Saxon Cemeteries of Caistor-by-Norwich and Markshall Norfolk.* London.

O'KELLY, M. J.

1970: Problems of Irish ring-forts. *The Irish Sea Province in Archaeology and History*, ed. D. Moore. Cardiff, 50–4.

OWEN, A. E. B.

1975: *Hafdic*: a Lindsey name and its implications. *English Place-Name Society Journal* VII, 45–56.

POOL, P. A. S.

1973: *The Place-Names of West Penwith*. Penzance.

REANEY, P. H.

1935: *The Place-Names of Essex*. EPNS XII.

1943: *The Place-Names of Cambridgeshire and The Isle of Ely*. EPNS XIX.

REDIN, M.

1919: *Studies on Uncompounded Personal Names in Old English*. Uppsala.

RICHARDS, M.

1970: Welsh entries in M. Gelling, W. F. Nicolaisen and M. Richards, *The Names of Towns and Cities in Britain*. London.

RICHMOND, I. A., CRAWFORD, O. G. S., and WILLIAMS, I.

1949: The British section of the Ravenna Cosmography. *Archaeologia* XCIII, 1–50.

RIVET, A. L. F.

1971: see Frere and Rivet.

RIVET, A. L. F. and JACKSON, K.

1970: The British section of the Antonine Itinerary. *Britannia* I, 34–82.

RODWELL, W.

1975: Trinovantian towns and their setting. *Small Towns of Roman Britain*. ed. W. Rodwell and T. Rowley. BAR 15, 85–101.

SANDRED, K. I.

1976: The element *hamm* in English place-names: a linguistic investigation. *Namn och Bygd* LXIV (1–4), 71–87.

SAWYER, P. H.

1958: The density of the Danish settlement in England. *University of Birmingham Historical Journal* VI, 1–17.

1962: *The Age of the Vikings*. London.

1968: *Anglo-Saxon Charters: An Annotated List and Bibliography*. London.

1974: Anglo-Saxon settlement: the documentary evidence. *Anglo-Saxon Settlement and Landscape*, ed. T. Rowley. BAR 6, 108–19.

SAWYER, P. H. ed.

1976: *Medieval Settlement: Continuity and Change*. London.

SMITH, A. H.

1928: *The Place-Names of the North Riding of Yorkshire*. EPNS V.

1937: *The Place-Names of the East Riding of Yorkshire and York*. EPNS XIV.

1956: *English Place-Name Elements*, Parts 1 and 2. EPNS XXV–XXVI.

1964–5: *The Place-Names of Gloucestershire*, Parts 1–4. EPNS XXXVIII–XLI.

STENTON, D. M. ed.

1970: *Preparatory to Anglo-Saxon England, Being the Collected Papers of Frank Merry Stenton*. Oxford.

STENTON, F. M.

1911: *The Place-Names of Berkshire*. Reading.

1924: Personal names in place-names. *Introduction to the Survey of English Place-Names*. EPNS I, Part 1, 165–89. Reprinted in Stenton, D. M. 1970. 84–105.

1939: The historical bearing of place-name studies: England in the sixth century. *Transactions of The Royal Historical Society*, fourth series, XXI, 1–19. Reprinted in Stenton, D. M., 1970, 253–65.

1941: The historical bearing of place-name studies: Anglo-Saxon heathenism. *Transactions of The Royal Historical Society*, 4th series, XXIII, 1–24. Reprinted in Stenton, D. M., 1970, 281–97.

1943: *Anglo-Saxon England*, first edition, Oxford.

1943b: The historical bearing of place-name studies: the place of women in Anglo-Saxon society. *Transactions of The Royal Historical Society*, 4th series, XXV, 1–13. Reprinted in Stenton, D. M., 1970, 314–24.

TENGSTRAND, E.

1940: *A Contribution to the Study of Genitival Composition in Old English Place-Names*. Uppsala.

TOLKIEN, J. R. R.

1963: English and Welsh. *Angles and Britons* (O'Donnell Lectures). Cardiff, 1–41.

WAINWRIGHT, F. T.

1962: *Archaeology and Place-Names and History: An Essay on Problems of Co-ordination*. London.

WALLENBERG, J. K.

1931: *Kentish Place-Names: The Charter Material*. Uppsala.

1934: *The Place-Names of Kent*. Uppsala.

WATTS, V. E.

1976: Comment on 'The Evidence of Place-Names' by Margaret Gelling. Sawyer 1976, 212–22.

WHITELOCK, D.

1952: *The Beginnings of English Society*. London.

1955: *English Historical Documents*, Vol. I, *c.* 500–1042. London.

WILLIAMS, I.

1949: see Richmond, Crawford and Williams.

Index